Children in F

Children in Families:
Research and Policy

Julia Brannen and Margaret O'Brien

 Falmer Press

(A member of the Taylor & Francis Group)
London • Washington, D.C.

UK   The Falmer Press, 4 John Street, London WC1N 2ET
USA   The Falmer Press, Taylor & Francis Inc., 1900 Frost Road, Suite 101, Bristol, PA 19007

First published in 1996

A catalogue record for this book is available from the British Library

Library of Congress Cataloging-in-Publication Data are available on request

ISBN 0 7507 0475 6 cased
ISBN 0 7507 0476 4 paper

Jacket design by Caroline Archer

Typeset in 10/12pt Bembo by
Graphicraft Typesetters Ltd., Hong Kong.

Printed in Great Britain by Biddles Ltd., Guildford and King's Lynn on paper which has a specified pH value on final paper manufacture of not less than 7.5 and is therefore 'acid free'.

To our children Patrick and Rosemary, Alex and Emil

Contents

Contents

Acknowledgments

The idea of this book emerged during a conference we organized in April 1994 under the auspices of the International Sociological Association Committee for Family Research and the Sociology of Childhood Group. We decided that the conference would be on the theme of children and families hoping that the event would provide a timely opportunity for dialogue between family sociologists and the growing number of sociologists researching and thinking about childhood. In the early 1990s, both of us had started research projects involving children and young people having previously taken adults as the main rapporteurs of family life. The international policy context of the conference, from which this book has grown, was informed by the 1991 UN Convention on the Rights of the Child and the 1994 International Year of the Family. Locally in the UK, new legislation on children (the Children Act 1989 and the Child Support Act 1991) was raising challenging questions concerning children in family life.

Our choice of contributions reflects the wide range of theoretical, empirical and policy-related issues about children in families in the 1990s. In the main the book contains chapters developed from a selection of the conference papers; we also invited Anne Solberg to add a methodological dimension which was not directly addressed by other contributions and Pat Allatt to examine parenting from the standpoint of children. Working on the book has been a stimulating experience enabling us to think creatively about the complex position of children in contemporary western societies and indeed in our own families.

Several people and organizations have supported us in writing this book. In particular we would like to thank all the contributors for their hard work and for providing us with so many insights into contemporary childhood and family life. The administrative staff at the Thomas Coram Research Unit and the Department of Sociology at the University of East London were very helpful both with the conference and in assembling the manuscript for the book. Finally, we would like to acknowledge the generous funding support given by the Economic and Social Research Council, the Nuffield Foundation and the Department of Sociology, University of East London.

Julia Brannen
Margaret O'Brien
July 1995

Foreword

Claims for a sociological paradigm of childhood are increasingly vocalized. Sociological interest in childhood is new — hardly much more than a decade ago a few scholars from Europe and North America, independently of each other, raised similar questions about the status of children and childhood in modern society. Cooperative international research and joint action have already emerged.

There is to be sure no agreement about the contents of the 'paradigm', but a common core of features defining the 'sociology of childhood' can be distilled: that childhood should be studied in its own right; that children should be the units of observation; that children themselves should talk about their own experiences; that childhood should be seen as a part of social structure; that children should be studied in the present not only in relation to their future as adults; that childhood be seen in an intergenerational context. On the other hand, one cannot speak of a consolidated 'paradigm' — far from it; there is, however, a serious and systematic search for coming to terms with childhood which, until recently, was both abandoned and neglected by sociology. I am not sure either that we should seek consolidation; rather we should be open-mindedly looking for new theoretical and methodological developments, and remember that a theory is fruitful only as long as it is contested.

The new sociologists of childhood have made 'mistakes'; as it is typical for new converts, we were perhaps exaggerating and unduly insistent on certain points. I am not sure that they should be regretted: from a tactical point of view a certain stubbornness was necessary in order to be heard; strategically, because boundaries needed to be established so as to clarify what was unique to a sociology of childhood and what made it different from adjacent disciplines. In a sense it was a search for legitimacy.

Among some of its more impatient representatives, complaints were sometimes aired: that we were not recognized as deserved; that we were looked upon as a cuckoo in the nest; that it was much harder for us than others to get funded, etc. Impatience in a tough world of competition leads to illusions. Illusionary or not, suspicion towards newcomers is both logical and understandable. Seen retrospectively — after a comparatively brief period — the much more remarkable and gratifying response was the genuine interest and cooperative spirit among colleagues from the already established sociological groups on youth and the family. Within the International Sociological Association (ISA) the desire of the newly formed Sociology of Childhood Group, that it should develop autonomously, was supported by neighbouring groups such as the Committee for Family Research and the Research Committee for Youth.

The present volume is an expression of the same obliging attitude. Not only was ISA's Thematic Group for the Sociology of Childhood (in the meantime elevated to a Working Group) cordially accepted as a junior partner in organizing the conference from which this book grew; its chairman was invited to write a foreword to the book. Most importantly, the book is a serious encounter between childhood sociology and family sociology with chapters written by authors from both 'camps'.

The editors are quite right in suggesting that there is no point in '*detach(ing) children from their family settings*'. Some sociologists of childhood may have gone too far in this direction while underscoring children's autonomy and their role as individuals (rather than family members) in many contexts outside the home. The same may however be said about family sociologists, at least conceptually. While children on the one hand are of course an indispensable ingredient of 'the family' for any family sociologist, the usage of the term 'family' has on the other hand too often come to be identified with 'parents'. Conventional phrases in both media and research such as: 'It is the task of the family to care for its children'; 'The family must socialize children'; 'The family should have more insight in the schools', demonstrates this. Strangely enough it has only recently begun to strike us that such phrases conceptually separate children from families, despite their contrary intent, *expresses verbis*, to be more concerned with children. This is not to say of course that parents should not care, socialize, have insight and so on.

In this context the suggestion to provide children with 'conceptual autonomy' — to use Barrie Thorne's apt phrase — makes sense. According to this recipe children's own being, having, and doing are accounted for, enabling children's lives and activities to be made visible. Indeed, it may even be the best way to bring children back into the family; as several chapters of this book clearly show, there is much to be gained from granting children subjectivity and agency, in this as in other contexts.

With reference to the subtitle of the book, 'research and policy', it is worthwhile to remind ourselves — and perhaps also to reassure politicians and public audiences — that a conceptual liberation of children does not necessarily imply their economic or political liberation. How far adults are ready to go in terms of granting children equal status with adults as participants in family and society is a political question, and there may be good reasons for not providing children with the same rights and obligations as adults. Given due respect to ethical problems that may be involved it is, however, much harder to justify denying children conceptual autonomy, i.e., for researchers not to deploy concepts that pertain to children's selves, lives and activities. Imaginative and relentless efforts to reveal children's life conditions and the status of childhood in the midst of competing adult interests may however have disturbing results, threatening the social order and the mythology surrounding childhood which is so dear to our past.

A democratic society is also an informed society. The new trends within childhood research wish to take this informed-ness seriously and exploit it on behalf of childhood and children. The support of family sociology for the new interest in childhood is an important step forward and the refocusing of research interests on '*children in families*' rather than on 'families with children', as it is nicely formulated by the editors, is a welcome sign. These interests are demonstrated with great imagination in this book, which promises much fruitful research cooperation in future about all family members and their varied relationships to the larger society.

Jens Qvortrup
President of ISA's Working Group for Sociology of Childhood

Chapter 1

Introduction

Julia Brannen and Margaret O'Brien

A central idea in assembling this volume was to put the spotlight on children and young people and their relationship to contemporary family life. The book has grown out of an international conference which we organized to celebrate the International Year of the Family in London, 1994 under the umbrella of the International Sociological Association's Committee for Family Research (see also Brannen and O'Brien, 1995).

Internationally, the period of writing is a time of increasing political concern and debate about the rights of children as a social category and as individuals (Lansdown, 1994). It is also a significant moment within sociology. In the emergent sociology of childhood, children are being conceptually liberated from passive dependency on adults and elevated to the status of social actor (James and Prout, 1990).[1] In common with childhood researchers, we have become conscious of the invisibility of children's perspectives and voices and the fact that children's worlds have typically become known through adult accounts.

To some our endeavour in writing a book about children in families may appear rather retrogressive reinforcing children's primordial link to families. For we agree with those who say that children have been conceptually constrained by, and substantively contained within, the social institutions of family and school rendering invisible their relationship to the wider social world (Alanen, 1990; Qvortrup, 1994). However, rather than detach children from their family settings, as some in the emergent sociology of childhood are disposed to do, we wish to recontextualize children within their families, to begin to prioritize their interests and perspectives, and to take account of the permeability of the boundaries between families and the outside world and the ways in which children negotiate these. We hope this book will be seen as a step in the right direction.

In contrast to researchers' treatment of children, research on young people has tended to locate them in institutional contexts and subcultures while the household domain which is a key arena in which transitions to adulthood take place has been neglected. However, with continuing high levels of youth unemployment, significant policy changes in reducing young people's access to welfare benefits, and the extension of education and training, young people have been pushed into greater economic dependence upon their families, a situation which has been reflected in a renewed research emphasis on the family life of young people (Jones and Wallace, 1992).

In editing the chapters and in discussing them with the authors and with one another, we have become conscious of the ways in which researchers have expressed their adult-oriented approach to family life through their particular neglect of children as research participants. The issue of whether or not to focus on children and to use them as research participants is of course, as with all research, related to the framing of the research questions. However it seems to us that the neglect of children in the study of family life has occurred not so much because children are not germane to research questions relating to the study of family life, but rather more because of researchers' assumptions about the appropriateness of including children. For some, children are assumed because of their age and immaturity to lack the necessary competence and abilities either to understand research procedures or to provide reliable responses. At the root of many researcher concerns are ethical issues. Researchers in their professional role are legally required by their professional codes to protect children in their status as minors. However in their other roles as parents or in positions of responsibility for children, researchers may also feel a strong need to protect children from the uncomfortable realities of life while at the same time discounting the extent to which children may be party to these. Confronting children's views and experience of adult care and authority may be uncomfortable and make researchers unconsciously fearful of doing so.

In refocusing on *children in families* rather than on *families with children*, we are conscious of risking the converse problem of underplaying parental perspectives and contexts. We have moreover asked ourselves how far it should be our task to 'balance' the two perspectives, a question which might have been framed rather differently had we been studying the relationships between other hierarchically related groups, for example employers and employees. Of course the problem can be overstated since in practice relatively few studies are designed to take account of the perspectives of both parents and children. In many ways the hypothetical problems are intractable; adopting a particular research focus inevitably overshadows other agendas. On the other hand, we are also conscious that, according to the social, cultural and political mores of our society, children *are* dependent upon parents in a variety of ways and for increasingly longer periods of the life course. The presence of parents as well as children in studies of family life is therefore critical.

The generational refocusing on children as well as parents, to which we hope this volume will make a contribution, is an important sensitizing exercise to the issues raised by taking children's accounts seriously. However the proof of the pudding will be in the eating when the relevant research has been done. Only then will it be possible to evaluate the difference made to studies of family life when children's interests and agency are prioritized.

Theoretical Perspectives on Children

The acceleration of economic change towards the end of the twentieth century alongside the increased fragility of couple relationships is a central backdrop to any consideration of the place of children in modern societies. Divorce and relationship breakdown are reshaping the lives of children. Analyses of demographic patterns in the UK (Clarke, this volume) and in America (Hernandez, 1995) show that recent cohorts of children, particularly from the 1970s onwards, are less likely to experience continuity in their household relationships over the life course. For Chris Jenks (this volume) the decline in commitment and trust previously generated through stable marriage and parental partnership has changed the nature of adults' relationship to children. He argues that the child has become a site of 'discourses concerning stability, integration and the social bond . . . The child is now envisioned as a form of "nostalgia", a longing for times past'. In this construction, portrayed also by Beck (1992) and Giddens (1991), the adult–child bond is constructed as primary, immediately satisfying, fundamental, and 'pure'. Jenks contrasts this contemporary vision of childhood with earlier constructions which placed more emphasis on the child becoming, growing, and maturing — a child of 'promise' when futures were more predictable.

> Oddly enough, children are seen as dependable and permanent, in a manner to which no other person or persons can possibly aspire. The vortex created by the quickening of social change and the alteration of our perceptions of such change means that whereas children used to cling to us, through modernity, for guidance into their/our 'futures', now we, through late-modernity, cling to them for 'nostalgic' groundings, because such change is both intolerable and disorienting for us'. (Jenks, this volume)

Jenks's argument resonates with that made by Zelitzer (1985) that, whilst increasingly economically useless, western children have become emotionally priceless, requiring from parents high investment and intense emotional involvement. The child of these theoretical accounts is vital in constructing adult identities. For Jenks the intensity of the adult gaze on and surveillance of childhood during the late twentieth century in part explains the 'discovery' of child abuse in this period. Whilst Jenks suggests that this concern with abuse is largely motivated by attempts to maintain a new nostalgic vision of the child, we suggest that it also indicates a protective and reparative stance on the part of adults towards individual children and children as a social group.

Jenks's portrayal of the postmodern child lies alongside discourses of children's rights which have gathered strength in the UK over the past fifteen years and more recently since the UK's ratification of the United Nations Convention on the Rights of the Child in 1991 (Roche, this volume). Essential to our understanding of modern childhood, particularly in the UK, is the diminution in parental, particularly paternal, rights over children and growth in the importance of parental duties, obligations and responsibilities towards children. It is clear that absolute paternal authority is no longer the main organizer of generational and gender relations in domestic and institutional life. However discourses of children's vulnerability and need for protection continue to coexist, sometimes uneasily, with discourses of children's right to empowerment and self-determination.

From a critical legal perspective, Jeremy Roche examines the meanings embedded in the new language of children's rights and exposes some of the tensions. Like other writers in the book he highlights how difference and heterogeneity in contemporary culture make consensus over children's rights difficult to achieve. He suggests how the old language of community has made children invisible and argues for the need to redraw its definitions and boundaries to take account of children. Roche is acutely aware that children's rights may conflict with the rights and responsibilities which attach to adults in their kin groups and communities who may have their own visions of children's best interests. His argument is that children belong to a multiplicity of communities and that cultural claims used in one community to justify the denial of children's rights have to give way when they clearly conflict with human rights norms. Moreover he suggests that where such conflict occurs it is important that insiders within the community concerned bring about the changes necessary.

At the heart of many of the problems about the notion of children's rights is the dominance of an individualizing language which presupposes an autonomous, unsupported individual, a concept which is peculiarly inappropriate with respect to children and more in rhythm with a multiply committed, self-determining adult. Some children's rights proponents, while they are to be lauded for freeing children from the conceptual categories of dependants and objects, tend to overstate the case in suggesting that children need to be liberated from the oppression of adults. This new way of constructing children may be as dangerous as its prior stereotype underplaying children's legitimate requirements for care and guidance from adult society. It is moreover an apparently genderless reconstruction of the child. As Gilligan (1982) has argued, the individual rights model is implicitly masculinist and underestimates the ways in which individuals not only have the right to separate themselves from, and assert themselves over, others but also have the right to be connected to others, to have responsibility for others and to seek responsibility from them. A key challenge is to fashion a conception of rights which promotes responsibility, trust and meaning between children and adults in their plurality of difference.

Difference, change and fluidity in contemporary life is also a starting point for James and Prout's analysis of childhood. They are critical of the conventional sociological approach which has portrayed children as being passively socialized by monolithic social institutions of family, state and education. Their model instead depicts a world of changing and differentially organized contexts, for instance from the hierarchically organized family to the less hierarchical (at least in formal terms) peer group setting. Their modern child is a 'strategic actor' using varying modes of action dependent on the nature of the context and as such is neither passively socialized nor thought to possess a unitary identity. James and Prout suggest that the child 'finds multiple expressions of the self through engagement with different sets of people in different social groups'. Some if not all contemporary children have a greater range of contexts to negotiate compared with children of previous generations; skills required to move easily between these different contexts and to integrate the consequent changes into self-identity become crucial for successful daily living. Of course it is also important to take account of the fact that children vary greatly in their access to the material and cultural resources upon which they need to draw in their negotiation of the complexities of modern life. Moreover children's gender is also likely to be central to their mode of negotiation (Thorne and Luria, 1986).

Studying Age

The core of the sociological case for a focus on children as active agents concerns the problematization of the developmental paradigm and the notion that 'age' is a biological given. Typically age is linked to the concept of children's dependency. As Hockey and James suggest, dependency is also socially as well as biologically constructed and contains elements of imagery and metaphor which serve to separate children as different from adults according to notions of naturalness, innocence and vulnerability (1993, p. 69). Childhood dependency is thereby contrasted with 'an individualistic knowledgeable, independence which is the mark of adulthood'. As Hockey and James note, there is a discontinuity rather than a continuity between child and adult social experience in western societies which contrasts with the process of socialization in many non-western societies. Evidence presented in Julia Brannen's chapter confirms this approach showing that adolescence is socially constructed in different ways according to the cultural origins of parents. UK origin parents see adolescence as an individualized pathway to adulthood whereby young people seek autonomy separating themselves from their families. By contrast those families from non-western origins emphasize the continuing connectedness of children to their families while also marking the social and biological processes of growing up.

Among families from western origins, children's experience of growing up is not uniformly a discontinuous process or a quest for independence from parents as Pat Allatt's chapter suggests. In a close examination of young people's own accounts Allatt reveals how parent–child relations are considered to be enduring at the same time as discontinuities brought about by life course transitions threaten the familial order. These continuities and discontinuities are expressed symbolically. For example, Allatt's chapter illuminates the concepts of home and parental concern as providing young people with a sense of attachment reaching back into the past and holding the potential for extension into the future. However it also suggests that young people may negotiate practices designed to take them away from home drawing upon other normative guidelines related to life course transitions.

Social constructions of age depend upon a dichotomy which is drawn between childhood and adulthood. However the consequences of this dichotomy often only become visible when age distinctions between adults and children are reconstructed, or rather come to assume less salience. Anne Solberg's chapter focuses on her experiences as a Norwegian childhood researcher. Solberg suggests that notions of what children 'are' focus centrally on their 'young age' which can over-determine the knowledge we gain about children. As her various research experiences testify, the age of children is rendered more or less relevant depending upon the context in which adult researchers encounter the children who participate in their studies. Solberg's critical methodological case is the situation in which the children she was studying became her social equals. This situation came about in a fishing community in northern Norway in which children were employed in work teams alongside adults attaching bait to fishing lines. In this work context children were treated as 'nothing special', as Solberg herself observed in her role of participant observer. This particular fieldwork situation enabled Solberg to create the necessary distance from her own preconceptions of what childhood means. Moreover it was critical to her development of a distinctive research strategy for studying children in other contexts and projects. In her subsequent research on children she adopted a position of 'setting age aside' which enabled her to study children without being encumbered by feelings of responsibility and protectiveness related to cultural constructions of childhood and her own personal responsibilities to children in her other roles. (This is not to say she was not bound by a professional code of ethics towards her research participants.) This research strategy of discounting age is therefore significant in constituting a theoretical as well as a methodological advance.

The Family Life Negotiations of Children and Young People

Demographic and social trends are reshaping the lives of parents and hence the living arrangements of children: shifts in childbearing age, changes in partnership, marriage and remarriage patterns, and the development of new reproductive technologies are domains where most research has focused. Lynda Clarke's chapter indicates the increasing variation in household type as parental relationships breakdown or fail to consolidate, and as parents enter into new partnerships. These patterns of household composition have implications for children's relationships both within and between households including relationships with non resident fathers, new step–parent relationships and step and half sibling relationships. With increasing household change and relationship breakdown, children are experiencing a wide variety of concurrent family relationships. Not only do children negotiate moves between a number of homes, they also experience change over the life course.

While cohort studies are able to address this complexity and indicate the nature of children's household trajectories, there is little UK research which considers how children themselves experience and define these changes. The chapter by Margaret O'Brien, Pam Alldred and Debbie Jones presents evidence concerning the ways in which children construct notions of 'proper families' and how they engage with these concepts and negotiate new meanings in the context of their own experiences when they diverge from the nuclear family stereotype. Their data show the importance of going beyond the household when examining children's experiences and representations of family life. For instance, when children were asked to make drawings of their families some included non–residential members, a pattern that was more common for children who had experienced parental separation. Interestingly these 'additional' family members were not usually non–residential fathers but other kin such as older siblings, cousins and grandparents who represented important emotional and material sources of support for children. In order to understand the nature of children's significant familial networks this study suggests that future research in this area should take care to enable child informants to construct their family worlds as they see them.

The empirical studies in this book also illuminate what it means to be a child or young person within the different cultures and communities that make up the fabric of contemporary family life. Miri Song's ethnographic investigation of children of Chinese origin living in families who own family-run, take-away food businesses highlights how parental work patterns help shape childhood and indeed construct childhood for some children as a time of responsibility. Participation in the family business, characterized by a 'family–work contract', was an implicit but central aspect of being a child in some of these families. Children's labour participation was grounded in shared assumptions of the work being a family project and, in some cases, was essential to family survival and strength but, more usually, seen as an investment for a shared future. Parental reliance and dependence on children was high in most of Song's study families — one child described how he and his brother were his parents' 'guide-dogs to the world'; in others children were less participant. Whilst most children expressed great empathy for their parents, Song found some evidence of ambivalence about the extent of parental dependence, showing perhaps that children wish to set limits to 'adult-like' activity in the context of contradictory discourses concerning what it means to grow up in western society.

The negotiated character of children's relationships with their parents in the face of competing norms about the transition to adulthood is a key theme in Julia Brannen's chapter. She argues that the public policy context of contemporary adolescence in the UK 'implies no ordered progression of increased rights and responsibilities'. It is not surprising therefore that in some of the families she investigated the relationship of adults to children was characterized by constant negotiation and renegotiation whereby communication rather than taken for granted rules became the mechanism of bargaining and control. This was typically the case in middle class households of UK origin, in contrast to Asian origin households where 'norms governing relations between parents and young people are renegotiated and rules as such disappear'. Any model of childhood has to contend with these actual features of contemporary family life where taken for granted assumptions for instance concerning parental authority are routinely contested by children.

Allatt's chapter, which focuses on the continuities in family life, suggests the ways in which young people's negotiations with parents in the context of their transitions to adulthood are also bound within a system of moral norms and reciprocities to which young people give meaning. Thus while many of the young people in Allatt's (and Brannen's) research find maternal worry about what they get up to outside the home irritating and constraining, they also see it as 'part and parcel of being a proper parent, symbolizing concern' (Allatt, this volume). Similarly, parents emerge as 'archivists of identity'; young people see parents as central to who they are and where they came from. Young people also located themselves at the centre of their parents' identities. This latter position is similiar to the stance of the children in O'Brien's study who felt that a household without children was not a family at all.

The empirical research in this volume on children in families has given centre stage to children's relationships with parents which will, we hope, complement sociology's emphasis on parental perspectives. However, clearly other aspects of children's experience of family life require further research, for instance their wider kin relationships and social networks, and their access to, and use of, household resources, for example space and material goods and the organization of their time (Ambert, 1992; O'Brien, 1995). Moreover the impact of child professionals on the negotiations between children and parents needs further investigation.

Economic and Social Policies on Children and Young People

Children are relatively less significant demographically both because of the continuing trend for families to have at most two children but also because of the ageing population as elderly people live longer. However while children are an increasingly scarce resource in society, society does not appear to value them accordingly in the way it distributes income to families with children. The findings discussed in the chapter by Kennedy, Whiteford and Bradshaw confirm this trend and show that welfare states do not necessarily treat children equitably with, or prioritize them over, other generations. Children's households are clearly more at risk of poverty than those of older people especially in the UK, USA, France, The Netherlands and Canada.

Most studies which examine these issues focus on households as defined in terms of parents rather than children. A consequence is that they underestimate the number of children who live in poverty (see Hernandez, 1995; Qvortrup, 1994). The chapter by Kennedy, Whiteford and Bradshaw is significant; in taking children as statistical units it treats children as key social actors both in the analysis and the presentation of the data.

There is considerable concern about the material plight of children in the developing and developed worlds. Wilkinson (1994), for instance, has charted an increase in child poverty in the UK between 1979–91 (using a definition of poverty to refer to household income less than half the national average). A recent report by Save the Children (1995) shows that nearly half of children under 5 years in developing countries live in absolute poverty.

Children's lives in families are influenced materially by the state of the economy and the labour market as they impact upon parents' employment patterns. The influx of mothers into employment, particularly those with young children, has been one of the most significant changes of the past three decades in the UK affecting children's care arrangements as well as their financial welfare. However the growth of mothers' employment does not benefit all households to the same extent with a growing gap between two full-time earner households and those with no earners, a polarized pattern of 'work rich' households and 'work poor' families (Gregg and Wadsworth, 1995; Harrop and Moss, 1994). The collapse of UK manufacturing industry and changes in the structure of the labour force in many countries have led to high levels of unemployment among families with children with increasing evidence of a heavy over-representation among unskilled fathers and lone mothers. In addition UK labour markets are increasingly 'flexible' leading to a decline in the number of permanent employment contracts together with a growth of self-employment and other working patterns, for example working from or at home especially among certain occupational groups (Brannen *et al.*, 1994). The chapter by Kennedy, Whiteford and Bradshaw shows substantial differences in the relative economic circumstances of children according to parental employment status in ten developed countries but also according to age and number of children, and household composition.

A concentration upon employment status and its financial rewards ignores the role of broader welfare policy and provision for children's well-being. Material welfare should not be limited to a discussion of the redistribution of cash incomes only and should include 'non-cash' benefits such as state and employer provisions of health, education and housing. Moreover, as Kennedy *et al.* (this volume) also recognize, they should take into account the impact of domestic work and responsibility, childcare provision and parental leave policies. This whole 'welfare package' contributes to families' command over resources and living standards and the share allocated to children. In practice the study by Kennedy *et al.* only included spending on health and education together with some data on housing in selected countries. But the chapter does raise the question, even if it only answers it partially, about the effect of a broader measure of income upon the well-being of children (and other population groups).

The material situation of children is contributing to their becoming an important political issue in the UK with calls for the redistribution of economic resources in favour of children (for example Young and Halsey, 1995). Some writers are speculating that current employment practices are preventing parents from spending sufficient dedicated time with their children and that children in the developed world are now beginning to experience 'time poverty' (Young and Halsey, 1995) or 'parenting deficit' as well as material disadvantages (Etzioni, 1993). In Scandinavian countries with very high maternal employment rates and high day-care coverage, the concerns are different focusing on the tensions between greater institutionalization of, and hence increased formal control over, children versus the child's need to be an individual (Nasman, 1994). On a more positive interpretation of the trend, others have argued that the provision of day care and extensive paid parental leave constitutes a partnership between employed mothers and the Welfare State (Leira, 1992).

Claims about children's rights and interests indicate the way in which the child question is not only taking over from the woman question but may also conflict with it. Moreover, as Oakley (1994) has explained so cogently, these are essentially political issues. Whilst women's studies and the Women's Movement originated through women's own realization of their position in society and their desire to change it, the 'uncovering of children's own perspectives and positions is complicated by the power relations of those who claim to be working on their behalf' (Oakley, 1994, p. 29). The question of who is to speak on behalf of the child is not easy to answer.

Social policies are created in the context of different political perspectives but do not necessarily reflect them. In the UK social policy context, children and young people have been deemed to be very much the private responsibilities of parents while the State has sought to limit its role. At first glance this appears to be the policy position in Greece. In this chapter Theodore Papadopoulos suggests that traditionally Greeks have a strong attachment to family. He also shows how the considerable modernization of Greece has done little to redistribute income to families with children. 'The family' in Greece continues to undertake a very important role in ideological, material and political terms (as in Spain, see Valiente, 1995). Above all it is the main vehicle for social mobility and families devote very large parts of their resources to their children's education and have developed a pattern of inter-generational responsibility for family welfare and family solidarity. The inaction of Greek social policy reinforces the model of the male breadwinner with women the sole carers of children and parents the main supporters of young people until they leave home (much later than in the UK) to get married. The UK appears to resemble Greece in that both governments fail to redistribute resources to families with children, as demonstrated in the chapter by Kennedy, Whiteford and Bradshaw. However to conclude that family life and welfare policy are similar in Greece and the UK would be extremely misleading.

Two chapters of the book consider policy changes which have taken place in the UK which have affected young people in the context of their relationships to their families. Like the chapter by Kennedy *et al.* the chapter by Hilary Land takes a macro-structural perspective. It is particularly significant for its broad historical sweep focusing on UK policy, defined in broad terms. Concentrating on young people as they move into adulthood and the recent policy trends according to which parents are required to support their children throughout their teens and into their early 20s, Land demonstrates the ways in which policies which used to form the bridges into adulthood have removed the supports. The chapter is also significant in taking a gender perspective. Some of the bridges which supported boys into adulthood have disappeared; the armed forces no longer provide employment for working class young men. These supports have crumbled as a consequent of global change such as demilitarization and because of changes close to home notably the demise of the British empire. Land also describes how the traditional female routes into adulthood have disappeared with the decline of servant classes (although there is some current resurgence of this phenomenon with the growth of two full-time earner households and a requirement for nannies). More recently, the recession and Britain's failure to invest in industry and to provide young people with the necessary skills have rendered young people dependent on parents with the simultaneous withdrawal of, and reduction in, welfare benefits both for young people and unemployed parents.

Selman and Glendinning's chapter is a more specific examination of the ways in which social policies affect particular aspects of young people's lives namely sexual behaviour and parenthood. They show the ambivalence of UK policy with respect to providing sex education with some policies aimed at limiting sexual behaviour while others express a reluctance on the part of government to interfere in the 'private' areas of family life. The chapter also puts social policy in the context of broader labour market policy. It suggests that the lack of training and job opportunities for young women bring about a situation in which motherhood is one of few alternatives available to them.

Both Land's chapter and the chapter by Selman and Glendinning suggest that the UK has a problem in positioning itself in relation to family life. At one level, family life is constructed as a private arena in which the State is reluctant to intervene. However, the growth and power of child experts continues to be marked in our society. A new and resonant ideology is that professionals should work in partnership with parents and, in child protection cases, the main drive is on reconciliation of birth families with children. At the same time it is abundantly clear that the overarching context of government policy (labour market, education, health, welfare and housing) is highly influential in shaping the nature of the partnership between parents and professionals.

Children and young people are located in a variety of domains. Researchers, professionals and policy makers have enclosed children conceptually in socialization terms within families and schools and the province of childcare experts. By contrast young people have been defined as a problem of social control with an emphasis on peer groups and the labour market. Increasingly children, rather than young people, are moving up the political agenda as adults advocate the rights of children to contribute to discussions concerning their welfare. Whilst these different discourses have points of agreement and points of difference, the relation of children and young people to their families will continue to be central. We hope that this volume of essays will make a contribution to social science debates concerning the place of children and young people in contemporary family life.

Notes

1   In the UK anthropologists were important forerunners in the study of childhood, notably the work of Charlotte Hardman (1973), and have had a significant impact on the methodologies adopted by sociologists.

References

ALANEN, L. (1990) 'Rethinking socialization, the family and childhood', in ADLER, P.A., ADLER, P., MANDELL, N. and CAHILL, S. (Eds) *Sociological Studies of Child Development: A Research Manual*, **3**, CT, JAI Press.

AMBERT, A.M (1992) *The Effect of Children on Parents*, New York, The Haworth Press.

BECK, U. (1992) *The Risk Society: Towards a New Modernity*, London, Sage.

BRANNEN, J. and O'BRIEN, M. (1995) *Childhood and Parenthood: Proceedings of the International Sociological Association Conference 1994*, London, Institute of Education.

BRANNEN, J., MESZAROS, G., MOSS, P. and POLAND, G. (1994) *Employment and Family Life: A Review of Research in the UK (1980–1994)*, Department of Employment, Research Series No. 41.

ETZIONI, A. (1993) *The Spirit of Community: The Invention of American Society*, New York, Simon and Schuster.

GIDDENS, A. (1991) *Modernity and Self-identity*, Cambridge, Polity Press.

GILLIGAN, C. (1982) *In a Different Voice*, Cambridge, MA, Harvard University Press.

GREGG, P. and WADSWORTH, J. (1995) 'More work in fewer households', in HILLS, J. (Ed) *New Inequalities*, Cambridge, Cambridge University Press.

HARDMAN, C. (1973) 'Can there be an anthropology of children?' *Journal of the Anthropological Society of Oxford*, **4**, 1, pp. 85–99.

HARROP, A. and MOSS, P. (1994) 'Working parents: Trends in the 1980s', *Employment Gazette*, **102**, 10, pp. 343–52.

HERNANDEZ, D. (1995) *America's Children: Resources from Family, Government and the Economy*, New York, Russell Sage Foundation.

HOCKEY, J. and JAMES, A. (1993) *Growing Up and Growing Old*, London, Sage.

JAMES, A. and PROUT, A. (1990) *Constructing and Reconstructing Childhood: Contemporary Issues in the Sociological Study of Childhood*, London, Falmer Press.

JONES, G. and WALLACE, C. (1992) *Youth, Family and Citizenship*, Buckingham, Open University Press.

LANDSDOWN, G. (1994) 'Children's rights', in MAYALL, B. (Ed) *Children's Childhoods Observed and Experienced*, London, Falmer Press, pp. 33–44.

LEIRA, A. (1992) *Welfare States and Working Mothers*, Cambridge, Cambridge University Press.

NASMAN, E. (1994) 'Individualization and institutionalization of childhood in today's Europe', in QVORTRUP, J., BARDY, M., SGRITTA, G. and WINTERSBERGER (Eds) *Childhood Matters: Social Theory, Practice and Politics*, Aldershot, Avebury, pp. 165–87.

OAKLEY, A. (1994) 'Women and children first and last: Parallels and differences between children's and women's studies', in MAYALL, B. (Ed) *Children's Childhoods Observed and Experienced*, London, Falmer Press, pp. 13–32.

O'BRIEN, M. (1995) 'Allocation of resources in households: Children's perspectives', *Sociological Review*, **43**, 3, pp. 501–17.

QVORTRUP, J. (1994) 'Childhood matters: An introduction', in QVORTRUP, J., BARDY, M., SGRITTA, G. and WINTERSBERGER, H. (Eds) *Childhood Matters: Social Theory, Practice and Politics*, Aldershot, Avebury, pp. 1–23.

SAVE THE CHILDREN (1995) *Towards a Children's Agenda: New Challenges for Social Development*, London, Save the Children.

THORNE, B. and LURIA, Z. (1986) 'Sexuality and gender in children's daily worlds', *Social Problems*, **33**, 3, pp. 176–90.

VALIENTE, C. (1995) 'Children first: Central government child care policies in post-authoritarian Spain (1975–1994)', in BRANNEN, J. and O'BRIEN, M. (Eds) *Childhood and Parenthood: Proceedings of the International Sociological Association Conference 1994*, London, Institute of Education.

WILKINSON, R. (1994) *Unfair Shares: The Effects of Widening Income Differences on the Welfare of the Young*, London, Barnardos.

YOUNG, M. and HALSEY, A.H. (1995) *Family and Community Socialism*, London, IPPR.

ZELITZER, V.A. (1985) *Pricing the Priceless Child: The Changing Social Value of Children*, New York, Basic Books.

Chapter 2

The Postmodern Child

Chris Jenks

Introduction

This chapter addresses the complex social constructions of childhood that have accrued through modernity and are now fracturing and reforming along different lines in modernity's wake. One sign of our times is the well documented increase in reported cases of child abuse in western society over the last thirty years; incidence has clearly increased.[1] While I do not attempt to provide a causal analysis or a morphology of this phenomenon here I do regard its recognition and election as indicative not just of the shifting character of the relationship that exists between adults and children but also of the condition of the wider society. From this basis I investigate the transition from a state of modernity into that of postmodernity and develop two models, or 'visions', of childhood which correspond to those structural forms. These visions are of 'futurity' and 'nostalgia' respectively. I conclude with a return to the issue of child abuse and suggest that our current heightened perception of the problem is understandable in terms of the loss of personal identity endemic in the postmodern condition.[2]

The Child in Modernity: 'Futurity'

Where did the modern child arise from? It was Rousseau who promulgated the manifesto of the child in modernity through *Emile* (1762), with its immanent, idealist, rational characteristics. Since that time western society, it is generally supposed, has not looked back. Rousseau forged an incontestable link between our understanding of the child and the emotions of the heart. He announced that humankind is naturally good and that it is only the constraints implicit in certain social structures or the corruption of some forms of social institutions that renders it bad. Children, who Rousseau regarded as the bearers of this 'goodness' in a primal condition, were properly to be educated and socialized according to 'natural' principles. Rousseau's 'savage' (a being wholly without the anthropological connotations of primitiveness), is a child highly charged with dispositions to love and to learn, and equipped with the propensity to become a good spouse, parent and citizen. Such an ideal being, the very image of modernity's child, is a stranger to avarice and is imbued with a natural altruism and kindliness. More than this, Rousseau's already overburdened creature is simultaneously the repository of all necessary wisdom. This child embodies an affective certainty which need not answer to objective, external criteria, and which is further insulated from scrutiny by Rousseau's implicit relativism and thus privatization of beliefs. We witness here the distillation of the principle of 'care' governing the modern relationship between adults and children but more than this we see the inauguration of the powerful commitment to childhood, in western society, as a form of 'promise'. A 'promise' of unimagined action, but also an extension of our own plans and a hedge against our own action as yet incomplete. Such a commitment has, for several generations, enabled us to indulge in pleasant reveries concerning tomorrow.

Once, it is assumed, we were unutterably beastly towards children (DeMause, 1976), at one time we did not attend to their specificity and difference at all (Aries, 1966), and for whole epochs we routinely abandoned them (Boswell, 1988), but following the optimistic illumination of the Enlightenment, children have become our principal concern, we have become their protectors and nurturers and they have become our primary love objects, our human capital and our future.

All of the neo-Enlightenment histories of infancy and maturation attest to this grand conceit, their analyses encourage our modern complacencies by regarding the archaeology of child-rearing with a disdainful backward glance. The brevity, ignorance, brutality and general ugliness of antiquity's parenting, we imagine, has been supplanted by a vision and attitude which has become crystallized into the form of a rational machine for nurture, the family and its macrocosm, the State. The modern family has become the locus for the confluence of politics and individual psychology, but beyond this it has emerged as both the primary unit for, and also the site of, governmentality (Donzelot, 1980; Rose, 1989), that is, it both absorbs and, in turn, distributes social control.

Through modernity childhood has gradually sequestered adult experience, it has claimed a greater duration within the total life experience, it has usurped and assumed greater and yet greater segments of adult labour: cognitive, affective and manual. Beyond this childhood has absorbed increased material provision and it has established this patterning of acquisitions as a 'natural' right policed by an ideology of care, grounded unassailably in the emotions. Adults, though primarily mothers, 'sacrifice everything' for their children and they, in return, are expected to experience 'the best time of their lives'. Adults have relinquished this space and this power in relation to a strictly moral dimension epitomized through the concept of 'dependency' but this, perhaps, disguises motivations of optimism, investment, and even a contemporary re-working of Weber's 'salvation anxiety'. Parental love and benevolent adult paternalism in general are not in question here, but rather the forms of social structure that accelerate their intensity and expand their currency. It is no great leap to see the absolute necessity and centrality of the modern nuclear family as the pivotal social space in this system of socialization.

The organization of this patterning of relationships and the emergence of a quasi superiority in the affectual attitude has, of course, not occurred in isolation, nor simply through the grand inspiration of Rousseau's romantic vision. The reconstruction of human relationality into the architecture of the modern family has been a recognizable complement to the division of labour through industrialization, not cynically planned, but not 'naturally' evolved either. The modern family has become the basic unit of social cohesion in advancing capitalism, and though loving and supportive in its self-image it has become the very epitome of the rational enterprise. Families are cellular, mobile, manageable and accessible to emergent forms of mass communication, unlike the extended families that preceded them. They are also self-sustaining, self-policing, discrete yet wholly public in their orientation and both biologically and culturally reproductive (Bourdieu, 1971; Donald, 1992; Jenks, 1993). They are a major component in the exercise of the contemporary principles of adaptation and integration; they are instrumental in their rationality by facilitating change while demonstrating stability to their members.

The modern family enabled the modern State to invest in 'futures'. The ideology of care both lubricated and legitimized the investment of economic and cultural capital in the 'promise' of childhood. Childhood is transformed into a form of human capital which, through modernity, has been dedicated to futures. The metaphoricity through which the discourse of childhood speaks is predicated on the absent presence of a desired tomorrow; with 'growth', 'maturation' and 'development' writ large at the level of individual socialization, and 'pools of ability' and a concern with the 'wastage of talent' at the level of formal state socialization. As children, and by way of children, we have, through modernity, dreamt of futures, and in so doing we have both justified and sought justification for modernity's expansionist urges in the post-Darwinian conflation of growth and progress.

The extant vision of childhood through the nineteenth and twentieth century had become one of 'futurity', and the much vaunted accretion of a 'caring', 'helping', 'enabling', 'facilitating' mode of nurture instances both the explicit awakening of a collective attitude more sensitive to children's needs, but also an implicit recognition of their worth and thus appropriate usage. The apparent gradual diminution of child abuse through the nineteenth century and on into the twentieth century can be seen as a considered shift from immediate to deferred gratification on the part of an increasingly enlightened adult society.

The Child in Postmodernity: 'Nostalgia'

Just as modern patterns of consumption have outstripped nineteenth century economics, the late-modern division of labour and its accompanying social structures have mutated beyond the communities and solidarities described by classical sociology. Thus everyday late-modern modes of relationality have outgrown the mid-twentieth century nuclear family. Things are not as they used to be and that is not a consequence of the erosion of the family, although this is what the rhetoric of contemporary politics often suggests in a variety of attempts to divert the level of problematic from the global and national to the local, and indeed the personal. Families have changed, as have the character of the relationships that they used to contain, and which, we should note, used to contain them (Wallerstein and Blakeslee, 1989; Giddens, 1991;

Beck, 1992; Stacey, 1990; Lasch, 1980). However this change is not causal, it is part of the set of emergent conditions that have come to be appraised as late- or post-modernity (Lyotard, 1986; Bauman, 1992; Smart, 1993). It is within this context that a new vision of childhood has arisen and one of the signposts towards this new vision is the seemingly unprecedented increase in child abuse in the late twentieth century. It is a vision very different from the 'futurity' of modernity.

Bell (1973), and later Touraine (1984, 1989), were perhaps the first to awaken our attention to the alteration in the traditional fabric of relations that made up modernity. Both these liberal, or indeed neo-Conservative, theorists revealed that traditional secular beliefs and taken for granted categories of community member-ship no longer prevailed. Bell, proclaiming an end to ideology, arguably instigated the era of the 'post-' with his thesis describing a change in both the mode and relations of production. The productive base, Bell and also Touraine informed us, had transmuted, through market forces and advances in technology, into the 'post-industrial', and the system of social stratification, long since recognizable in terms of polarization had, through a series of social movements, thickened at the waist to contain a middling service class such as to diffuse conventional class antagonisms, and altered into the 'post-capitalist'. These two concepts, Bauman stated:

> have served the purpose well: they sharpened our attention to what is new
> and discontinuous, and offered us a reference point for counter arguments
> in favour of continuity. (Bauman, 1992, p. 217)

Previously assumed points of attachment of the individual with the collective life, like social class, work group, local community and family, were now seen to be los-ing their adhesion in line with the demands of a post-Fordist mode of production, global economies and networks of communication, and the exponential inroads that techno-science continues to make into the previously located centres of know-ledge and authority. Individuals are now much more recognizable through their imme-diate location and project than through their group affiliations or previously established identity. The new experience of history at both the individual level and the level of institutions, is one of discontinuity rather than of continuity.

The living through of modernity, a practice stemming from a firm belief in enlightenment and emancipation, gave rise to a confident cultural attitude of 'being in control'. This was a control based on: the possibility of objective knowledge through rational process; the primacy of centred, communicating selves; and the conviction that difference was reconcilable through analysis and discourse. Such bases ensured that the ensuing attitude was both sustaining and comfortable. This attitude was deeply rooted in the necessity, the viability, and the moral certainty of 'progress'. Human progress committed social action to the perpetual struggle for higher forms of life. Contingency, the condition that ruled the pre-modern (the 'savage' before Rousseau), was now part of a strategic calculus waited in the favour of homo sapiens by the guarantees provided by our applied sciences.

The excitement and the purpose of social being, the dreams and the promise embedded in our children, were all to reach for the stars, to control more and more of the wantonness of the cosmos, and to produce human culture as the triumph of finitude over infinity. What could not be achieved today could be set in train for tomorrow. The sufferings and deprivations and ignorance of our parents were certainly not going to be visited on the next generation, our future, our children. There would be no repeat of the Holocaust, but instead mass education and mass consumption.

That the natural has become tamed, through modernity, ensures that all phenomena become both social and historical. In this sense the pre-modern contingency inverts and all phenomena become dependent upon human conduct, including their forms of knowledge and interpretive procedures. Despite the fact that nature occasionally strikes back, with a Los Angeles earthquake for example, its character is anticipated and its impact minimized. A new omnipotence was released into the human attitude, instancing perhaps a 'second passing' of the deity: the first recorded by Nietzsche irrationalism; the second etched onto the public memory by Hiroshima. However as Heywood stated:

> This is not just to do with the problems attendant on the nature of modern weaponry and warfare, of global industrialization, of the revolutionary, 'deconstructive' impact of capitalist market systems on all aspects of human relationships . . . At a deeper level it is related to the termination of nature and tradition in late-modernity.

and he continued that this has been expressed:

> . . . in terms of the appearance of a fully socialized nature, marking the emergence of human power as globally decisive and unchallenged, without equal, limit, confining shape or *telos*, its old adversaries — nature and the 'second nature' of traditional cultures now having been vanquished. The possibility, indeed the necessity, of radical self-formation confronts individuals, institutions and whole societies. Opportunities to fulfil the emancipatory promise of enlightenment are balanced by the potential for social, ecological, political and cultural calamities on an unprecedented scale. (Heywood, 1995, p. 6)

These observations are informed by Beck's (1992) concept of a 'risk society', and they exemplify (Giddens's (1991) tightrope between 'ontological security and existential anxiety'. Within these tendencies of late-modernity, personal actions and personal aspirations take on a different form. The previously centred, continuous self of modernity becomes more of a reflexive project involving disparate interactional planes rendered coherent through a revisable narrative of self-identity. And, in the same manner that institutions hold together through the ingenious practice of 'crisis management', the reflexive project of the self sustains through the artfully renewable strategies of auto/biographical stories. The late-modern calls forth a constant, reflexive, re-presentation of self (Goffman, 1971). This is, of course, critical to the experience of being a child but, more significantly, critical in terms of how adults now understand and relate to children.

The social spaces occupied by adults and children have changed, not just in place but in character, and the spaces previously allocated to fixed identities of adults, and children, and families have transmogrified. But this spatial dimension of social experience is not alone in its new-found versatility, its pacing has changed as well. Following a stable period of historical inevitability, we are now also witnessing innovations in the vocabulary of time which drastically alter our relation to a whole set of cultural configurations, established under modernity's motif of 'progress'. As Virilio (1986) has put it:

> The loss of material space leads to the government of nothing but time . . . In this precarious fiction speed would suddenly become a destiny, a form of progress, in other words a 'civilization' in which each speed would be something of a 'region' of time. (p. 141) . . . The violence of speed has become both the location and the law, the world's destiny and its destination. (Virilio, 1986, p. 151)

This impacts directly upon our vision of the child. Through modernity time itself was measured and contained, it came to be expressed in minutes, days, weeks, years and in categories such as generations. We marked out our personal ability, responsibility, functionality, mortality and general expectations of self, and others, through such divisions. We elected a periodic framework within which we might assemble unconnected events and ascribe to them the status of achievement or 'progress'. Generations have been gathered by such devices and the coincidental accumulation of social action has been defined under the detached title of a particular era (Chaney, 1994) — like, for example, the 'swinging 1960s'. Although the formal divisions on the clock and calender are unchanged our collective expectations of appropriate chronological advancement have altered: people make late entry into education; marriage is not a necessary temporal goal and is also a repeatable experience; families are established at the limit of a woman's band of fertility and by men of an age ensuring that they will not see their children through adolescence; occupational careers are interrupted and individuals opt for early retirement; vast numbers of people experience a lifetime of unemployment. The previously indelible normative markers of social experience (in the form of 'achievement' and 'status') are becoming relativized, sometimes through the pressure of material circumstances but equally because of the expression of a proliferation of new and different senses of 'purpose'. Indeed, 'purpose' is no longer linked to 'progress'. The higher forms of life, to which modernity since enlightenment aspired, were the utopias of freedom, equality, goodwill, peace and prosperity, all long since recognized for their unattainability and their ideological content. Such utopias are now treated as mere ciphers, as hazy images deriving from the reveries of 'futurity', the dreams dreamt through children and through their childhood promise. When we return to real, active people, we witness not dreams, nor yet the realization of nightmares, but a pragmatic state of disenchantment. Rather than a life spent in pursuit of utopias the late-modern condition is one of the avoidance, or minimization, of dystopias. Horizontal strategies for the annulment of convention occur, a process of de-traditionalization. Alternative lifestyles are so common and widespread as to find difficulty in expressing their alternativeness 'to'. For example, gross financial materialism lives alongside holistic medicine, health foods, body culture, astrology, narcotic addiction and dealing, arcane 'New Age' belief systems, serial killers and single-parent families. This is no list of pathologies but a glimpse at the many facets of the late-modern experience, some are bizarre and criminal, others are benign or simply diverting. All of these expressions, and many others, are met in the street and all are now shadows of the mainstream.

In the context of this decline in collective aspiration, or 'disenchantment' (Beck, 1992) with the sense of purpose previously exercised by the concept of 'progress' [what Lyotard (1986) refers to as the death of a meta-narrative] people are resourceful in their search for both alternative reasons for being and also new points of attachment to a collective life. Although, as Giddens (1991) argues, the late-modern individual may be less well imbued with a strong sense of the fixity of the inside and of cultural inheritance and may therefore have developed a robust adaptive strategy of bargaining and negotiation with the outside, it is nevertheless the case that members of a late-modern society continue to seek out both coherence of self-identity and continuity with the past.

The classical sociological actors who populated Durkheim's emergent 'organic solidarity' at the end of the previous century, were perpetually insecure in the face of the potentially destructive 'anomic' forces inherent in modernity's form of the division of labour. Their external response was to develop a secular credo of interdependency, but their internal response was to re-establish a supportive mosaic of 'mechanical solidarities' in the form of work groups, professional guilds, churches and families. This inward search for coherence and continuity sustains into late-modernity but, as I have argued, these nineteenth century sources of integration are not so readily available. However, there are two visible indices of the maintenance of an inward pilgrimage within late-modernity. The first, I suggest, is the obvious growth and, at the same time, destigmatization of psychotherapy in western societies. Psychiatric and psychotherapeutic regimes tend to be conducted through regressive narratives with individuals 'finding their way' through the excavation of roots and attachments from the past — the 'inner child'. The second index is the real child, that is our new vision of the child and our practical relationship with it.

Late-modern society has re-adopted the child. The child in the setting of what are now conceptualized as postmodern cultural configurations, has become the site or the relocation of discourses concerning stability, integration and the social bond. The child is now envisioned as a form of 'nostalgia', a longing for times past, not as 'futurity'. Children are now seen not so much as 'promise' but as primary and unequivocal sources of love, but also as partners in the most fundamental, unchosen, unnegotiated form of relationship. The trust that was previously anticipated from marriage, partnership, friendship, class solidarity and so on, is now invested more generally in the child. This can be witnessed empirically in a number of ways: through the affectual prolongation of adolescence; the disputed territory that children constitute during parental divorce; the uprating of children's status through the modern advances in children's rights (like the 1989 Children's Act in the UK); the modern iconography of the child in Third World aid politics and in western campaigns against addiction and criminality; and the enhanced interest in men's relationship to children and of men in children — a development marked by the growth of sociological research into masculinity and fatherhood since the 1980s.

The instability and necessary flexibility of all forms of relationship, other than that between adult and child, through late-modernity make them unreliable repositories for 'the inside', whether in the form of feelings, altruism or sociality itself. As Beck has stated:

> The child is the source of the last remaining, irrevocable, unexchangeable primary relationship. Partners come and go. The child stays. Everything that is desired, but not realizable in the relationship, is directed to the child. With the increasing fragility of the relationship between the sexes the child acquires a monopoly on practical companionship, on an expression of feelings in a biological give and take that otherwise is becoming increasingly uncommon and doubtful. Here an anachronistic social experience is celebrated and cultivated which has become improbable and longed for precisely because of the individualisation process. The excessive affection for children, the 'staging of childhood' which is granted to them — the poor overloved creatures — and the nasty struggle for the children during and after divorce are some symptoms of this. The child becomes the final alternative to loneliness that can be built up against the vanishing possibilities of love. It is the private type of re-enchantment, which arises with, and derives its meaning from, disenchantment. (Beck, 1992, p. 118)

Oddly enough, children are seen as dependable and permanent, in a manner to which no other person or persons can possibly aspire. The vortex created by the quickening of social change and the alteration of our perceptions of such change means that whereas children used to cling to us, through modernity, for guidance into their/our 'futures', now we, through late-modernity, cling to them for 'nostalgic' groundings, because such change is both intolerable and disorienting for us. They are lover, spouse, friend, workmate and, at a different level, symbolic representations of society itself. As Scutter stated in an analysis of children's literature:

> . . . the child is characteristically associated with values that *seem* to be in opposition to those ascribed to adults, just as Peter Pan seems to be set in antithesis to the adult growing world. But the contemporary child and adolescent . . . again and again proves to be a superior repository of those values the adult world ascribes to but falls short of. The child makes a better adult. (Scutter, 1993, p. 12)

Although this work is from within a literary textual world it is highly instructive. Peter Pan's Neverland is no longer a recalcitrant state from which children have to be prised to get on with 'futures', it is, what was: love and care, reciprocity and sociality.

Scutter continued: . . . Neverland is actually not a child realm but an adult realm.'
(Scutter, 1993, p. 12)

We need children as the sustainable, reliable, trustworthy, now outmoded
treasury of social sentiments that they have come to represent. Our 'nostalgia' for
their essence is part of a complex, late-modern, rearguard attempt at the resolution
of the contradictory demands of the constant re-evaluation of value with the pro-
nouncement of social identity.

As we need children we watch them and we develop institutions and programmes to watch them and oversee the maintenance of that which they, and they
only, now protect. We always have watched children but once as guardians of their/
our future and now because the relationship has become inverted in a subtle way, they
have become the guardians, the curators of the 'good' in relationships. Our expanded
surveillance has, needless to say, revealed more intrusions into their state of well
being. The abuse of children, in all its manifestations, which include physical (Kempe
et al., 1962), sexual (Finkelhor, 1979) and psychological (Garbarino and Gilliam, 1980),
has clearly 'increased' through the magnification and breadth of our late twentieth-
century gaze. This is evidenced from two sources.

Firstly, with reference to a shift in Kempe's perspective (Kempe and Kempe,
1978), the 'invention' of child abuse in the 1960s seems to transform into a 'discovery' of child abuse in the 1970s. The prevalence of child abuse as a social practice, far from spontaneously re-generating in the second half of the twentieth century,
had, in fact, been relatively stable, which is testified to by Kempe's renewed interest
in the historical dimension of the phenomenon. However, the incidence of child
abuse during that period, in terms of reported and recorded occurrence, was to be
treated as a novel phenomenon, an expanding phenomenon, and a phenomenon
worthy of further explanation in itself.

Secondly in Dingwall *et al.* (1983) who, in making an essentially ethnometh-
odological point concerning the routine practices of rate-producing agencies, examine the psychological and social processes by which social workers decide whether
or not children are being abused. Dingwall *et al.* develop the concept of professional strategies and put forward two models, the 'pessimistic' and the 'optimistic'.
The former, it is suggested, is that which is adopted by social workers in the face of
governmental, media, local and public pressure (for example, during the moral panic
created by the 1987 Cleveland 'affair' in the UK) and consists of a 'better safe than
sorry' approach, involving all children being regarded as potentially abused, which
in turn leads to a dramatic increase in reported cases. The 'optimistic' strategy which
derives from a different climate of expectation, or, ironically, emerges as a reaction to
the backlash often caused by the former strategy, involves actual abuse being regarded,
by social workers, as the least plausible diagnosis of a family problem.

Nevertheless, the dramatic increase in the reported occurrence of child abuse
during late-modernity is not reducible solely to the improved technology of our
scrutiny nor just to our diligence, however enforced. It is due to the intensity of the
collective response to those very late-modern conditions. What is being so jealously
preserved through the new, 'nostalgic', vision of the child is the meta-narrative of
society itself. The story of the postmodern child and its abuse makes up a palimpsest.

To abuse the child today is to strike at the remaining, embodied vestige of the social bond and the consequent collective reaction is, understandably, both resounding and vituperative. The shrill cry of 'abuse' is a cry of our own collective pain at the loss of our social identity. The source of blame for this abuse whether projected into the form of psychopaths, perverts, devil-worshippers, colluding mothers, men, or even incompetent social workers should really be sought in the way that we have, over time, come to organize our social relationships.

Conclusion

With the acceleration of the pace of social change towards the end of the twentieth century, the individual witnesses a diminution of their points of attachment to a collective life, or at best a recognition of the utterly transitory nature of such points of attachment. With the dispersion, fragmentation and de-traditionalization of established sources of judgment, such as the cognitive, the ethical and the aesthetic, the individual experiences increasing discontinuity between previously held interests, beliefs and commitments and those of any coherent group. Politics becomes mediated by speed and authority by risk. Where classical sociology had pointed to the remedy for disintegration resting with the establishment of an ethic of interdependency, no such positive altruism or pragmatic reciprocity are now available options. The current experience of subjectivity is a fierce tension between dependency and independency.

> It was specifically in bourgeois society that an association between age and dependence was established . . . Liberated from the necessity of labour yet excluded from the adult social world, childhood became an increasingly puzzling phenomenon. Its sequestration was justified on the grounds of children's 'immaturity' and 'helplessness', on their evident need to be 'looked after'. (Ferguson, 1990, p. 11)

However, dependency is no longer a taken for granted feature of the relationship between adults and children what with demands for charters of children's rights, with children 'divorcing' from parents, and the increasingly cynical backdrop of 'abuse', topicalized here, policing the exercise of all and any control between adults and children. And it is certainly the case that dependency is no longer a respectable feature of any relationship between adults. Independence, it would seem, has become the dislocated mark of personhood in the postmodern life, a criterion which frees the self from the outmoded constraints of the old order but precludes an analysis of the successful mechanisms of cultural reproduction inherent within that structural order. As Coward (1993) put it:

> We apply the term 'abuse' so widely that we are in danger of misrepresenting modern relations of social power . . . Excessive concentration on abuse

puts a question mark over dependency but does not allow us to understand or criticise power. Instead it criticises character types — the abuser
and the abused, the perpetrator and the victim — and pathologises their
relationship. Abusers are now seen as the ultimate villains, more sinister
than any who benefit from the real inequalities of society. (Coward, 1993)

Dependency rests on a need and an authority in the provision of that need —
abuse requires the misuse or corruption of that authority. The postmodern diffusion
of authority has not led to democracy but to an experience of powerlessness; this is
not a potential source of identity but a prescription for victimization. Children, I am
suggesting, figure largely as symbolic representations of this welter of uncertainty,
both literally and metaphorically.

Political correctness, another postmodern regulator of experience, is a blanket
strategy for the resistance to the imposition of any form of authority (primarily in
linguistic form) and the current 'climate of abuse' derives from a sustained confusion
between power and its legitimation.

Children have become both the testing ground for the necessity of independence in the constitution of human subjectivity but also the symbolic refuge
of the desirability of trust, dependency and care in human relations. In this latter
role 'childhood' sustains the 'meta-narrative' of society itself and abuse, both real
and supposed, expresses our current ambivalence towards and impotence in the face
of constantly emergent structural conditions. As we see less coherence and sustained
meaning in the experience of our own subjectivity and our relationships with others,
we witness more symbolic abuse of children.

We are compelled to care about the well-being and prospects of other
peoples' children as a condition of preserving our nationhood. If the value
placed on national life recedes, displaced by an ethos of autonomy and dis-
sociation, our relations with children and each other change profoundly.
Children lose their collective status, and are no longer the ancestral and
progenitorial bond of national continuity. Instead, they become the private
presences whose entry into the world is occasioned by the pursuit of private fulfilment. The child of choice becomes the responsibility of the adults
who choose. The life quality and life chances of children increasingly reflect
the arbitrary fortuities of family origin and genetic endowments. (Novick,
1994, pp. vii–viii)

Notes

1   Extrapolations from the official statistics provided by the NSPCC and the Department of
    Health show that the total number of children on child protection registers in England
    and Wales increased from 11,844 in 1978 to 45,200 (England only) in 1991.
2   Much research attests to the discrepancy between incidence and prevalence of cases of child

Chris Jenks

abuse that this argument draws upon. See Corby, 1993; Parton, 1985; Freeman, 1983; Straus and Gelles, 1986; Finkelhor, 1984; and Kempe and Kempe, 1978.

References

ARIES, P. (1962) *Centuries of Childhood*, London, Cape.

BAUMAN, Z. (1988) 'Is there a postmodern sociology?', *Theory, Culture and Society*, **5**, pp. 2–3, 6, 217–237.

BAUMAN, Z. (1992) *Intimations of Postmodernity*, London, Routledge.

BECK, U. (1992) *Risk Society: Towards a New Modernity*, London, Sage.

BELL, D. (1973) *The Coming of Post-industrial Society: A Venture in Social Forecasting*, New York, Basic Books.

BOSWELL, J. (1988) *The Kindness of Strangers: The Abandonment of Children in Western Europe from Late Antiquity to the Renaissance*, Harmondsworth, Penguin.

BOURDIEU, P. (1971) 'Systems of education and systems of thought', in YOUNG, M. (Ed) *Knowledge and Control*, London, Collier-Macmillan.

CHANEY, D. (1994) *The Cultural Turn*, London, Routledge.

CORBY, B. (1993) *Child Abuse: Towards a Knowledge Base*, Buckingham, Open University Press.

COWARD, R. (1993) 'Culture obsessed with abuse', *The Observer*, 6 June 1993.

DEMAUSE, L. (Ed) (1976) *The History of Childhood*, London, Souvenir.

DINGWALL, R., EEKELAAR, J. and MURRAY, T. (1983) *The Protection of Children: State Intervention and Family Life*, Oxford, Basil Blackwell.

DONALD, J. (1992) *Sentimental Education*, London, Verso.

DONZELOT, J. (1980) *The Policing of Families*, London, Hutchinson.

FERGUSON, H. (1990) *The Science of Pleasure*, London, Routledge.

FINKELHOR, D. (1979) *Sexually Victimized Children*, New York, Free Press.

FINKELHOR, D. (1984) *Child Sexual Abuse: New Theory and Research*, New York, Free Press.

FREEMAN, M. (1983) *The Rights and Wrongs of Children*, London, Francis Pinter.

GARBARINO, J. and GILLIAM, G. (1980) *Understanding Abusive Families*, Cambridge, MA, Lexington Books.

GIDDENS, A. (1991) *Modernity and Self-identity*, Cambridge, Polity Press.

GOFFMAN. E. (1971) *Relations in Public*, London, Allen Lane.

HEYWOOD, I. (1995) 'An art of scholars: Negation and particularity in paintings by Ryman and Richter', in JENKS, C. (Ed) *Visual Culture*, London, Routledge.

JENKS, C. (Ed) (1993) *Cultural Reproduction*, London, Routledge.

KEMPE, R. and KEMPE, C. (1978) *Child Abuse*, London, Fontana.

KEMPE, C., SILVERMAN, F., STEELE, B., DROEGEMUELLER, W. and SILVER, H. (1962) 'The battered child syndrome', *Journal of the American Medical Association*, **181**, pp. 17–24.

LASCH, C. (1980) *The Culture of Narcissism*, London, Abacus.

LYOTARD, J. (1986) *The Postmodern Condition: A Report on Knowledge*, Manchester, Manchester University Press.

NOVICK, M. (1994) 'Foreword' to O'NEILL, J. *The Missing Child in Liberal Theory*, Toronto, University of Toronto Press.

PARTON, N. (1985) *The Politics of Child Abuse*, Basingstoke, Macmillan.

ROSE, N. (1989) *Governing the Soul*, London, Routledge.

SCUTTER, H. (1993) 'Representing the child: Postmodern versions of Peter Pan', Paper presented at 'Issues in Australian childhood' conference, QUT, Brisbane.

SMART, B. (1993) *Postmodernity*, London, Routledge.

STACEY, J. (1990) *Brave New Families*, New York, Basic Books.

STRAUS, M. and GELLES, R. (1986) 'Societal change and change in family violence from 1975 to 1985 as revealed by 2 national surveys', *Journal of Marriage and Family*, **48**, pp. 465–79.

TOURAINE, A. (1984) 'The waning sociological image of social life', in *International Journal of Comparative Sociology*, **25**, 1, 2.

TOURAINE, A. (1989) 'Is sociology still the study of society?', *Thesis Eleven*, **23**.

VIRILIO, P. (1986) *Speed and Politics*, New York, Semiotext(e).

WALLERSTEIN, J. and BLAKESLEE, S. (1989) *Second Chances*, London, Bantam.

Chapter 3

The Politics of Children's Rights

Jeremy Roche

In this chapter, I explore some of the difficulties associated with the language of children's rights. I do so from a critical legal perspective rather than that of sociology or social policy. As a result much of what follows draws on case law and statute as well as on Anglo-American jurisprudence. This is part of an ongoing project of assessing the social and legal consequences of enhanced rights of participation given to young people. To this end I first review some recent developments in the field of child law in order to consider how the law responds to the child's self-defined wishes and interests. Second, I examine how notions of community have been, and are, used to justify the silence and invisibility of children. Third, I examine the tensions which arise when talking about rights at the same time as acknowledging cultural difference. While the language of children's rights is politically and socially important, at the same time it must be open to the heterogeneity of modern industrialized society.

In conclusion, I outline why the language of children's rights is nevertheless necessary and valuable. The idea of children's rights as moral claims to be respected as human beings (from which positive rights for children might spring), can emphasize both the need for, and the inevitability of, the redrawing of boundaries and the connected constant redefinition of community; both are linked with the idea of 'public conversation'.

Children and the Law: From Silence to Speech

Since the International Year of the Child in 1979 there has been a transformation in the debates surrounding children's rights (Freeman, 1983a; Franklin, 1986; Freeman and Veerman, 1992; and Alston *et al.*, 1992). A number of legal and organizational developments reflect the ongoing nature of the public debate around children e.g., the setting up of the Children's Legal Centre, the launch of Childline, revised Department of Health Guidance to local authorities on the registration of childminders and their use of corporal punishment and the government's ratification of the United Nations Convention on ,the Rights of the Child in December 1991.

Yet, there is no core children's rights agenda — the politics are complex and contradictory. The child's right to be protected can be seen to clash with the right to self-determination, and the child's right to have contact with both parents on relationship breakdown can be seen (and exploited) as a device under which men are enabled to continue to control the lives of their ex-partners (see Smart and Sevenhuijsen, 1989). For some the emphasis is on the child's right to participate as a good in itself and that society should endeavour to facilitate such participation whenever and wherever it is practicable.

In England and Wales, prior to the passing of the Children Act 1989, the House of Lords had ruled in the landmark case of *Gillick v West Norfolk and Wisbech A.H.A.* [1986] A.C.112 that parental rights gave way to the 'mature minor's' right to decide. It was the radical judgment of Lord Scarman in Gillick that best expressed the judiciary's willingness to recognize a child as a developing and potentially rational decision-maker in his/her own right. Lord Scarman stated:

> I would hold as a matter of law the parental right to determine whether or not their minor child below the age of 16 will have medical treatment terminates if and when the child achieves a sufficient understanding and intelligence to enable him or her to understand fully what is proposed.

However, alongside this symbolically and practically important development in jurisprudence increasing poverty blights the lives and opportunities of children robbing them of their social rights (Miringoff and Opdycke, 1993; Children's Rights Development Unit, 1994), and parents are still being allowed to assault their children. The Department of Health has recently revised its guidance to local authorities to allow childminders to 'smack' children they look after as long as the child's parents consent (Department of Health, 1994). Nevertheless, despite what may be termed the 'retreat' from Gillick led by Lord Donaldson, the law can be seen as increasingly concerned to take the child's wishes and feelings and self-defined preferences into account whenever possible.[1]

The Children Act 1989

The Act set out to repair a number of procedural and substantive failings of the law. It envisioned a more accountable professional practice and, in some respects, can be seen as 'privatizing' children's issues (see Bainham, 1990 and Roche, 1991). It is arguable that despite its association with promoting children's interests and, in a more limited sense, their rights, the Act is centrally concerned with the powers and duties of the concerned adults. The Act's jurisprudence appears to support this view — recent decisions preserving the ability of adults, judges and social workers, to intervene 'free' of the irksome constraints of the language of the statute.[2]

Nevertheless three aspects of the Act and the new rules of court reveal its radical potential: the child's ability to commence or defend proceedings on his/her own behalf i.e., without the appointment of a 'next friend' or guardian *ad litem*; the duty on the solicitor in certain circumstances to take instructions directly from the child rather than the guardian *ad litem*;[3] and the child's ability to apply to the court for leave to apply for a section 8 order.[4]

The Child's Right to Participate

In law a child is a person under a 'disability'.[5] Under the Family Proceedings Rules, r 9.2, a child may only prosecute family proceedings by a next friend or guardian *ad litem* unless r 9.2A applies. Rule 9.2A provides that a child may prosecute or defend proceedings without a next friend or guardian *ad litem* in two sets of circumstances. First, where a minor wishes to commence proceedings, or to be a party to proceedings, which are not specified proceedings they may do so with the leave of the court. Second, where a solicitor has accepted their instructions having considered, in the light of their age and understanding, that they are able to give instructions. However, in *Re CT* (A Minor) (Wardship: Representation) [1993] 2 F.L.R. 278 the Court of Appeal held that it is ultimately a matter for the court, not the solicitor, to decide whether the child has the requisite understanding. In *Re S* (a minor) (independent representation) [1993] 2 F.L.R. 437 the issue was whether the child should be allowed to conduct the remaining stages of the proceedings without a guardian *ad litem*. Here Sir Thomas Bingham M.R. emphasized that the test was not age, but understanding, and that where the issues raised by the case required insight, which only maturity could bring, then the court would be less likely to allow the child to conduct the proceedings without a guardian *ad litem* or next friend.

Conflict Between the Child and the Guardian Ad Litem

Where in public proceedings there is conflict between the child and the guardian *ad litem* the child's solicitor may be required to take instruction directly from the child. In *Re H* (A Minor) (Care Proceedings: Child's Wishes) [1993] 1 FLR 440 the court held that a solicitor's failure to take instructions exclusively from the child client, who had sufficient understanding to give instructions, when there was clearly a conflict between the child and the guardian *ad litem* 'constituted a fundamental forfeiture of the child's right'.

Applying for Section 8 Orders

Under the Act a child has a 'right' to apply to the court for leave to apply for a section 8 order.[6] The court may only grant leave if it is satisfied that the child has sufficient understanding to make the proposed application. The response of the courts to such applications has been to issue a Practice Direction which states that in future all such applications should be heard in the High Court (see the Practice Direction [1993] 1 F.L.R. 668). Recent cases testify to the unease of the courts faced with a mature, participating child.[7] Now, in order to succeed in an application for leave to apply for a section 8 order, the child applicant will have to convince the court not only that he/she has the requisite understanding laid down by section 10(8) of the Act but that the application gives rise to an issue which it is proper for the court to determine *and* it has a reasonable chance of success.

If children's rights are to have any practical consequence children must not be left at the mercy of the willingness of adults to act on their behalf. Without the right to have more open access to the legal system and to participate in proceedings which affect their lives children's rights will always be conditional. This is a key challenge facing the legal system in its dealings with children and young people.

Insofar as the Children Act allows the child, in certain circumstances, unmediated access to a lawyer and to the courts it can be seen as going some way towards meeting the UK government's obligations under the United Nations Convention on the Rights of the Child (UNCRC). Article 12 of the UNCRC provides that children, who are capable of forming their own views, should have the right to express those views freely in all matters affecting them and these should be given due weight in the light of the child's age and maturity. In particular, children should be provided with the opportunity to be heard either directly, or through a representative, in any judicial and administrative proceedings affecting them.

While the Children Act 1989 can be seen as providing new avenues whereby some children can express their own interests not all children will be able to do so. Either because of age or disability many children will not be able to participate directly in proceedings which concern them. However the practice of some lawyers and welfare professionals reveals that changes in the representation of children's views and interests are taking place (see Liddle, 1992 and King and Young, 1992). However Burman has reservations about such a development:

> The problems with determining children's 'best interests' become most evident where the children, for reasons of age or disability, are unable to make their own opinions clear. One strategy for dealing with this is to appoint child advocates. However . . . what this does is to create a further layer of professionals through which the same set of ideas about children and families is circulated. For what resources can a child advocate draw upon except those already popularised by the childcare and welfare 'experts', then recycled as the child's putative wishes? (Burman, 1994, p. 74)

Even if the space for the child's participation is limited and that, for younger children in particular, the representation of their interests can result in an enhancement of professional power and standing, it must be acknowledged that the child has such an opportunity now and that, where the child is being represented, the adult contestants involved will be engaged in a struggle over meaning and social relations. For some it will involve acknowledging the interconnectedness of our lives, of no longer seeing the relationships that children have with significant adults as inevitably hierarchic. We need to consider what kind of childhoods we as a community desire. A commitment to the development of the voices of children being heard is in itself a sign of who we want and imagine ourselves to be. Likewise a community that accepts some assaults on children as instances of 'loving discipline' (a phrase used recently to justify the 'smacking' of children) has its own images of self and childhood (see *London Borough of Sutton v Davis* [1994] 1 FLR 737).

Images of Community: Family Privacy

The idea of community has appeal conjuring up images of tolerance and shared understandings. However, notions of community can be used to exclude and its rhetoric to mask real and substantial intra-community conflicts (see Milne, 1992). The idea of 'family privacy' is one powerful instance of community. Family life is justified and conducted on terms different from that of civil society (Elshtain, 1989). Goldstein, Solnit and Freud in *Before the Best Interests of the Child* argue that:

> The child's need for safety within the confines of the family must be met by law through its recognition of family privacy as the barrier to state intrusion upon parental autonomy in child rearing. (Goldstein *et al.*, 1979, p. 9)

The family as a community should be left to itself. Yet children may fare badly in this community — the 'barriers' justified on the basis of children's natural dependency on their parents or the negative consequences of intervention. In the context of public law the question of state intervention is often described as a 'line drawing' exercise (Freeman, 1983b). No-one is claiming that the family should enjoy absolute autonomy: even Goldstein *et al.*, do not argue that. The family is not 'free' of outside intervention or support. There is a host of professionals 'policing the family' (Donzelot, 1979; Parton, 1991). Yet, for many reasons, the idea of family privacy has a firm hold on our imagination in western society (see Mount, 1982). At the same time there is an awareness that victory for the family might mean defeat for its more vulnerable members — historically women and children. In the realm of private law similar issues are raised. For example, in order to protect her 'family values' Mrs Gillick wanted the law to declare unlawful the advice given by the Department of Health and Social Security regarding the circumstances in which a medical practitioner could give confidential contraceptive advice and treatment to a minor. The complaint in essence was that the law should uphold her authority as a parent, not undermine it. *The Times* editorial (entitled 'Gillick's Law', 1985) observed:

> The main contention on one side is that the law ought to be arranged *so as to lend support to those parents who are conscientiously doing their duty to care for the health and morals of their children* . . . to lead them to a proper understanding and right use of the sexual drive, as the parents understand these things. (*The Times*, 1985) (my emphasis)

However if we pretend that the family is harmonious the result might be that its 'marginal' members will suffer. The question is, in the face of conflict, what mechanisms should be available for its resolution. The imagery of children's rights is one vehicle whereby the reality of conflict, be it in the home, the school or wherever, will be voiced and made visible — thereby opening up a new politics and reshaping communities. To acknowledge conflict and to seek the use of law may 'shift the balance of power in an already violent situation' (Minow, 1987, p. 1902). In her analysis of the politics and history of family violence in Boston Gordon states:

Most of the invitations for intervention came from women and secondarily children. In other words, the inviters were the weaker members of family power structures . . . The effect of social workers' involvement was sometimes to change existing family power relations, usually in the interest of the weaker family members. (Gordon, 1989, p. 296)

Gordon argues that part of the anxiety surrounding social work interventions into the family is based on a misconception of the family as a homogeneous unit and concludes by observing:

The very inequalities of power that make the state oppressive create the need for state responsibility for welfare, and these inequalities include gender and age as well as class . . . an accurate view of this 'outside' intervention into the family must consider, as the clients so often did in their strategic decisions, both external and familial forms of domination. (Gordon, 1989, p. 299)

Family privacy has functioned as a bolster to male power leaving women and children in a subordinate position. Much recent writing has emphasized the struggles waged by women against male power and the male bias in law (O'Donovan, 1993). Perhaps the problematic feature about the children's rights movement is that it does not allow us to assume either that families always know best or that the interests of child and mother are always identical (Federle, 1994).

Children have no choice about the family to which they belong — as Friedman notes:

For the child maturing to self-consciousness in her community of origin, typically the family–neighbourhood–school–church complex, it seems uncontroversial that 'the' community is found, not entered, discovered, not created. (Friedman, 1992, p. 110)

Children are unavoidably constituted by the lives they lead in these given communities. Their social identity is inextricably bound up with their place. The identity of the child is not singular. There are, and will be, conflicts between the different communities which the child inhabits. As the child grows up these conflicts will increase. Social life is a process of differentiation of identities in which children move between different communities and negotiate their identities accordingly. As children enter 'communities of choice' the potential for conflict and redefinition is heightened.

Culture and Children's Rights: Unfamiliar Voices

Notions of right and responsibility are linked to the particular communities to which people belong. Parekh tells a story of a Bangladeshi man attempting to enter

Britain with two children. At first he told the immigration officer that the two boys were his but later it transpired that they were his dead brother's sons. He argued:

> that his dead brother was not really separate from him, that their children had all grown up together . . . that each adult in the family had a moral obligation to look after the children of all of them, that this was how his society was constituted, and that he had additionally given a pledge to his dying brother to treat his children as his own . . . he saw no difference between his own and his brother's sons . . . Since the quota of two children had not been exceeded, he could not understand why it mattered. (Parekh, 1992, p. 170)

The officer accused him of making a fraudulent claim and they were deported. One reading of this story is that it illustrates cultural difference, differing images of family life and obligation. For some while children are valued, quite properly it will be adult visions of their best interests that will predominate. Yet the language of children's rights as deployed for example in the United Nations Convention on the Rights of the Child imagines distinguishable interests and separate concern for the wishes and feelings of children.

Social identities are multiple and multi-layered: the fact of belonging to different communities has within it the possibility of conflict and negotiation (see Keith and Pile, 1993). Friedman argues in the context of a feminist critique of communitarian theory:

> The problem is not simply to appreciate community *per se* but, rather, to reconcile the conflicting claims, demands, and identity–defining influences of the variety of communities of which one is part. (Friedman, 1992, p. 108)

It is, of course, not just a question of hierarchy within the family or community but hierarchy among communities: some central, some on the margin. Writing in the context of racism and sexual violence Crenshaw observes that one response to the racism of the majority population is to abide by a code of silence.

> Although abiding by this 'code of silence' is experienced by African Americans as a self-imposed gesture of racial solidarity, the maintenance of silence also has coercive dimensions. (Crenshaw, 1993, p. 420)

This coercion becomes most visible when someone 'breaks the code'. Oppression and disadvantage may only become public when someone breaks ranks, 'betrays' the community and, as a consequence, the racism of the majority population will be often confirmed. Yet, as Alston observes, there are many cases in which cultural arguments continue to be used to justify the denial of children's rights (Alston, 1994, p. 20). He argues that 'cultural considerations will have to yield whenever a clear conflict with human rights norms becomes apparent' (Alston, 1994, p. 21). However, some claims command more attention than others, some will be in harmony with the worldview of the majority culture.

Boyden, in her discussion of international rights and the welfare of children, writes:

> Some of the measures for child welfare — advocated often on humanitarian grounds — have the effect of isolating children further from their family and community and increasing their social and economic disadvantage. Innovative responses to the problems of childhood that are sensitive to customary law and practice and meet the needs of children — *that they themselves identify* — are rare. On the other hand, judgmental or repressive responses, involving elements of containment and correction are all too common. (my emphasis) (Boyden, 1990, p. 208)

Kent, addressing the question of universal right and differences in tradition and culture, writes:

> I want to show respect for others' views of what is right and wrong, but I also want to act with integrity, with respect for my own views of what is right and wrong. I want to take account of others' ways, but ultimately my action must be based on my own values and understanding of the situation. (Kent, 1992, p. 339)

Kent's argument is that respect for cultural diversity should not, and does not have to, lead one into moral relativism. His opposition to infanticide does not evaporate in the face of a longstanding traditional practice of infanticide. The fact that he is confronted by a culturally sanctioned practice, of which he disapproves, raises questions of strategy not substance. An-Na'im takes this argument further:

> To be effective in changing the beliefs, attitudes and behaviour of the relevant population, the proposed alternative perspective must be perceived by that population to be consistent with the internal criteria of legitimacy of the culture, and appreciated as relevant to their needs and expectations. (An-Na'im, 1994, p. 67)

He continues by observing that this requires that the proponents of change must be insiders and deploy arguments that have a resonance within that culture (*ibid.*, pp. 67–8). Otherwise the project will fail, and deserve to, in that it neglects the differing social contexts in which children live their lives. An-Na'im emphasizes the importance of approaching issues from the 'inside' not from outside — in order to avoid the self-imposed silences within minority communities from closing down channels of communication (see Crenshaw, 1993). A more constructive response is to work with oppositional groups (as An-Na'im advocates) — groups which are themselves both of their community and for a redefinition of their community. This is jeopardized, not advanced, by the use of tainted and culturally insensitive images.

The diversity of child-rearing practices poses a challenge for children's rights activists. It is one thing for us to declare that children have certain rights, it is quite another to persuade the different communities in our society of the rightness of this declaration especially when it can be read as undermining key beliefs and values and when the very language of rights, let alone children's rights, is seen as inappropriate in the context of notions of family life in the respective communities.

Children and Rights

The difficulties associated with the use of the language of community, historically and in the present, are clear (see Frazer and Lacey, 1993). The ideal of family life presupposes that children are part of, and brought up in, a loving and respectful environment: but this is not always the case. What kind of community is created and joined which is built upon the denial of a voice to children and curtails their participation? It is important to think in terms of shifting identities and communities, those bound together not by prescription but by tolerance and dialogue. Frazer and Lacey observe:

> We experience ourselves as embodied and socially-situated beings with multiple ties and commitments. Human life outside the context of human society, interaction and interdependence is evidently impossible. (Frazer and Lacey, 1993, p. 56)

Such a position might be seen to be antithetical to the language of rights insofar as rights language is seen to be an individualizing and alienating language. However such might not be the case. Olsen argues that the 'dominant conception of right presupposes an autonomous individual' and as children are not only not autonomous but also dependent such language appears particularly inappropriate. Olsen draws on the work of Minow (Minow, 1986) to argue that, within a feminist approach, it is possible to fashion a conception of rights which recognizes that rights are not just about the State–citizen relation but also about promoting more respectful relationships and interactions between people. With reference to children's rights this translates to:

> Rights that promote the ability of children 'to form relationships of trust, meaning and affection with people in their daily lives and their broader communities'. (Olsen, 1992, pp. 207–8)

Such relationships presuppose a participating and listened to child; it is not just a question of autonomy. Recently the Scottish Law Commission has recommended that before a parent makes a major decision affecting a child she 'shall, so far as is practicable, ascertain the views of the child concerned regarding the decision, and shall give due consideration to those views, taking account of the child's age and maturity.' (Scottish Law Commission, 1992).

Can struggles around rights advance the interests of children? Some see struggles for rights as valuable to those on the margins of society, for example women and ethnic minority groups, and as part of a strategy of meaningful inclusion rather than exclusion (Minow, 1987; Williams, 1991). Minow argues that the reality of the distribution of social power results in the law and legal processes having potentially very different meanings for people. The public violence of law (Sarat and Kearns, 1991) can be and has been used to challenge private violence. For many women and children the law's silence on domestic relations meant subjection to the power and violence of husbands and fathers. Law's silence did not, and does not, mean an absence of power; it meant, and means, the absence of a mechanism to challenge *private* power. Can children be participants in a struggle against the abuse of power, private as well as public? There are many examples of children taking action in pursuit of their own self-defined interests (see Hoyles, 1989). Such self-help will not always involve recourse to the law, for example rather than applying for a section 8 order (see the cases noted above) many children will simply run away to a 'safe house' (see Roche and Briggs, 1990). There are a growing number of children's organizations which are dependent on the participation of children and which can be seen as representing their interests for example the National Association of Young People in Care, the Children's Express and initiatives to involve children more in their communities (see Henderson, 1994).

New Conversations?

Parents should not always take priority over concern for the rights and welfare of children; children should not be silenced by, or for, their family. Families and communities can act to the disadvantage of children: indeed this is precisely the issue. The recognition of the possibility of the child having interests which are independent of their parents and community leads us to a consideration of how such interests might be expressed and how the wider community should facilitate and respond to such a voice. This brings us to a consideration of an 'inclusive politics of children's rights'.

The language of rights can make new stories heard in public and with far-reaching consequences (Scheppele, 1989; Delgado, 1991); it is one mechanism which permits the constitution of community. It is not the only one and it will not flourish on its own, outside of other developments. For example, in the case of children's rights, the activities of a range of organizations committed to promoting the interests of different children may dictate the direction and pace of change. Nevertheless rights talk as a critical public language is part of the process.

Children, of course, live in differently constituted households, in particular communities which are fundamental to their identities (inseparable from notions of their welfare and rights). In much of the children's rights literature 'the family' is assumed to be the western, nuclear family. There is little or no sense of other family forms or cultures. Within western society there is a plurality of family lives in which the boundaries of authority and responsibility differ.

Just as there is a variety of family lives and cultures so too is there a variety of childhoods according to dimensions of culture, class, gender and race. Children, of different backgrounds may make varying demands of adults regarding education, health, religion, marriage as well as regarding with whom they are allowed to associate. There is no single voice of childhood and there is no single audience. The dialogue between, on the one hand, the child's advocate and the child as advocate, and, on the other, adults and professionals will have to confront the issues of social difference and conflict of interests. Any such 'contest' will take place in a context of changing understandings of childhood which acknowledge and value the awkward voices. The words of Mary Dietz, writing on feminism and citizenship, have a resonance here:

> the power of democracy rests in its capacity to transform the individual as teacher, trader, corporate executive, child, sibling, worker, artist, friend or mother into a special sort of political being, a citizen among other citizens. (Dietz, 1992, p. 75)

Conclusion

The law and courts have not always responded well to the idea of children's rights. The retreat from Gillick (noted above) and the caution that characterizes the law in this sphere (O'Donovan, 1993) suggest that the law is limited in its ability to embrace the language and spirit of children's rights. But in a complex, fragmented society understanding requires dialogue, a public conversation among those involved. Once children are enabled to speak and be heard we may have to participate in new conversations (Minow, 1986; Stainton Rogers and Stainton Rogers, 1992). Children are talked about. What needs to change is how they are talked about and how children can connect with, and participate in, such conversations.

Those without the privilege of control of material resources, economic wealth and power (i.e., children) have only words and bodies with which to resist power's claims. The language of rights, citizenship and democracy may be a critical resource, 'the only capital' available. This language does not 'belong' to any one group or class; it is a constantly contested language whereby private and public experiences and interests are exchanged:

> In society meanings are not fixed, they are prizes in a pitched conflict among groups attempting to constitute their social identity by transforming the communicative tools that link their members together and set them apart from others. (Bowles and Gintis, 1986, p. 157)

This raises issues of community, identity and belonging: it is about who is 'in' and who is 'out'. Williams writes:

> For the historically disempowered, the conferring of rights is symbolic of all the denied aspects of their humanity: rights imply a respect that places

one in the referential range of self and others, that *elevates one's status from human body to social being.* (my emphasis) (Williams, 1991, p. 153)

The child's right to a voice, to participate must be part of this process: it is only through respect for children and their perspectives that a real community of interests, which includes all those who live within it, can come into being. Perhaps children's claims to rights, whether made by themselves or by committed adults, and the detail of these demands will become part of an enlarged democratic political process in which the focus is on citizenship, relationships and dialogue (see Young, 1990). Young's image/metaphor of the city which she uses to explore the possibility of 'social relations of difference without exclusion' seems appropriate here:

If city politics is to be democratic and not dominated by the point of view of one group, it must be a politics that takes account of and provides voice for the different groups that dwell together in the city without forming a community. (Young, 1990, p. 227)

Similarly, a commitment to children's rights requires a respect on the part of the majority (adult) traditions to the different lives led by our children and their different, and at times awkward, voices in the private as well as the public world. There will be inconsistent stories. Such new conversations will be difficult because, despite the cosiness of the word, they will not take place between equals and because in this post-modern world our traditional reference points of right and wrong have been eroded (Cahn, 1993). This is why children's rights are important and why their politics is so difficult and energetic.

Notes

1 See his judgments in *Re R* (A Minor) (Wardship: Consent to Treatment) [1992] 1 FLR 190 and *Re W* (A Minor) (Consent to Medical Treatment) [1993] 1 FLR 1.
2 For example, warning against an over-legalistic interpretation of the 'threshold criteria' in section 31(2) (*Newham L.B.C v AG* [1993] 1 FLR 281), the reference to the 'tyranny of language' in *Re M* (A Minor) (Care Order: Threshold Criteria) [1994] 2 FLR 577 and the High Court overriding the 'right' of a mature minor to refuse to submit to a medical assessment (*South Glamorgan C.C. v W and B* [1993] 1 FLR 574). This case concerned the exercise by a 'mature minor' of her right under the Children Act 1989 to refuse to submit to medical or psychiatric examination or assessment. Here Brown J. gave leave to the local authority to invoke the High Court's inherent jurisdiction in order to override the 15-year-old girl's refusal.
3 The guardian *ad litem* is an officer of the court and is appointed to represent the child's best interests. The guardian *ad litem* is not an advocate for the child in the sense of taking instructions from the child as a lawyer would. Rather he/she advises the court as to the course of action that would best advance the child's welfare.
4 There are four section 8 orders: contact, prohibited steps, residence and specific issue orders. These orders are pragmatic in that they are designed to resolve a particular dispute

regarding the child's upbringing and the exercise of parental responsibility; they do not fundamentally alter the powers and duties of those with parental responsibility for the child.

5 Part IX of the Family Proceedings Rules 1991, SI 1991/1247 which contains these new provisions is entitled 'Disability'.

6 Section 10 of the Act deals with who has a right to apply for a section 8 order and who requires the permission of the court before being able to apply.

7 See *Re SC* (a minor) (leave to seek residence order) [1994] 1 F.L.R. 96 and *Re C* (a minor) (leave to seek s.8 orders) [1994] 1 F.L.R. 26.

Case

Re C (a minor) (leave to to seek s.8 orders) [1994] 1 Family Law Reports 26
Re CT (a minor) (wardship: representation) [1993] 2 Family Law Reports 278
Gillick v West Norfolk and Wisbech Area Health Authority [1986] Appeal Cases 112
Re H (a minor) (care proceedings: child's wishes) [1993] 1 Family Law Reports 440
London Borough of Sutton v Davis [1994] 1 Family Law Reports 737
Re M (a minor) (care order: threshold criteria) [1994] 2 Family Law Reports 577
Newham London Borough Council v AG [1993] 1 Family Law Reports 281
Practice Direction [1993] 1 Family Law Reports 668
Re R (a minor) (wardship: consent to treatment) [1992] 1 Family Law Reports 190
Re S (a minor) (independent representation) [1993] 2 Family Law Reports 437
Re SC (a minor) (leave to seek residence order) [1994] 1 Family Law Reports 96
South Glamorgan County Court v W and B [1993] 1 Family Law Reports 574
Re W (a minor) (consent to medical treatment) [1993] 1 Family Law Reports

References

ALSTON, P. (1994) 'The best interests principle: Towards a reconciliation of culture and human rights', *International Journal of Law and the Family*, **8**, pp. 1–25.

ALSTON, P., PARKER, S. and SEYMOUR, J. (Eds) (1992) *Children, Rights and the Law*, Oxford, Clarendon Press.

AN-NA'IM, A. (1994) 'Cultural transformation and normative consensus on the best interests of the child', *International Journal of Law and the Family*, **8**, pp. 62–81.

AVINERI, S. and DE-SHALIT, A. (Eds) (1992) *Communitarianism and Individualism*, Oxford, Oxford University Press.

BAINHAM, A. (1990) 'The privatisation of the public interest in children', *Modern Law Review*, **53**, 2, p. 206.

BOWLES, S. and GINTIS, H. (1986) *Democracy and Capitalism*, New York, Basic Books.

BOYDEN, J. (1990) 'Childhood and the policy makers: A comparative perspective on the globalization of childhood', in JAMES, A. and PROUT, A. (Eds) *Constructing and Reconstructing Childhood: Contemporary Issues in the Sociological Study of Childhood*, London, Falmer Press, pp. 184–215.

BURMAN, E. (1994) *Deconstructing Developmental Psychology*, London, Routledge.

CAHN, N. (1993) 'Inconsistent stories', *The Georgetown Law Journal*, **81**, pp. 2475–531.

CHILDREN'S RIGHTS DEVELOPMENT UNIT (1994) *UK Agenda for Children*, London, CRDU.

CRENSHAW, K. (1993) 'Whose story is it anyway?: Feminist and antiracist appropriations of Anita Hill', in MORRISON, T. (Ed) *Race-ing Justice, En-gendering Power*, London, Chatto and Windus, pp. 402–40.

DELGADO, R. (1991) 'Storytelling for oppositionists and others: A plea for narrative', in PAPKE, D. (Ed) *Narrative and Legal Discourse*, Liverpool, Deborah Charles.

DEPARTMENT OF HEALTH (1994) *Guidance on Registration of Childminders and Smacking of Children*, London, HMSO.

DIETZ, M. (1992) 'Context is all: Feminism and theories of citizenship', in MOUFFE, C. (Ed) *Dimensions of Radical Democracy Pluralism, Citizenship, Community*, London, Verso, pp. 63–85.

DONZELOT, J. (1979) *The Policing of Families*, London, Hutchinson.

ELSTHAIN, J. (1989) 'The family, democratic politics and the question of authority', in SCARRE, G. (Ed) *Children, Parents and Politics*, Cambridge, Cambridge University Press, pp. 55–71.

FEDERLE, K. (1994) 'Rights flow downhill', *International Journal of Children's Rights*, **2**, p. 344.

FRANKLIN, B. (Ed) (1986) *The Rights of Children*, Oxford, Basil Blackwell.

FRAZER, E. and LACEY, N. (1993) *The Politics of Community: A Feminist Critique of the Liberal-Communitarian Debate*, Hemel Hempstead, Harvester Wheatsheaf.

FREEMAN, M. (1983a) *The Rights and the Wrongs of Children*, London, Frances Pinter.

FREEMAN, M. (1983b) 'Freedom and the Welfare State: Child-rearing, parental autonomy and state intervention', *Journal of Soc Welfare Law*, pp. 70–91.

FREEMAN, M. and VEERMAN, P. (Eds) (1992) *Ideologies of Children's Rights*, Dordrecht, Nijhoff.

FRIEDMAN, M. (1992) 'Feminism and modern friendship: Dislocating the community', in AVINERI, S. and DE-SHALIT, A. (Eds) *Communitarianism and Individualism*, Oxford, Oxford University Press.

GOLDSTEIN, J., FREUD, A. and SOLNIT, A. (1979) *Before the Best Interests of the Child*, New York, Free Press.

GORDON, L. (1989) *Heroes of their Own Lives: The Politics and History of Family Violence*, London, Virago.

HENDERSON, P. (Ed) (1994) *Children and Communities*, London, Community Development Foundation/Children's Society.

HOYLES, M. (1989) *The Politics of Childhood*, London, Journeyman.

JAMES, A. and PROUT, A. (Eds) (1990) *Constructing and Reconstructing Childhood: Contemporary Issues in the Sociological Study of Childhood*, London, Falmer Press.

KEITH, M. and PILE, S. (Eds) (1993) *Place and the Politics of Identity*, London, Routledge.

KENT, G. (1992) 'Little bodies international dimensions of child prostitution', in FREEMAN, M. and VEERMAN, P. (Eds) *Ideologies of Children's Rights*, Dordrecht, Nijhoff.

KING, P. and YOUNG, I. (1992) *The Child Client*, Bristol, Jordans.

LIDDLE, C. (1992) *Acting for Children: The Law Society's Handbook for Solicitors and Guardians ad Litem Working with Children*, Law Society.

MILNE, B. (1992) '. . . We just grew apart', *Childright*, **86**, May, p. 14.

MINOW, M. (1986) 'Rights for the next generation: A feminist approach to children's rights', *Harvard Women's Law Journal*, **9**, pp. 1–24.

MINOW, M. (1987) 'Interpreting rights: An essay for Robert Cover', *Yale Law Journal*, **96**, 8, pp. 1860–2017.

MIRINGOFF, M. and OPDYCKE, S. (1993) 'The index of social health: Monitoring the social well-being of children in industrial countries', A report for UNICEF, Fordham Institute for Innovation in Social Policy.

MOUNT, F. (1982) *The Subversive Family*, Jonathan Cape.

O'DONOVAN, K. (1993) *Family Law Matters*, London, Pluto.

OLSEN, F. (1992) 'Children's rights: Some feminist approaches to the United Nations Convention on the Rights of the Child', in ALSTON, P., PARKER, S. and SEYMOUR, J. (Eds) *Children, Rights and the Law*, Oxford, Clarendon Press.

PAREKH, B. (1992) 'The cultural particularity of liberal democracy', *Political Studies*, **XL**, Special Issue, p. 160.

PARTON, N. (1991) *Governing the Family Child Care, Child Protection and the State*, Basingstoke, Macmillan.

ROCHE, J. (1991) 'The Children Act 1989: Once a parent always a parent?', *Journal of Social Welfare and Family Law*, **5**, pp. 345–61.

ROCHE, J. and BRIGGS, A. (1990) 'Allowing children a voice: A note on confidentiality', *Journal of Soc Welfare Law*, **3**, pp. 178–92.

SARAT, A. and KEARNS, P. (1991) 'The jurisprudence of violence', in SARAT, A. and KEARNS, P. (Eds) *The Fate of Law*, Ann Arbour, Michigan University Press.

SCHEPPELE, K. (1989) 'Forward: Telling stories', Michigan *Mich. L. Rev.*, *Law Review* **87**, p. 2073.

SCOTTISH LAW COMMISSION (1992) *The Report on Family Law*, HMSO Edinburgh No. 135.

SMART, C. and SEVENHUIJSEN, S. (1989) (Eds) *Child Custody and the Politics of Gender*, London, Routledge.

STAINTON ROGERS, R. and STAINTON ROGERS, W. (1992) *Stories of Childhood: Shifting Agendas of Child Concern*, Hemel Hempstead, Harvester Wheatsheaf.

THE TIMES (1985) 18 October.

WILLIAMS, P. (1991) *The Alchemy of Race and Rights*, Cambridge, Harvard University Press.

YOUNG, I. (1990) *Justice and the Politics of Difference*, Princeton, Princeton University Press.

Chapter 4

Strategies and Structures: Towards a New Perspective on Children's Experiences of Family Life

Allison James and Alan Prout

Introduction

When we were asked to contribute perspectives on the sociology of childhood to a meeting of family sociologists it seemed at first rather paradoxical.[1] Paradoxical because, during the last fifteen to twenty years, those researchers working towards establishing the independent intellectual integrity of a sociology of childhood have engaged in a counter-endeavour: that of, wresting the study of children out of the familial context of socialization within which, for so many years, it was traditionally located (Alanen, 1992). Traditional texts on the family, invariably made but passing mention to children, subsuming their experiences of family life under index entries such as 'child-rearing', 'socialization' and 'education' or, alternatively, linking children with other adult-centred activities, viz, children 'and conjugal roles', 'and experts', 'and importance to parents' and children 'and punishment' (Anderson, 1971). Clearly, whilst children might have been seen within family sociology they were certainly not meant to be heard.

The late 1970s marked the end of the eclipse of the study of children and childhood by family sociology. Sociologists and anthropologists began to construct an independent sociology of childhood, a task which has now begun to produce results in the establishment of childhood as a separate empirical topic in both sociology and social anthropology. Although we have perhaps yet to realize fully the ambition voiced in those early days, of seeing a shelf in the bookshop marked childhood studies alongside those other new shelves for ageing and gender studies, nonetheless the sociology of childhood has made a reputable beginning. These developments might lead to the conclusion that the study of childhood has now, at last, come of age. After its unruly adolescence and disassociation, nay even disaffection, with the family, it is now grown up, set to return as a mature and reflective adult to be reunited with its parents. But whether or not this will represent the return of an acquiescent prodigal son or daughter remains to be seen. As this chapter argues it may offer, instead, a radical challenge, one which enables new perspectives to be brought to an understanding of the structure and process of family life.

Our task in this chapter, then, is to document developments in the sociological and anthropological study of childhood and to indicate the directions within which the sociological study of children is now moving, one of which is to engage with the sociology of the family. The family, we would argue, is becoming an important site within which child studies can be (re)located, not as a naturalized place derived simply and unproblematically from close affection and ties of kinship, but rather, as we shall go on to demonstrate, one among many of the social environments within which children literally find themselves. That is to say, the family represents a social context within which children discover their identities as 'children' and as 'selves' (James, 1994). Thus, we would argue, the ethnographic approaches which characterize contemporary sociological and social anthropological research into what children think and do, offer a mature, more sophisticated avenue for exploring processes of socialization, processes for which the family is an important context.

The agency which, through metaphor, we are attributing here to the sociology of childhood and to the family is neither incidental nor unintentional. As we shall show, what is new in the sociological study of childhood, is the very attribution of agency to children. And it is a discussion of what this agency might look like — how we might think about children as social actors and theoretically account for this — which forms a central part of our discussion. To continue the metaphor: perhaps the separation of the study of childhood from that of the family was also no accident. Like many children striving for independence in western societies, perhaps the sociology of childhood was only able to establish its autonomy through making a radical break with the family?

Our discussion of the coming of age of the sociological study of children and childhood centres, therefore, on the ways in which it might now be possible to conceptualize children in relation to their own, and indeed other, families. This arises out of our recent concern to account for variation and variety in children's social relationships as they move between different social domains. Discussed fully elsewhere, (James and Prout, 1995) our intention here is to look closely at how we might conceive of children's strategies and actions within the domain of the family through drawing on recent ethnographic fieldwork. In doing so we not only wish to demonstrate the scope and application of this new direction in the sociological study of childhood, in terms of both research and social policy, but also to relocate children back in the bosom of the family. But, this time, they will be active subjects.

Children, Childhood and the Family

The history of the sociological study of children and childhood begins with the concept of socialization, a concept which allocated the family a major influential role. The family, alongside the school, was seen as a major site for the socialization of children and, in studies until the 1960s, the question of the agency of children — the possibility that children might be studied as independent social actors — was rarely raised. Indeed, traditional socialization theory actively played down children's roles in two main ways.

First, children were seen to be the passive recipients of culture, rather than active participants in it. They were positioned simply as its disembodied vehicle in the next generation, as if, through socialization, culture was literally able to be imprinted upon the child. Within traditional accounts of socialization, for example, can be found little discussion of the ways in which social roles are taken on or learnt about; it was simply assumed that they are. So too, was there little recognition that the manner in which children themselves take on the part of 'being a child' might bear some relationship to the child's own understanding of what that role comprises. Thus, often no adequate explanation was proffered to account for the considerable variation in children's experiences of childhood both between and within cultures. It was assumed that children simply 'take on' the mantle of childhood, destined, in their turn, to become adult socializers of other children through later 'taking on' the familial role of parent (Prout and James, 1990). Although it was acknowledged that the manner of this transition to adulthood — this taking on — is extremely diverse historically, cross-culturally and inter-culturally, rarely were these differences credited with significance.

This oversocialized perspective on childhood's role in cultural reproduction (Wrong, 1961), which remained in vogue until the late 1960s, can therefore be held partly responsible for ensuring the continued subjugation of the study of children within family sociology, representing, as it did, the culmination of three centuries of rumination on the nature of childhood (Hockey and James, 1993, pp. 63–6). Out of the early Puritan conception of children as conceptually 'other', as being different from adults and therefore in need of rigorous cultural training, grew the notion that such differences were fundamental to the biological, rather than sociological, condition of childhood. Children's difference from adults simply reflected children's developmental lack. And, by the beginning of the twentieth century these western philosophical perspectives on children's nature were overlaid by the emerging scientific discourse of developmental psychology, a perspective which gave prominence to biological and psychological explanations of children's everyday *social* experiences (Prout and James, 1990).

Despite evidence gleaned from anthropological work in the 1930s–40s, which showed that the biological aspects of childhood might be seen as a context for rather than a cause of children's immaturity (Mead, 1928, 1963; Benedict, 1935), the inevitable outcome of this dominant developmental perspective was that children's agency became obscured. Biological development was held to be the key to children's growing up.[2] Children as competent actors — as people who could make decisions, argue against or indeed comply with social rules — was given little emphasis in explaining the process of becoming social. 'The child', indeed any child, was cited as an unproblematic representative of a largely undifferentiated category and until the late 1970s, therefore, children's experiences were still largely regarded as accountable in terms of the social roles allocated to the category of 'child'.

One of the casualties of this perception of 'the child' as a non-participant in the process of socialization was children themselves. As Armstrong (1983) has documented when children *did* make their social presence felt, by adopting patterns of behaviour which contravened the cultural codes and social rules which they were supposed to be so passively absorbing, questions were asked about the extent of these children's normality. Were they still children or were they children of a different kind? Thus, for example, it was partly the inability of socialization theory to explain why individual children 'failed' to become social which stimulated interest in the study of deviancy and which, in medicine, was associated with the increasing surveillance of the total child population. Regarded initially as evidence of a distinct bodily pathology — children who were delicate, nervous, over-sensitive, maladjusted — the anti or non social child came by the mid-twentieth century to be regarded as instancing wider social ills such as those associated with nominally dysfunctional families (Armstrong, 1983, p. 18).

Thus, although the unitary category of 'the child' had become fragmented by the mid-twentieth century — there were now identifiable subcategories of battered children, deprived children, sexually abused children — and, as Armstrong points out, the normality of 'the (ordinary) child' was becoming increasingly precarious too. Liberating certain sections of the child population from the constraints of the category of child had not therefore yielded them increasing agency; it had merely 'othered them' in a new, perhaps more stigmatizing, manner by frequently locating their difference within the body of the family, rather than the body of the child. Recent work on public perceptions of children and violent crime suggests that such a view remains highly influential today (James and Jenks, 1994). When children step over the boundaries of what it is to be a child — children abusing other children or children behaving like adults do — although blame may still be located within the child itself, attributed to its idiosyncrasy or malfunction, more commonly explanations are sought in the home environment. Rarely, if ever, are questions raised as to the adequacies of our own understanding of what childhood is; more rare still is any admission of the poverty of our knowledge about the everyday lives of children in or outside families.

Within sociology, however, the 1970s marked a watershed in the study of childhood through the emergence of the 'ethnography of childhood' movement. In a radical departure from traditional socialization perspectives, this challenged the hegemony of developmental psychology through claiming that childhood is socially constructed. Its main thrust was that the ways in which children are thought about vary cross-culturally and through time and that, therefore, the biological base of childhood should not be awarded any over-determining role in explaining how particular children live through that period in the life course known as childhood. Stimulated by the work of the French historian Phillipe Aries, published in 1962 and its subsequent critiques (for example, Pollock, 1983; Wilson, 1980), this debate became inextricably bound up with a focus on children's agency as researchers rallied to the call for explorations of the autonomous social worlds of children which would yield a child's eye view of the world (James and Prout, 1990).

Charlotte Hardman's work of 1973 represents one of the earliest of these accounts. In it she suggested that children might be seen as a muted group in society, a phrasing carefully chosen to illustrate the dominating presence of adult-centred world views in children's social lives. Children, she argued, can be seen as 'people to be studied in their own right, and not just as receptacles of adult teaching' (1973, p. 87). By beginning from a view of children as competent social actors in the social world, rather than as passive spectators of it or, more darkly, its malleable victims, Hardman's work thus engages directly with the vitality and visibility of children in the social world. And in doing so it represented a radical departure from traditional socialization studies, through its direct engagement with the world view of a group whose ideas and practices are often dismissed in the moment of their trivialization by a more powerful adult world. It was a shift in perspective which not only gave to children an agency which hitherto had been lacking, it also permitted the dismantling of the monolithic category of 'the child'. It would now be possible to account sociologically, rather than just pathologically, for variation and differences in the lives children lead.

By the 1990s, therefore, the study of childhood had moved from being the study of children as passive beings structured by the social context of the family or the school to the study of children's active part in that structuring. In essence a shift away from an emphasis on structure to one on agency, this change had been partly facilitated by the symbolic removal of children from their families. It was, seemingly, a necessary accompaniment. If children were to be studied in their own right then 'the family' had to be conceptually distanced for, within many families, children's rights often come second place to the right of parents to control and order the home environment. To study children 'in their own right' seemed more possible in contexts which were maximally under children's rather than adults' control: in the street or in the playground. That is to say, if in this new perspective, social structure was to be understood through children's own experience of it, it seemed appropriate to study children in contexts within which they could freely reflect on these experiences without fear of restraint.

Unsurprisingly, therefore, much early empirical work took place as school ethnographies. No doubt partly because of ease of access to schools as research sites (and the difficulties of carrying out research with children in the familial context) it is also important to note that in western cultures, the school provides one of the main contexts within which children's informal peer culture flourishes. Thus, it is one environment where children's agency can most easily be seen to predominate.

But this marginalization of institutional structures such as the family in accounting for the processes whereby children learn about the social world, simply will not do. First, although the abandonment of the family was perhaps an inevitable consequence of the shift towards recognizing children's agency, nonetheless, for most children 'the family' (together with the school) provides one of the more important social and emotional contextualizations of their everyday lives. Second, whilst the emphasis upon agency allows us to acknowledge the temporal flow of children's lives and, in contrast to traditional socialization theory offers the possibility to address questions of social and cultural change, it does not always permit us to properly account for the constraints which children themselves experience as a consequence of their membership of the category of 'child'. The family, for example, may operate many informal controls over children's activities through reference to their status as children, rather than as sons or daughters. Thus, as we have noted elsewhere, exploring children's agency divorced from one of its prime contexts of operation fails to give a satisfactory account of the totality of children's experiences:

> A more satisfactory theoretical perspective would be one which could account for childhood as a structural feature of society *in the moment* of its impinging upon children's experiences in daily life and, conversely, the reshaping of the institution of childhood by children through their day to day activities. In essence, it would address both structure and agency in the same movement. (James and Prout, 1995)

What we wish to suggest now is how we might begin to tackle such a 'double pronged' approach.

Social Environment, Hierarchy and Boundary

Our recent engagement with this problem (James and Prout, 1995) develops the insights of cultural theory outlined in the work of the social anthropologist Mary Douglas. In particular it makes its starting point her grid-group theory which we use as an attempt to explore the dynamics of social interaction found in very different environments.[3] This allows us to embrace children's experiences as both subjective agents and the recipients of other people's socializing through the institutions of family, school and the State. In short, it allows us (after some modification) theoretically to reunite children with their families without abandoning the recent advances made in the sociological study of childhood.

Douglas's argument is first that social environments range from ones which have strong classificatory 'grids' or, as we term it hierarchies, to those which are loosely ordered with little in the way of differentiating hierarchies. Second, all social environments also have implicit ways of regulating group belonging, what we term boundaries; again there is a wide range to be found between two extremes, from social contexts which are strongly bounded and to which entry and/or exit is strictly controlled to those which have a more open access and weaker boundaries. When combined these concepts create a four-field space and, Douglas argues, all social contexts can be located somewhere within it. Thus, although the range of possibilities is infinite all social contexts will exhibit weaker or stronger degrees of hierarchy and weaker or stronger degrees of boundedness.

The applicability of these ideas for understanding children's experience of different social contexts lies, we suggest, in its potential as a tool to inform and guide ethnographies. Not to be used as a ready-made description of social environments, it rather opens up the possibility of exploring children's agency in the very moment that children themselves are learning about and coming to grips with the constraints and possibilities of the very differently structured environments they encounter in their everyday lives.

For example, a better understanding of *children's* experiences of family life, rather than the familial experience *per se*, might be gained by considering the different kinds of constraints which hierarchical (grid) and boundary structures (group) within different families might place upon children's social experiences. We would begin to acknowledge and theoretically account for the very many different family environments in which children live — for example, lone-parent families, large extended families, step-families, reconstituted families. All of these represent different ways of belonging to 'the family' for children, facilitating different forms of social action by children both within and outside the family environment.

Moreover, within these different kinds of families there will be a range of diverse cosmologies shaping the day to day flow of family life: families which place high premiums on discipline and punishment at one extreme and, at the other, those whose lack of hierarchical orders is more reminiscent of the swinging 1960s than the back to basics 1990s. The experience of family life of children from these very different kinds of home environments would, we suggest, again be quite dissimilar and permit children access to very different perspectives on social action with ramifications beyond the family environment.

In short, then, what the use of this approach offers is one way of beginning to explore children's experiences of different family environments and of individual children's experiences of the different kinds of social environments that they experience as they move, for example, beyond the boundaries of the family itself, venturing into other peoples' families or other institutional settings such as schools. With this twin perspective 'children's socialization' can be examined as the highly creative experience it in fact is. No longer is it necessary to see children's experience of 'the family' as a necessary function of either a particular structural family form nor simply the outcome of particular parenting practices. Neither does it entail any implicit ranking of family forms on an absolute scale against which children's experiences of childhood can be judged — for example, middle class as against working class family contexts — as was sometimes the case with more traditional socialization approaches. Through combining an emphasis upon children's agency with a focus on the structuring of social environments children can be seen as the strategic social actors that they are.

Strategic Action

What our approach draws attention to — indeed forces attention on — is the different experiences of 'childhood' which different children have. It therefore also raises questions about the different constraints which children encounter in this process; not only between one family and another — my family, his family, their family — but also about children's experiences as they move between one social environment and another, social environments through which 'childhood' is daily experienced by children — the street, the school, the playground. In the mundane course of their everyday lives children move between different environments with (amongst other features) different hierarchy and boundary characteristics. How do children deal with, and make sense of, these experiential shifts? How do they learn the different styles of behaviour which each environment may encourage or require and how do they learn which kinds of action are appropriate to which kinds of context? Such questions invite others: through the life course, how do children learn new styles of agency appropriate to the new environments they encounter: as infants, rather than babies; as adolescents rather than children; as young adults rather than teenagers.

Clearly, children manage to achieve different degrees of the necessary strategic flexibility to ensure their transition between social domains but what traditional socialization perspectives cannot provide is any theoretical account of how it is that they do so. In this section we consider the extent to which our approach offers such an account through allowing exploration of children's competence as strategic social actors.

Childhood and Fractal Identities

Let us imagine a child ethnographically observed in the different social environments that make up the shifting contexts of their social lives: at home, in school, in the playground etc. If we were to do this it would be possible to see how different modes of action (that is to say different ways of being an agent) might be being employed in these different settings. Going further we might argue that different children could be understood in terms of their strategic flexibility in moving between social environments characterized by the different sectors of the hierarchy–boundary diagram. For example, children might be seen as moving between the age-bound hierarchy of the school, the more fluid and shifting social context of a youth club and then entering a tightly bound family household. What sorts of agency engage with which kinds of structures and to what extent is children's consciousness shaped as a multi-subjective set of 'selves' by the experience of moving between these different social environments (James, 1994)?

Like other writers such as Strathern (1987) and Adam (1988) we find metaphors drawn from chaos mathematics useful in communicating a sense of complexity to social environments.[4] The celebrated Mandelbrot Set (Gleick, 1987), for example, is a complex and intricate diagram of a fractal curve. It has the extraordinary property of being infinitely recursive; each point of its complex shape recapitulates the shape as a whole, and each point of the recapitulated shape does the same — *ad infinitum*. So, perhaps, with social environments: each part of the complex social pattern can be thought of as recurring through social structure, in organizations, groups and networks, in individual interaction and in the multi-subjectivity of individual actors. Children might be thought of as having multiple identities and subjectivities, each both an effect and a cause of the environments within which they engage.

Seen in this light the actions of individuals become susceptible to the same analysis as groups, an idea that has been applied by Strathern (1991) and Wagner (1991). The latter expresses the notion through his term 'fractal person'. This is someone who:

> . . . is never a unit standing in relation to an aggregate, or an aggregate standing in relation to a unit, but always an entity with relationships integrally implied. (Wagner, 1991, p. 163)

Actions by a person in a social setting might, therefore, be seen as having the same characteristics of, for example, the hierarchy–boundary pattern which we made our starting point. Indeed, action becomes based upon strategies related to particular social environments. Since in practice, however, no-one strategy can meet all the requirements of ongoing social life, mixed and shifting strategies will be found. All the actors in the situation more or less understood all the strategies of action and all more or less skilfully employed all of them — not withstanding their possible tendency to occupy, and identify with, one particular position and its associated strategy of action.

Within traditional socialization theory and sociological studies of childhood prior to the later 1970s children were seen to be simply constrained by the environments within which they found themselves. What the emergent paradigm within the ethnography of childhood has begun to see is the possibility of understanding children as complex actors in, and interpreters of, a complex world. What is needed now, we suggest, is to examine the variety of forms of engagement which children have with the hierarchies, the boundaries and other features of the social situations in which they are located; to trace how their knowledge of those environments becomes translated into the strategies of action which they use — sometimes effectively, sometimes not — as engaged and embedded but also mobile actors confronting different social settings.

For example, whilst much research has shown how gender operates as a highly structuring feature in children's social lives, imposing a rigid separation between boys and girls, variability in the ways in which gender differences are articulated and experienced by children themselves through social encounters has been more rarely discussed. A glimpse of the shifts in the significance of gender is offered by James's (1994) ethnography. This shows, for example, that whilst 7-year-old English girls might play with boys at home and maintain cross-gender friendships in that setting, within the school a rigid demarcation of age and gender comes into operation. For the school day such social interactions are suspended. One such cross-gendered friendship was for example, terminated and rekindled each day at the school gate.

A more explicit consideration of the differences between the structured environments of the family and the school which encourage or inhibit such strategic action by children would add considerably to this account, allowing us to see the social contexts within which children's agency is embedded. James's main focus on agency, while providing a welcome caution against assuming the constancy of gender as a significant difference in children's lives, does not explore on what grounds and in what ways particular choices about gendered friendships are made by children.

In the same ethnography, account is given of a rare cross-gender friendship which flourished within the school among two 9-year-old children. Explanation of this focused again on the children's perspective alone, with the boy's friendship with a girl seen by his class mates as further demonstration of his ambiguity within the larger group of boys: tall, strong and bookish in inclination, this boy, teased as one who had a friend-who-is-a-girl, might just possibly be the admired boy who had a girlfriend. The other boys could not be sure. What perhaps we see here is a moment in a complex process in which children explore strategies of action and create ambiguous, shifting and multiple identities.

Recognition of the necessary strategies of action which are needed within particular social environments *and* the circumstances in which they can be cross-cut, mixed and even reversed, both have an important bearing on the success with which children learn to 'take on' social roles. Although all children acquire knowledge of the social world through various kinds of social interaction, through media and through more explicit instruction, not all children recognize the subtle biases which are to be found in different social environments. Not all children learn the skills necessary to switch or mix behaviour or styles of action between different social environments. At school this difference in ability may illuminate much about the position of the outsider, the friendless child or the bully's victim and may also explain why the same child may, at home, be a favoured offspring. Such a child has less competence and flexibility as a strategic social actor. What our framework begins to explore is the processes of such phenomena.

Conclusion

In contrast to the approach outlined here, traditional socialization theory posits a finite model of agency: the child at home, in the street and at school is in all respects the same child. In our approach this same child, finds multiple expressions of the self through engagement with different sets of people in different social groups. Whether these are age mates or members of the family each interaction both contributes to, and is an expression of, that child's belonging because outside of that engagement the 'group' — be it family or gang — has no life. Whether family relations are strictly controlled or allowed free expression, they are but the outcome of the ways in which a particular idea of 'the family' is constituted through social encounters. Thus it can be seen that the strategies and styles of behaviour which children adopt across and between different social environments are both the context for, and the outcome of, children's experiences of belonging. Socialization can only be glimpsed, therefore, in the moment and context of its accomplishment, just as, in a very real sense, the family is only accomplished through contextualizing the lives of children. Thus in allowing us to explore how styles of agency change as children mature and as children move between different social environments sociology can at last re-insert children in families whilst not awarding 'the family' any priority in shaping the outcomes of socializing processes. And if, as we are suggesting, childhood is a key site for studying the formation of both agents and agency, then the ethnographic study of children should continue to provide an opportunity for exploring processes of cultural reproduction, socialization and change, processes in which the family has a key part to play.

Notes

1   This chapter was first given as the opening address to the Conference of the International Sociological Association's Committee for Family Research, London 1994.

2   The relationship between nature and culture in the constitution of childhood is discussed in Prout, 1994.

3   We use Douglas's grid-group approach strictly as a convenient but creative starting point which highlights two putatively important dimensions of social environments. We do not wish in any way to exclude other dimensions or modes of analysis. In the argument that follows three key theoretical differences separate our position from that of Douglas. First, that the possibilities generated by hierarchy–boundary combinations are not necessarily stable — indeed they are necessarily unstable. Second, that the implicit argument of scale made by conventional grid-group theory (that the 'big' social environment holds the 'small' actor in place) is also unnecessary. Third, and as a consequence of the former two arguments, that the theoretical humanism (holding that actors are an irreducible point outside of the social field) implicit in much grid-group writing should be reformulated. These theoretical points are developed in James and Prout, 1995. Grid-group theory is discussed, *inter alia*, in: Douglas, 1973, 1982 and 1992.

4   The argument we are making here is similar to that of Strathern (1987). She uses another concept of chaos mathematics (Cantor's Dust) as a metaphor for the process by which each part of a social whole reproduces the whole. Similarly, Adam (1988) calls on the example of the holographic plate, each fragment of which contains not a part but the whole of the image inscribed in it. The picture of social life which emerges from these considerations is a complex patchwork of groupings which merge into, contain and recall one another.

References

ADAM, B.E. (1988) 'Social versus natural time: A traditional distinction re-examined', in YOUNG, M. and SCHULLER, T. (Eds), *The Rhythms of Society*, London, Routledge.

ALANEN, L. (1992) *Modern Childhood?: Exploring the Child Question in Sociology*, Jyvaskyla, University of Jyvaskyla.

ANDERSON, M. (1971) (Ed) *Sociology of the Family*, London, Penguin.

ARIES, P. (1962) *Centuries of Childhood*, London, Jonathan Cape.

ARMSTRONG, D. (1983) *Political Anatomy of the Body: Medical Knowledge in Britain in the Twentieth Century*, Cambridge, Cambridge University Press.

BENEDICT, R. (1935) *Patterns of Culture*, London, Routledge and Kegan Paul.

DOUGLAS, M. (1973) *Natural Symbols*, Harmondsworth, Penguin.

DOUGLAS, M. (Ed) (1982) *Essays in the Sociology of Perception*, London, Routledge and Kegan Paul.

DOUGLAS, M. (1992) *Risk and Blame: Essays in Cultural Theory*, London, Routledge.

GLEICK, J. (1987) *Chaos: Making a New Science*, London, Cardinal.

HARDMAN, C. (1973) 'Can there be an anthropology of children?', *Journal of the Anthropology Society of Oxford*, **1**, 2.

HOCKEY, J. and JAMES, A. (1993) *Growing Up and Growing Old: Ageing and Dependency in the Life Course*, London, Sage.

JAMES, A. (1994) *Childhood Identities*, Edinburgh, Edinburgh University Press.

JAMES, A. (1995, in press) 'On being a child: The self, the group and the category', Paper to be presented at the Association of Social Anthropologists Conference, Anthropology and Consciousness, St Andrews University, Scotland.

JAMES, A. and JENKS, C. (1994) 'Public perceptions of childhood criminality', Paper presented to ESRC Seminar Series 'Childhood and Society', Keele University, July.

JAMES, A. and PROUT, A. (1995) 'Hierarchy, boundary and agency: Towards a theoretical perspective on childhood', in AMBERT, A. (Ed) *Sociological Studies of Childhood*, New York, JAI Pres.

JAMES, A. and PROUT, A. (1990) 'Re-presenting childhood: Time and transition in the study of childhood', in JAMES, A. and PROUT, A. (Eds) (1990) *Constructing and Reconstructing Childhood: Contemporary Issues in the Sociological Study of Childhood*, London, Falmer Press.

MEAD, M. ([1928] 1943) *Coming of Age in Samoa*, London, Penguin.

MEAD, M. (1963) *Growing Up in New Guinea*, London, Penguin.

POLLOCK, L.A. (1983) *Forgotten Children: Parent–Child Relations from 1500 to 1990*, Cambridge, Cambridge University Press.

PROUT, A. (1995) 'Nature–culture dualism: Reflections on childhood, social constructionism, the body and technology', Paper to the ESRC Seminar series 'Childhood and Society', Keele University, December.

PROUT, A. and CHRISTENSEN, P. (1995, in press) 'Children and medicine use: Theorizing the cultural differences', in BUSH, P., TRAKAS, D., PROUT, A. and SANZ, E. (Eds) *Children, Medicine and Culture*, Bingham, NY, Haworth Press.

PROUT, A. and JAMES, A. (1990) 'A new paradigm for the sociology of childhood?', in JAMES, A. and PROUT, A. (Eds) *Constructing and Reconstructing Childhood: Contemporary Issues in the Sociological Study of Childhood*, London, Falmer Press.

STRATHERN, M. (1987) *Partial Connections*, Savage, Maryland, Rowman and Littlefield.

STRATHERN, M. (1991) 'One man and many men', in GODELIER, M. and STRATHERN, M. (Eds) *Big Men and Great Men: Personifications of Power in Melanesia*, Cambridge, Cambridge University Press.

WAGNER, R. (1991) 'The fractal person', in GODELIER, M. and STRATHERN, M. (Eds) *Big Men and Great Men: Personifications of Power in Melanesia*, Cambridge, Cambridge University Press.

WILSON, A. (1980) 'The infancy of the history of childhood: An appraisal of Phillipe Aries', *History and Theory*, **XIX**, 2, pp. 132–53.

WRONG, D. (1961) 'The oversocialized conception of man in modern sociology', *American Sociological Review*, **26**, pp. 184–93.

Chapter 5

The Challenge in Child Research: From 'Being' to 'Doing'

Anne Solberg

During my career as a child researcher, I have, from time to time, had questions and comments from my colleagues, experienced in gaining knowledge about the social world from adults, concerning methodological issues in the study of children.[1] A common assumption underlying most of these enquiries has been that studying children is significantly different from studying adults. Doing research which involves the use of informants of young age presupposes, they seemed to assume, a special knowledge about children and competence in some particular child-centred techniques.

For a long period I rejected such comments without giving them much consideration. My own experience from doing interviews and participant observation with people of different ages, was that studying children was nothing special. Therefore, in my view, there was no need to discuss matters of methodology with particular reference to young informants. Increasingly I have however reached the conclusion that some issues are worthy of attention. My interest is not directed primarily to questions of method in a narrow sense, as techniques, but to the broader issues of how knowledge arises in the research process, and in particular to our own role as research instruments. The study of children and childhood seems to confront us with a twofold challenge with regard to the problem of ethnocentrism. Like other researchers sharing a culture, we risk being ethnocentric. Because we are positioned within that culture as occupying adult roles, notably in families, we may have difficulty in obtaining the necessary distance to reflect on adult ways of conceptualizing children and childhood.

The work of other researchers who have drawn attention to methodological issues in child research have influenced my own interest in these matters. I share the preoccupation, common amongst child researchers, with the question of what kind of knowledge it is possible for adults to gain about children (Alanen, 1988, 1992; Kitzinger, 1990; Thorne, 1987; Waksler, 1986).

My methodological interest derives also from the discovery in my own research that reflexivity may be an important source of knowledge. The exploration of the interaction between researcher and researched, and the special case of adult–child interaction, may throw light on adult–child interaction in general, and therefore tell us something about how childhood and age are constructed in contemporary society. It seems to me that the potential for gaining knowledge about social reality by studying one's own research relations is largely unused by social scientists with an interest in children and childhood (for an exception see Baker, 1983).

The growing body of social science literature concerning children's life conditions and personal experiences includes however valuable accounts of the data gathering process and reflections on the role of the researcher, which may represent a useful point of departure for such analyses (for example, Fine and Sandstrom, 1988). A main objective of the present article is to direct attention to what I see to be an obstacle to making full use of this potential. There is a tendency among social scientists experienced in researching children to stress the importance of considering the age-specific personal qualities of this group of informants.

Although one obviously has to approach a 4-year-old differently from a 14-year-old, in ordinary social interaction as well as in research encounters, I suggest a certain reluctance among researchers with respect to drawing conclusions about these differences, because this may maintain and strengthen our prior assumptions about how children 'are'. If we want to gain knowledge about the shaping of childhood in contemporary society and the significance of age and status within different contexts and situations, we should avoid letting such assumptions influence our approach. I recommend instead a certain ignorance of age. This implies greater emphasis on the situational contexts within which children act and that we move our attention away from 'being' to 'doing'.

In exploring these issues I shall make extensive use of my own research experiences with children which have covered a variety of methodological approaches: participant observation in a study of children's work in the fishing industry in northern Norway; a national survey of children's work using prestructured questionnaires; and a qualitative study of the organization of everyday life of children in families with open-ended interviews. These research encounters have varied from highly structured environments with few opportunities for informants to influence the research to relatively open settings with greater possibilities to do so. In addition, they have ranged from studying children in a work context outside the home to those in which children were positioned within families.

Exploring Research Relations in Participant Observation

Whilst my first fieldwork experience was in a setting where no young people were present, namely a mental hospital, it threw up methodological problems and challenges similar to those which I encountered in my first research project with children in a fishing community.[2] This experience may have influenced my reluctance to conclude that studying children is any different from studying other people. I shall briefly explore my research relations in these two different settings, paying attention both to how I gained trust from the participants and to how I engaged with the analysis of the social system.

My first months in the mental hospital were extremely difficult. I could not find any clues or patterns to pursue in a sociological analysis and, even worse, I did not feel at all comfortable being present in this setting. In spite of great efforts to present myself and explain my presence, I never felt that the independent research role which I tried to play was fully accepted. The patients in particular seemed to be confused about how to classify me. However with time and change of setting, my relationship to both patients and attendants improved significantly and, obviously related to this, research questions 'emerged' before my eyes almost instantly. The significant change was a move from a hospital ward to a department of occupational therapy, where the patients were engaged in producing bandage compresses for the pharmaceutical industry.

I learned three lessons from these experiences. The first was that research roles are negotiated. An important reason why my efforts to play an independent role did not succeed was that the members of the institution would not allow me such a role. We did not reach any 'agreement' about my position. Secondly, I learned that mistakes can be productive. The confusion deriving from doubt about how to classify me was productive in my understanding of how deeply the two groups of patients and attendants were separated on the hospital ward. My third lesson was that my relation to the participants improved greatly when we had work in common as a medium of interaction. I felt much more relaxed about being present and about talking to my informants when we all shared in the production of bandages. Similarly my co-workers seemed to be quite comfortable with me being there; some explicitly stated that they appreciated having someone to talk to.

However, this talking-while-working relationship with the patients was soon disturbed by the attendants who turned to me, increasingly often, for assistance in speeding up productivity. They were worried about how to keep to agreed delivery dates, negotiated with the management of the hospital and the recipient of the bandage compresses. I was quite disturbed by this demand and resisted adapting my research role to fit in with the organizational constraints of the hospital. But I found it difficult to reject direct requests for assistance, even if it sometimes implied that for periods of time I moved physically away from the patients. I noticed a change in my attention from being primarily occupied with the situation of the patients to being increasingly occupied with the dilemmas of the attendants. At this point in my fieldwork I perceived the situation of the two groups to be very different, and I complained that I was unable to balance my involvement. Later I realized that my involvement with the attendants contributed to my understanding of the relation between the groups in important ways. The pressure on production and the bad communication within the organization as a whole meant that the department of occupational therapy shared some of the characteristics of an ordinary place of work, and the relation between patients and attendants resembled human relations outside the hospital. Work seemed to diminish the relevance of madness.

An important reason for choosing, several years later, to study children's work by taking part in that work myself was the experience gained from the mental hospital, namely that a work role was a highly productive research role. In a fishing community in northern Norway, the work of baiting longlines (which involves putting pieces of bait on to hooks attached to long fishing lines) offered excellent opportunities to enter such a research role. Firstly, there was an extensive demand for labour, and anyone who had some spare time, local people or visitors, were welcome to take part as long as there was space in the workplace. Secondly, the work was simple; no long training was necessary to master baiting, evident in the fact of the young age of some of the baiters. Thirdly, baiting was highly flexible; there were no fixed working hours and, I was told, the baiters could choose whether to turn up or not and decide themselves on how much work to do. I also learned that it was easy to talk while doing the work, since the work was done by hand and no noise from machinery disturbed conversation. Altogether, this context seemed well fitted for getting information about the position of children in the work system.

Entering the baiting role implied acquiring particular practical skills, as well as knowledge about the system of negotiations on which the baiting of longlines is based. The first steps in my baiter career I learned by watching, listening and imitating others, as well as by breaking rules that were previously unknown to me but were made explicit through others sanctioning deviant behaviour. Elsewhere I have described this process in detail (Solberg, 1994, pp. 165–71).

As my fieldwork proceeded, my research role was shaped through further negotiations. As in the mental hospital I felt a growing commitment to sharing the workload with my co-workers when the demand was extensive. Initially my reason for taking part in the baiting was to enter a position from which I could watch the working children closely, interact with them and gain first-hand knowledge about the work. When asked to take a second tub of longlines or return the next day, I was flattered to be taken into account as a 'real' baiter, and accepted the request if it fitted into my research plans. Little by little I found it hard not to comply with the requests without having a good reason. I soon learnt that exchanges about what reasons were 'good' and how to rank them were central when the tubs of longlines were distributed.

A reason not to bait which was never questioned concerned the children's school attendance. However, at the end of the school-day — at about two o'clock — being young was not seen as a 'good reason' for staying away. Just as work seemed to diminish the relevance of madness in the mental hospital, the status of worker seemed to make the status of child subordinate in the baiting setting. In both situations I had problems making my status as a researcher relevant. Both social systems subordinated all other statuses to that of worker. Through reflecting on my own experience in the role as sociologist in these two settings, it was possible to see how work had a formative influence on the patterns of interaction in both of them.

I was more aware in the fishing community than I had been in the hospital about how my interpretations changed during the fieldwork. When entering the workplace for the first time, the mixture of age groups struck me as rather special. Workers, ranging in age from about 8 to 60 mingled as they prepared the tubs of longlines for fishing. In spite of the differences in age they did exactly the same kind of work. Their working tools were identical too, except for one item. The shortest of the workers had specially made crates to stand on in order to achieve the right height for work.

The differences in age, which appeared initially so significant to me, weakened during my observation of, and participation in, the work. The similarities between us appeared increasingly apparent to me as the days passed. Whether schoolchildren, housewives, retired fishermen or researchers, we 'grew' alike through baiting the same kind of hooks. One episode in the first days of fieldwork stands out for me as a critical case of the 'disappearance of age'. A boy of about 11 years was complaining to his parents about the work. He repeatedly asked what time it was, and I learned he wanted to leave the work place to join in the Bingo at school. When no-one seemed to take notice, he turned to his mother and asked her to complete his tub. To me his voice sounded 'childlike', and I noticed he was rather thin and considerably shorter than myself. Had she heard him? She obviously had. By continuing her work she demonstrated to all of us, what we (including her son) already knew, that if she took over his tub she could not at the same time complete her own, and the entire baiting work would be delayed. In relation to this, she implicitly said, our different ages do not matter. At that moment I saw him grow. I asked myself, as Ariès (1962) did, whether 'childhood' existed in this situational context.

Much later my interpretation of this and similar episodes broadened. From being occupied with the observation that concepts of what children can do and what childhood is about varies in contemporary Norwegian society, I became increasingly engaged with the ways in which the meaning of childhood and age are made the subject of negotiations. Rather than pointing out that 'age and status do not matter' within the work situation, my attention was now directed to *how* 'age matters' and the verbal and non-verbal exchanges involved in 'deciding' this. In the situation referred to above, the boy tried to make age a relevant category since this would give him some personal benefit, but it did not succeed. Generally, requests to be exempt from work were ignored on account of being young and wanting to engage in leisure activities. This does not imply that in distributing the tubs consideration was not taken of the workers' wishes to take part in outside activities, nor that children had no way of escaping work commitments. They certainly had, for example, by not turning up at the baiting place at all and, therefore, stating rather distinctly their own position.

These experiences based on participant observation formed the point of departure for my suggestion that child researchers should pay close attention to the research process in encounters between researcher and researched. Within both these settings work structured the interaction in ways that helped me to set aside previously taken for granted assumptions. In both places being a co-worker implied interacting on a fairly equal basis. Even if my position in the fishing community was special, my role as a beginner in some important ways resembled the role of other beginners such as children. Also, reflecting on the negotiations in which I was involved, explicitly about how many tubs to bait and implicitly concerning the extent to which my status as a researcher should be made relevant, gave me additional clues for understanding the negotiations in which children took part in this setting and the degree to which 'age' is a valid category.

Exploring Research Relations in Interviewing

With increasing interest within the social sciences in children's activities and subjective experiences, a growing number of researchers have turned children into informants.

A common point of departure for many of these researchers is that posing questions to children raises particular methodological problems, which have to be handled carefully if valid knowledge is to be produced. Attention is directed to the problem of understanding the child's world, seen as an inner world or culture. The relationship between researcher and researched is seen to be influenced more by issues of power–powerlessness than in other research relations, producing problems both of validity and ethics. The point that studying children raises special methodological questions is made with particular reference to structured and standardized approaches. The underlying argument here is that children are easily influenced, and that children's cultures are difficult to grasp with these methods.

My own experience of interviewing children covers both highly structured and less structured interviews. In neither did I make any special efforts to adjust the encounters to any assumed 'child-like' qualities of my informants. On the contrary, I ignored or bracketed child-oriented proposals. By letting children answer pre-structured questionnaires, I questioned the assumption that some techniques are better suited to studying children than others.

Questionnaires

In order to gain knowledge about the extent and distribution of a broad range of children's work activities, inside as well as outside the market, a sample of 800 five and six graders (11–12-year-olds) living in different parts of Norway was selected.[3] The methods were highly monitored and standardized. The interview took place during school-time in the class-room, and while the children were sitting at their desks. The researchers replaced the teacher for two school hours in order to monitor and assist the children in filling out a questionnaire.[4] Instructions were given before the actual process started, in front of the class, as well as to the children individually. During the interview, the children asked for assistance in the proper way of doing so in the school setting, by raising their hands.

Our choice of schools as a means of gaining access to children was based on sampling considerations. Choosing school classes means being able to get all or most children of a certain age in a particular area. The method also provided an opportunity to interview children in groups, a time-saving procedure. However, at the same time, we were conscious that within the school setting teachers ordinarily defined children's responses as correct or incorrect. In relating to the researchers, we feared that the children might be inclined to answer in line with what they assumed to be a 'correct' answer, rather than in accordance with their actual experiences. A main challenge for us was, therefore, to avoid making the children perceive the questionnaire as a test. To this end our strategy was, firstly, to express verbally, while introducing the interview, that the children were the experts on the matters which interested us. They seemed immediately to sympathize with our point of departure for this investigation; namely the lack of knowledge about children's work activities within social sciences. They also seemed to accept as a matter of course, that they were the ones who were chosen as best informants. Perhaps more importantly, we also tried to indicate through the actual structure of the questionnaires, that the correct answers were to be found in the concrete everyday life experiences of children. We did so by specifying, in a very detailed manner, the different work activities about which we wanted information, and directed the informants' attention to the issue of whether they had ever taken part in the task. If they had participated, they were further required to 'anchor' their experience in the past; had they performed the task yesterday, last week, last month, and so on.

The fact that the topic of the investigation was not 'school work' might have had some influence on the children's acceptance of the questionnaire as something other than a test. If the interviews had been conducted in the home-setting, the subject of work, and particularly of housework, might have made them give socially acceptable responses or report 'helpful' behaviour. It is probably easier to be aware of the influence of the school setting, and take action to reduce it, than it is to be conscious about how a home setting influences the interaction between researcher and researched. I shall return to the home setting later.

Several clues suggested that 'work', defined in terms of eighty household tasks, was of concern to our informants. Through their answers they indicated that these work activities belonged to their everyday experiences. During the interviews the children also expressed, both verbally and by their eagerness in filling out the questionnaires, that they found reporting on these activities of great interest. Of course, this positive reception should be viewed in the light of the children's alternative time use; taking part in the investigation exempted them from two hours of lessons.

We recognized an ethical problem connected with children's consent to take part in the study. In order to gain admission to the school to carry out the study, consent from several authorities was required: local education authority, headteacher, class teacher, parent–teacher association, and lastly the children's parents. But the children themselves, who were to be interviewed, were not asked to give their consent.[5] The right to refrain from participating in social science investigations has been strongly emphasized and particularly so with reference to children. Our experience from the school interviews made us recognize not only children's right to say 'no', but also their right to say 'yes'. Among the very few children who did not gain permission from home and had to leave the classroom to stay in the library during the administration of the questionnaire, there were some who looked as if they would have preferred to stay.

I have emphasized the point that in developing our technique to obtain information from a large number of children about a variety of household tasks, we largely ignored the 'child-oriented' advice to adjust our approach to the particular qualities of our young informants. However, we did not, of course, ignore the setting within which the questionnaire was administered. Our technique was designed to fit into the school setting, and would probably function rather well for other groups within similar settings, for example students and military recruits. It might be difficult to make use of the same technique in interviewing adults, who do not ordinarily find themselves in similarly regimented circumstances, and therefore are not as trained, like children are, to receive instructions. However, apart from discomfort about being instructed, which is likely to vary among groups of adults, adults would probably manage just as well as school children. People not able to read or write, because they have not learnt to do so or, for other reasons, would need special guidance.

Open-ended Interviews

In a further project I followed up the questionnaire study, broadening the concept of work to include what may be called 'hidden work' (see Wadel, 1979), for example negotiations over the sharing of work and managing single-handed. Through explorations of how children's families organize their everyday life, we hoped to gain some understanding of how children and their parents 'decide' what it means to be a child in a family.[6] As our interest was here in interactions and 'chains' of activities, and the actor's own reflections about these matters were essential, an exploratory approach seemed obvious. A 'life-mode interview', developed by Haavind (1987) and her associates, seemed useful for our purposes, and was applied in separately conducted interviews with members of ten families; mothers, fathers and children (Solberg and Danielsen, 1988; Solberg, 1990, 1994).[7]

My starting point in doing these interviews was to approach my informants from different generations in basically the same way. The life-mode interview seemed well-fitted for turning children and their mothers and fathers into 'sociological equals'. However, I experienced some problems in carrying this out. There were no difficulties due to any 'child-like' qualities of the child, or in our methods. Rather, the problem was about my own ability to relate as a sociologist to all my informants, and not to 'fall back' on relating as an educator — or as a mother — to those of young age. As I will show, my own professional code forced me to conduct the interviews according to the principle of approaching adults and children as equals. But also my partners in interaction during the interviews — the children themselves — supported my efforts to stick to the initial contract, and guided me back on 'track' when I had trouble in doing so. In other words one might say that, during the interview, interviewer and interviewee took part in exchanges at different levels, not only about the subject of investigation but also about how to interact.

Compared to the research encounters in the classroom, the interactions in the study of families was far less structured. Like all exploratory studies I approached every research encounter without knowing what would be the exact content of the conversation. The researcher's way of structuring the verbal exchanges in the life-mode technique lies in instructing the informant to give information in a particular way, by providing a detailed record of what happened the day before, using time as an organizing principle and moving slowly through the day from the moment of getting up to going to bed. The informant acts as the guide on the 'tour' through yesterday. However, the situations and events paid attention to can be seen as joint 'decisions' reached through negotiations. As the interviewer, I influenced these decisions by requesting more details about situations I found to be of special interest. For their part, the informants 'persuaded' me to become more interested in some parts of their stories than others by voice and mimicry. One of the themes which we agreed to pay particular attention to was the early afternoon when the children were at home with no adults present (Solberg, 1990, 1994). My own response to the children's accounts probably contributed to the children's emphasis on this part of the day.

Negotiations were also conducted concerning 'who is talking to who'. I shall illustrate the point by exploring aspects of the research encounter with one of my child informants, Annette. At a particular stage, I recognized in the interview that the young age of my informant was about to be made significant, not by Annette herself, but by me, in a way that would have been unproductive if I had not stopped myself.

My interview with Annette was one of my most successful child interviews. Annette looked enthusiastic at being invited to share her everyday life experiences, and very soon caught on to what I required namely a detailed account of what had happened the day before. The interview took place in Annette's bedroom, in the three-roomed flat she shared with her mother and younger sister in a suburb of Oslo. A significant part of the interview with Annette was about how she made use of the home and her efforts to secure her private territory: objects that did not belong there, sounds that were unwanted, and people who were not invited. She frequently pointed to her younger sister as a source of disturbance. Her sister played music which 'clashed' with the sounds that pleased Annette, left behind objects in Annette's room which proved she had been illegally present, and begged to be let inside when Annette excluded her.

In between these concrete accounts of yesterday and about what usually happened, Annette made some remarks about her little sister. She passed off these comments as statements of fact about her sister's character. On several occasions I was about to pick up on these comments. I felt it would be 'good' for Annette if she was helped to talk about something pleasant which the two of them had done together. I wondered how I could help her to do so. This impulse to guide Annette to give a more 'balanced' picture of her relationship to her sister did not last long however. I held myself back realizing that I was about to step away from my role as researcher, and that I was about to take on the role of an educator or mother.

Two matters were of particular importance in my 'withdrawal'. Firstly, my professional code prevented me from following my initial impulses. Comparing my encounter with Annette with my previous encounter with her mother was helpful in this respect. When I was introduced to Annette, I had already interviewed her mother. The two generations of females talked in a similar way about how they managed their everyday life, and appeared to me as two separate agents and, at the same time, as important negotiating partners in the life they shared. Seeing them side by side it seemed quite evident to me that I should respond to Annette in the same way that I had done with her mother, that I should listen carefully to their stories and show interest in them, without judging whether the content was 'fair' or not.

Secondly, my partner in the interaction supported me by responding in accordance with the same general rules which I had applied in the interview with Annette's mother. Annette did so by 'sticking' to the same way of talking as her mother had done on the day before. Her remarks about her younger sister's qualities were simply a 'sidetrack' in her account. Holding myself back from turning the relation to her sister into an educational issue, she continued on her 'main track' undisturbed. What I was about to do, if I had not stopped myself, was to move from my position as a sociologist to the position of an 'ordinary' adult, or rather an educator, and by doing so, turning Annette from being an informant into a minor in need of guidance (Waksler, 1986).

Concluding Reflections

The growing body of social science literature on children and childhood includes valuable reflections on methodological issues: basic epistemological questions, including what kind of knowledge researchers positioned as adults can get about children, as well as empirically based accounts of 'how I did it'. Further steps need to be taken in bridging the gap between these levels. The present article aims at taking such a step by exploring in some detail my own varied experiences of researching children. From this vantage point I shall try to draw conclusions about, and recommendations for, ways of gaining valid knowledge about the everyday life of children and the shaping of contemporary childhood. A central point here is how to bracket my own taken for granted assumptions of what children do and what childhood is like.

One such tentative conclusion is that some 'ignorance of age' may be helpful in setting aside prior assumptions. I noticed, on reflection, that this was the case in my own research. In the fishing community my concepts of childhood and age were modified through *experiencing* a situational context in which children to some extent were treated as 'nothing special'. This encounter with what to me was an exotic phenomenon created the necessary distance to make me reflexive about childhood. I had previously discussed concepts of work mainly in relation to concepts of adulthood, while concepts of childhood had belonged to the realms of play and socialization. Studying children and their work in this context allowed me to make a first break with the traditional concept of what children are, what children can do and what 'age' itself means.

I used 'ignorance of age' as a *technique* (although I did not see it as such until much later) in broadening my concept of work in the questionnaire study. In northern Norway it was necessary for me to pay close attention to the process of production, simply to learn what was going on. This focus on 'doing' implied a certain ignorance of the 'doer'. Looking in the same way for example at children taking part in activities which I had previously categorized as 'helping at home' made me recognize their productivity. To decide whether to conceptualize a task as work and include it in the questionnaire, I 'replaced' in my mind a child doing that activity with an adult. If the term 'work' seemed appropriate with an adult performer I would apply it to children as well. In conducting open-ended interviews with children I recognized that some ignorance of age was part of my professional code.

Other researchers present conclusions and advice that differ from mine. Generally recommendations for studying children include advice about the ways in which children differ from adults. For example, Fine and Sandstrom (1988) have examined methodological problems in ethnographic research with children and emphasize the problem of the authority adults in general possess over children. However, although they share the general assumption in ethnographic research that all groups should be treated as equals to the researcher, they stress the point that elimination of the power differential between children and adults may be ethically inadvisable (Fine and Sandstrom, 1988, p. 26). Researchers are reminded to take into consideration that 'children are "immature" . . . and not at the age of legal responsibility' (Fine and Sandstrom, 1988, p. 26). Thus, if children place themselves in danger, the participant observer has a moral obligation to take action to protect them, deriving from children being 'mischievous, sometimes aggressive, and occasionally cruel' (p. 26). Researchers are given warnings that 'Children of this age not only behave in ways that are unknowingly dangerous, but also knowingly and consciously behave in ways that are outside the rules set by adults. They even behave in ways that are morally wrong' (p. 55). The point is underlined 'that the researcher has to recognise that preadolescents will be exploring the boundaries of proper behaviour' (op.cit. p. 56).

I read in Fine and Sandstrom's account methodological recommendations at two different levels which to some extent are in opposition to one another. At one level the authors offer the opportunity to share their experiences about studying children by participant observation in particular settings. To me advice which derives from fieldwork experiences obviously is useful for researchers planning to carry out research in similar situational contexts. In addition, reflections on interactions between researcher and researched during ethnographic fieldwork, as in other kinds of data gathering, may constitute a valuable source for exploring the topic of research. For example, reflections about different fieldwork experiences may form a useful starting point for comparisons of how age is acted out in different situational contexts. Fine and Sandstrom's fieldwork seems to have been carried out in a setting in which age matters significantly, namely a baseball camp, a setting which is relatively unstructured and where the researcher was the only adult present, very different from the fieldwork setting in my fishing study. However, at another level, their fieldwork account may be read as a recommendation about how to study children in general. They emphasize age-specific qualities of the baseball players as if they were universal, which encourages a reading of the text at a very general level. This reading may act as a brake against making fuller use of the potential for knowledge at a lower level, by guiding our attention away from questions concerning how the parties involved 'decide' about how and to what extent age is to be made relevant within different situational contexts. The line of thought underpinning notions about how children 'are' arises out of the traditional developmental paradigm of psychology namely that children pass through particular stages on their way to adulthood, which have to be taken into consideration by those studying them.

My tentative conclusion to 'ignore age' does not imply any claims that children do not possess qualities different from adults. Rather my suggestion is that our concepts of such qualities should not influence ways of approaching children in social

science research. It should be open to empirical investigation to explore the significance of age and status within different contexts and situations, to explore 'doing'
rather than 'being'. My exhortation not to take account of age is meant as a recommendation to researchers to make an effort to set aside what we already 'know'
about how children and adults differ when they embark on fieldwork.

Notes

1   This article is based on experiences from several investigations of modern childhood and
    its conceptualization carried out over the last twenty years in Norway. Here questions of
    methodology are highlighted. For more substantial information about these studies I refer
    readers to Solberg, 1990 and 1994. Readers with knowledge of the Scandinavian language
    may also turn to Solberg and Vestby, 1987; Solberg, 1987; Solberg and Danielsen, 1988.
2   This study was done within a well-established sociological tradition which emphasized the
    situational context within which people act (Goffman, 1961). In this research tradition it
    is the norm to employ the same model of interpretation with all people and disregard
    the fact that high-ranked participants conceptualize low-ranked participants in particular
    ways. This tradition has still a weak position as far as child research is considered (but see
    Thorne, 1987 and Waksler, 1986), which indicates that it might be easier to bracket peo-
    ple's madness than their youth.
3   From an early stage in the data analysis, children's work in their own household, and
    particular tasks ordinarily categorized as 'housework' occupied my special attention. Partly
    this interest derived from the finding that this kind of work stood out as the most ordinary
    and most common work activity. Another reason for my special interest in children's house-
    work was that I wanted to emphasize that children contribute to the domestic division of
    labour, and to expose this fact to public statistics and social scientists who have ignored
    children's domestic production. (Solberg and Vestby, 1987; Solberg, 1994)
4   'Work activities' were defined by us to mean eighty concrete tasks, and the children were
    asked to mark for every one of these tasks whether or not they had ever taken part in
    that activity. When ticking a 'yes' for a particular task, they were instructed to respond
    to several follow-up questions; for instance when was the last time they performed the
    activity, how often and how much time they usually spent in doing the activity. Alter-
    natively, when ticking a 'no', they were told to go on to the next question. For further
    information about the questionnaire technique, see Solberg, 1994, p. 184.
5   We have no information about how decisions about children's participation in the invest-
    igation were made in the homes. In cases where parents had put a 'no' on the form which
    each child brought home to obtain permission, this 'no' might have been influenced by
    the children's own reluctance to take part. Our impression was however that refusals
    expressed first and foremost the parents' wishes.
6   The term 'child families' is directly translated from the Norwegian term *barnefamilier*. I am
    referring here to families in which one or more children are among the members. I prefer
    this to the English term 'Families with children' (corresponding to the Norwegian *familier
    med barn*) which focuses on the adults who *have* children among their other belongings.
7   This approach, which was initially designed for adult informants, has been further developed
    and successfully employed with children aged 8–9 (Gulbrandsen, 1994) and as young as
    4 years old (Andenæs, 1991).

References

ALANEN, L. (1988) 'Rethinking childhood', *Acta Sociologica*, **31**, pp. 53–67.

ALANEN, L. (1992) *Modern Childhood?: Exploring the 'Child Question' in Sociology*, Jyväskylä, Institute for Educational Research (Publication series A, Research reports 50).

ANDENÆS, A. (1991) 'Fra undersøkelsesobjekt til medforsker?: Livsformsintervju med 4–5-åringer', *Nordisk Psykologi*, **43**, pp. 275–92.

ARIÈS, P. (1962) *Centuries of Childhood: A Social History of Family Life*, New York, Vintage.

BAKER, C.D. (1983) 'A second look at interviews with adolescents', *Journal of Youth and Adolescence*, **12**, pp. 501–19.

FINE, G.A. and SANDSTROM, K.L. (1988) *Knowing Children: Participant Observation with Minors*, New York, Sage. (*Qualitative Research Methods*, **15**).

GOFFMAN, E. (1961) *Asylums*, New York, Doubleday.

GULBRANDSEN, M. (1994) 'Kulturens barn: En utviklingspsykologisk studie i 8–9-åringers sosiale landskap', Manuskript, Oslo, Universitetet i Oslo, Psykologisk institutt.

HAAVIND, H. (1987) *Liten og stor: Mødres omsorg og barns utviklingsmuligheter*, Oslo, Universitetsforlaget.

JAMES, A. and PROUT, A. (Eds) (1990) *Constructing and Reconstructing Childhood: Contemporary Issues in the Sociological Study of Childhood*, London, Falmer Press.

KITZINGER, J. (1990) 'Who are you kidding?: Children, power and the struggle against sexual abuse', in JAMES, A. and PROUT, A. (Eds) *Constructing and Reconstructing Childhood: Contemporary Issues in the Sociological Study of Childhood*, London, Falmer Press.

SOLBERG, A. (1994) *Negotiating Childhood: Empirical Investigations and Textual Representations of Children's Work and Everyday Life*, Nordic Institute for Studies in Urban and Regional Planning, Dissertation 12, Stockholm: Nordplan.

SOLBERG, A. (1990) 'Negotiating childhood: Changing construction of age for Norwegian children', in JAMES, A. and PROUT, A. (Eds) *Constructing and Reconstructing Childhood: Contemporary Issues in the Sociological Study of Childhood*, London, Falmer Press.

SOLBERG, A. and DANIELSEN, K. (1988) *Dagliglivets Organisering i Familier Med Store Barn* (Everyday Life in Families with Children of School-Age), Oslo, NIBR (NIBR-rapport 1988, 22).

SOLBERG, A. and VESTBY, G.M. (1987) *Barns Arbeidsliv* (The Working Life of Children), Oslo, NIBR (NIBR-rapport 1987, 3).

SOLBERG, A. (1987) 'Barn arbeider, hvorfor ser vi det ikke?', *Sosiologi idag*, **1**, pp. 25–99.

THORNE, B. (1987) 'Re-visioning women and social change: Where are the children?', *Gender and Society*, **1**, pp. 85–109.

WADEL, C. (1979) 'The hidden work of everyday life', in WALLMAN, S. (Ed) *Social Anthropology and Work*, London, Academic Press.

WAKSLER, F.C. (1986) 'Studying children: Phenomenological insights', *Human Studies*, **9**, pp. 71–82.

Chapter 6

Demographic Change and the Family Situation of Children

Lynda Clarke

Introduction

The demography of the family in most developed western countries has changed substantially since the beginning of the 1970s and looks likely to continue to do so. Revolutionary changes in ideas about birth, marriage, divorce, child-rearing, gender and death have been so dramatic that they have been termed by some the 'Second Demographic Transition' (Lesthaeghe, 1991). None of these changes in western family life had been predicted. The most obvious manifestation is that living arrangements have changed dramatically in the past two generations. The changes in demographic behaviour are a subject of great complexity and heated debate. Traditionalists believe the family is collapsing while modernists welcome the new opportunities and equality for women. These choices for parents and gains for women may be at the expense of their children.

What does family change auger for children? Low fertility, population ageing and the frailty of relationships bequeath uncertain prospects for children. If the life cycle transitions of adults have become more frequent, less strictly patterned and more complex what has happened to the family life of children? Despite the importance to the functioning of the economy and society in general, little is known about the stability of the contemporary family or household nor the amount of time individuals spend in co-resident groups. The evidence is disparate but is beginning to be assembled.

The aim of this chapter is to examine trends in the demographic framework of society that affect children and to take a first step in understanding their impact on children's family lives to date. Most previous work in Britain has examined family change in relation to adults. Work in other countries, especially America, has appreciated the importance of children for some time (Hofferth, 1988; Furstenberg *et al.*, 1983; Bumpass, 1984; McLanahan and Bumpass, 1988). These have recently gained centre stage (Bumpass, 1990; Rendall, 1994), culminating in the publication of an important account of American childhood over the last fifty years (Hernandez, 1995). This review, from the Chief of the Marriage and Family Statistics Branch of the US Bureau of Census, draws attention to the dramatic changes in the family life and material resources available to children and makes a forceful case for the need to address children's welfare. Until recently, the perspective of children had been largely overlooked in research on the impact of family change in this country, apart from a few studies dating from before the changes in family formation and union stability gained momentum (Brown, 1986; Haskey, 1983). Interest has been growing recently, however, to the conference from which this book arose is testimony and there have been a number of demographic studies on the effect of family disruption on children (Haskey, 1990 and 1994; Clarke, 1992; Kiernan, 1992; Ni Brohlchrain *et al.*, 1994). Children are becoming a priority for research and policy development in many countries following reports by national and international organizations focusing on children's needs, notably the UN Convention on the Rights of the Child (UN Report, 1994; UK Council for UN International Year of the Family, 1994; Utting, 1995).

Demographic Change Affecting Children

Contemporary trends benefit from being placed in a longer term perspective. It is worth remembering, before we consider the most recent British changes, that the 'traditional' nuclear family is somewhat of a misnomer. Its origins are relatively recent and its existence has coincided, to a great extent, with unusual social circumstances, in the form of world wars. The most salient features of this 'modern' family arose in Britain in the twentieth century and, for many, not until after the Second World War. Previously, life was far from certain, stable and predictable. The history of the West's population in the last century has been marked, above all, by the mastery that has been established over both mortality and fertility. Pre-twentieth century marriage breakup rates parallelled modern ones but were due to death rather than divorce. Also, given that death in the past was largely independent of parental status while divorce is significantly correlated with childlessness, the proportion of children affected must have been considerably higher than at present (Anderson, 1983). Another facet that throws current patterns into a different light is the high proportion of children who became orphans. A child born in 1851 stood a 1 per cent chance of orphanhood (both parents dead) by the age of 10 and a 6 per cent chance by the age of 25. In contrast, only 1 per cent of the cohort born in 1946 lost just one parent by the age of 25 (Anderson, 1983). Also, the proportion of children living outside a 'traditional' two parent family was almost the same in 1851 at it is has been recently; about one child in eight under the age of 15 lived with a lone parent, a figure similar to that found by the 1981 census (Anderson, 1994).

The Birth of Children

The separation of marriage and childbearing, which is not unrelated to developments in cohabitation, has been an important demographic motor in the 1980s for creating dramatic changes in family structure. The proportion of all births that occur outside marriage has more than trebled, from 9 per cent in 1976 to nearly 31 per

Table 6.1: *Birth rate within and outside marriage by age of mother, 1981, 1986, 1991*

England and Wales

	Year			**Age of Mother**			
		Under 20	20–24	25–29	30–34	35–39	All ages
Extra marital	1981	13.7	27.8	33.7	26.0	11.9	19.7
Rate per 1,000	1986	21.3	38.2	43.1	35.8	17.2	28.9
unmarried women	1991	28.0	54.4	56.1	48.7	26.0	40.7
Marital rate	1981	324.8	204.3	161.5	76.9	23.3	88.8
per 1,000 married	1986	360.9	209.8	167.2	90.1	26.2	86.3
women	1991	264.0	189.2	172.5	102.3	33.9	84.6
Ratio of	1981	0.04	0.14	0.21	0.34	0.51	0.22
extra marital	1986	0.06	0.18	0.26	0.40	0.66	0.33
rate to marital	1991	0.11	0.29	0.33	0.48	0.68	0.48

Source: OPCS Birth Statistics, 1991, Series FM1, No. 21, Table 3.1

cent (30.8 per cent) in 1992. The growth in extra-marital childbearing is partly a result of the older average age at marriage and the larger cohorts of the 'baby boom', women born in the late 1950s and early 1960s, increasing the proportion of single women in the population (Ermisch, 1990). Also, marital childbearing has been postponed and somewhat depressed, which has tended to exaggerate the effect of childbearing outside marriage. Even taking these factors into account, the evidence points to a noticeable and increased propensity for children to be born outside marriage, a tendency which is by no means confined to those with teenager mothers (Kiernan and Wicks, 1990).

Table 6.1 shows the extra-marital and marital fertility rates for women of different ages in 1981, 1986 and 1991. It also shows the ratios of these rates in the bottom rows, which indicate the propensity for children to be born outside marriage if born to mothers of different ages. The ratio is larger for children born to older women, suggesting a greater tendency for children to be born outside marriage if they have older rather than younger mothers. The ratio is very low for teenage women because of the very high fertility rates of the small minority of married teenagers compared with the fertility of the large majority of single teenagers. The ratio of extra-marital to marital fertility rates increased by about 50 per cent for children born to mothers of all ages combined in both the early and late 1980s, with a noticeable increase for children born to mothers aged 20–24 between 1986 and 1991. Not only has the number of births outside marriage increased dramatically in the 1980s but the propensity for children to be born outside marriage appears to be increasing. It is not only a function of the larger proportion of single women in the population.

What is interesting is that an increasing majority of these births outside marriage are being registered by two parents and by parents living at the same address (see Table 6.2). The proportion of joint registrations has risen from 58 per cent of all births outside marriage in 1981 to 74 per cent in 1991. Moreover, more than

Table 6.2: *Births outside marriage*

England and Wales

		Age of Mother				
Year	All ages	Under 20	20–24	25–29	30–34	35 and over
		Percentage of births outside marriage				
1980	11.8	42.6	13.2	6.0	5.8	9.5
1985	19.2	64.8	24.6	10.6	9.0	11.8
1991	30.2	82.9	44.9	21.1	15.9	18.8
		Jointly registered births as a percentage of all births outside marriage				
1980	57	46	57	66	71	70
1985	65	57	66	70	72	73
1991	74	65	75	78	79	80
		Percentage of jointly registered births with parents at same usual address				
1985	72	56	71	79	81	80
1991	73	58	73	79	81	81

Source: OPCS Birth Statistics, 1991 Series FMI, No. 21, Tables 3.1 and 3.10

seven out of ten of the joint registrations made in 1991 (73 per cent) were made by parents living at the same address. In other words, over a half (54 per cent) of all births outside marriage in 1991 were jointly registered by parents living at the same address, presumably cohabiting.

Families based on cohabitation or legal marriage could be considered to be the same as far as children are concerned. There are, however, important official distinctions and evidence of differing characteristics. It is true that there appear to be few differences in the socio-economic characteristics of childless, married and never-married or previously-married cohabiting couples but there seem to be marked differences between married and cohabiting families. On most of the available meas-ures, the never-married, cohabiting couples with children are more disadvantaged than their married counterparts (Kiernan and Estaugh, 1993; McRae, 1993). The cohabiting relationship can be regarded as having similarities to a mutual contract, being based on cooperation and lacking some of the formal obligations of mar-riage. This could be a crucial difference when considering the care of children. Early results from the British Household Panel Study suggest that cohabiting couples may be more than four times as likely to split up as married couples (Buck *et al.*, 1994). But this analysis is crude in that it does not control for age, presence of children, and length of relationship (Murphy, 1995). Certainly, evidence from other countries indicates that cohabiting unions break down more frequently than marriages (Leridon, 1990; Hoem and Hoem, 1992; Jensen, 1994). Also, fathers in cohabiting families have no automatic parental rights to children, even if they are registered as the father of the child. A recent survey found that few cohabiting parents took active steps to

Lynda Clarke

Table 6.3: Birth by status of mother, 1983, 1987, 1991

England and Wales   **Percentage**

| Year | Inside marriage | | Mother's Status | Outside marriage | |
| | Total Births (= 100%) | | Sole Registration | Joint Registration | |
				Same address	Different address
1983	629,134	84	6	7	3
1987	681,511	77	7	11	5
1991	699,217	70	8	16	6

Source: OPCS Birth Statistics, 1991, Series FM1, No. 21, Table 3.1

secure these paternal rights because they were unaware that a specific legal step needed to be taken (McRae, 1993). If there is a greater risk of family break-up for cohabiting unions, then this weaker tie with fathers can be a critical difference for children in such unions.

A significant proportion of children born outside marriage (46 per cent) are to mothers who, on the available evidence, appear to be lacking the support of the child's father. Nearly three out of ten children born outside marriage are registered by their mother alone, while two out of ten are registered by both parents but by parents who do not live together. Are these sole registrations evidence of a missing father? It might be that these mothers are cohabiting but that their partner's details are not requested at registration. It is interesting that the proportion of all births that are sole registrations has changed very little during the last ten years, unlike the proportion that are joint registrations (Table 6.3). We do not know the family circumstances of these children, particularly whether their father is present in their life, nor for those children who are jointly registered by parents giving different addresses. We can only guess. We do know that at least 16 per cent of all children born in 1991 were to cohabiting couples, possibly more, but we do not know what happens to the family circumstances of these children after birth (Table 6.3).

It should be remembered that the majority of children are still born to married parents. Major changes in childbearing behaviour, apart from the increase in child-bearing outside marriage, is the postponement of parenthood and decrease in family size. Children, especially first children, are becoming more likely than in the past to have older parents. Couples marrying since the late 1960s have been delaying starting their families. Teenage fertility rates in Britain are still among the highest in Europe but are exceeded by those in the United States (Babb, 1995). There has been, however, a decrease in the fertility rates of women in their 20s and an increase in those of women in their 30s and 40s, especially for first births rates (Jones, 1992). Later childbearing has not compensated for the shortfall at younger ages, at least not for women born between 1935 and 1950 who have completed their childbearing. Further declines in completed family size are projected for more recent cohorts of women; for example, women born in 1955 are projected to have on average 1.99

children compared with the 2.19 already achieved by women born in 1945 and the 2.36 for women born in 1940 (Jones, 1992). These trends reflect the increasing likelihood that recent generations of women nearing the end of their reproductive span will remain childless. A higher proportion of women born since 1945 are childless at each age (Babb, 1955). There is growing conformity to the two-child family ideal, both in terms of actual family size and expectations about future numbers of children (Central Statistical Office, 1995).

This delayed childbearing, increased fertility for the over 30s and increase in childlessness have important ramifications for the future place of children in families and their care. Children are less likely today to share the companionship of siblings or wider kin. Contact with cousins, aunts and uncles will become less common for the children whose parents may be only children or whose parents' sibs have not had children. This means that these family members will not be present to provide support at times of family disruption nor will children learn at first hand about parenting. On the positive side, children will not be competing with other siblings for family resources, both material and human.

Children's Experience of Family Disruption

The instability of family life is the most publicized facet of family life in recent times. The family and marriage are said to be under threat from the recent increase in the likelihood of marital disruption or relationship breakdown. We do not know how cohabiting relationships compare with marriage in terms of stability but the record on marriage in this country is far from 'till death us do part'. Britain has one of the highest divorce rates in western Europe (Eurostat, 1993). It has been estimated that, if the divorce rates prevailing in 1979/1980 were to continue, one in five children would experience a divorce of their parents by the age of 16 (Haskey, 1983). This was confirmed in an estimate based on children's experience in the early 1980s, where 22 per cent of children would expect to experience the divorce of their parents (Clarke, 1992).

One effect of this increase in divorce is the growth in the number of lone parent families over the past two decades so that currently about one in five families with dependent children is a lone-parent family (Haskey, 1993a; Haskey, 1993c; OPCS, 1993a). The United Kingdom has the highest proportion of lone-parent families in the European Community (Roll, 1993). Nine out of ten of these are lone mothers and about two-thirds of them have previously been married. Lone parenthood is often not a permanent situation for many mothers and their children, being terminated by cohabitation or marriage. An increasing proportion of marriages are remarriages for one or both partners, which means the creation of stepfamilies for children of a remarrying parent.

The most recent General Household Survey (GHS) in 1991 asked both men and women for the first time about the presence of stepchildren, which has produced the estimate that 8 per cent of families with dependent children were stepfamilies (OPCS, 1993). We know that remarriages are at greater risk of breaking down than first marriages (Haskey, 1988) but we do not know whether different types of reconstituted family have different risks of breaking down (Kiernan and Wicks, 1990). Evidence from the United States suggests that risks increase with the complexity of the reformed families (White and Booth, 1985). For example, couples where only one partner has been married before and there are no children have the lowest risk of breakdown, whereas couples where both partners have been married previously and have children from their previous marriages have the highest risk (Kiernan and Wicks, 1990).

The increase in remarriage and cohabitation after the breakdown of a relationship and the resulting increase in reconstituted families are likely to have produced families with increasingly complicated familial ties. It is likely that this complexity will grow with the passage of time if relationships continue to fail and be replaced with alternative liaisons. The consequences of these changes in adult marital and childbearing behaviour for children's family lives are nor clear nor the consequent risks for their welfare.

Children's Family Circumstances

Data on Children

There is no direct information on the different living arrangements of children at birth nor in changes in these following a birth outside marriage or marital breakdown. In Britain information on the different family circumstances of children at birth is largely limited to that collected at birth registration. Little is known about the child's exact living arrangements or changes in these following a birth outside marriage or marital breakdown. Retrospective information from mothers about children loses track of any children from whom mothers have parted and gives no information about the children whose mothers have died or have not been interviewed for any other reason. We need such longitudinal information if we are to answer important questions about how adult behaviour impinges on the lives of children. We do not know, for example, how many cohabiting parents separate as this is not recorded in official divorce statistics, although the early results from the British Household Panel Study suggest that they may be less stable than families based on marriage (Buck et al., 1994), which would confirm findings reported from some other countries. These results have recently been questioned, however (Murphy, 1995). It is only when we have such information that we can estimate the effect of such changes in adult marital behaviour on their children.

Most data are analysed and collected in relation to adult circumstances and are not focused on children. There are constraints on our ability to track children's family circumstances but we can discern their living arrangements according to their mother's marital status from retrospective marital and birth history data from national surveys. We can estimate the living arrangements of children at one point in time, their mother's marital status at their birth and any changes in her marital status since their birth. This does not allow us to know about the support children obtain from

Table 6.4: *Distribution of children aged under 16 according to living arrangements, 1979–91*

Children aged 0–15 of women aged 18–49   **Great Britain**

Current living arrangements of child	1979*	1981	1984	1987	1991	1991
Living in the Household with:						
Both natural parents currently:						
• married	83	81	78	77	68	71
• cohabiting	1	1	1	2	3	3
Natural mother and 'stepfather' + currently:						
• married	4	6	7	7	7	4
• cohabiting	1	2	2	2	3	3
Lone mother:	9	9	10	10	17	17
Total	98	98	98	98	98	98
Living Apart from Mother:						
• with father	1	–	–	–	–	–
• adopted, fostered, relatives, non–relatives	1	–	–	–	–	–
• at special school or home	x	–	–	–	–	–
Total	2	2	2	2	2	2
Base = 100%	6842	7148	5446	5332	5185	5185

Note: 1991 includes premarital cohabitation
Source: 1979 General Household Survey report. All other years derived by author from the General Household Survey.

people with whom they do not live but may regard as their family. It does, however, give us information on co-residents who must play a central role in the children's lives. We wish to emphasize that we are primarily concerned here with the living arrangements of children and not with their wider family relationships.

Trends in Children's Current Living Arrangements

A first step in unravelling the effect of family change on children is to refocus the data collected on adult's current living arrangements from the perspectives of children. Some of the impact of recent trends in marriage, cohabitation, births outside marriage, separation and divorce on the family circumstances of children can be seen in Table 6.4.

Table 6.4 shows the decreasing proportion of children aged under 16 years who are living with both natural parents who are married to each other, from 83 per cent of all children in 1979 to only 68 per cent in 1991. The table also shows a doubling of the proportion living with a lone mother or in a stepfamily, from 9 per cent to 17 per cent and 5 to 10 per cent respectively. Over this period an unchanging proportion of children, 2 per cent, lived apart from their mothers. In 1982, the last time the GHS asked the whereabouts of children not living with their mothers, roughly half of these children were living with their fathers and the other half with other relatives and non–relatives. Less than 0.5 per cent were in institutions.

These estimates have been derived from women's birth and marital history data from the GHS in the appropriate years. It is difficult to say whether these estimates are similar to those found in other countries because of both a dearth of estimates based on children and differences in the definitions of family types. Evidence from the United States, however, suggests that Britain has not yet reached the low levels of intact two, natural parent families seen there. But it is important to remember that the ethnic profiles of the two countries are very different (Hernandez, 1993).

Children Living with Natural Parents

An interesting development in the GHS is that dates of premarital cohabitation have been included in the marriage histories since 1989. Table 6.4 also shows that in 1991, the most recent year for which these data are available, the inclusion of premarital cohabitation boosts the estimated proportion of children living with both natural, married parents from 68 to 71 per cent with a consequent decrease from 7 to 4 per cent in the proportion living in a married stepfamily. All but one of the estimates in Table 6.4 had overestimated the proportion of children living with stepfathers, and underestimated the proportion living with natural married parents, because their mother was not married to the father at their birth. There was no way of telling prior to 1989, therefore, if she was pre-maritally cohabiting with the natural father of the child in question, whom she married at a later date.

It follows that more children may be living with their natural parents than shown even in Table 6.4 because women are not asked if the man with whom they are now living, in legal marriage or otherwise, is the natural father of their child(ren). We can determine this fact only if the woman was living with the natural father at the birth of the child. Further, a proportion of children may have been born into a two-parent, cohabiting relationship which has broken down. This is unknown because of the lack of a cohabitation history in the GHS. There is evidence that some children's families can be exceedingly complex. In a recent exploratory analysis of 1991 data from the National Child and Development Survey, a longitudinal study with study members aged 33 years in 1991, Ferri classified thirty-six different family types by a combination of relationship to partner, past marital history and relationship to children (Ferri, 1994).

Older teenagers were less likely than younger children to be living with their mother and to be living with both natural parents. For example, only 63 per cent of teenagers aged 16–18 were living with both natural, married parents compared with 71 per cent of children under the age of 5, and 14 per cent of them were living apart from their mother compared with only 1 per cent for the youngest age group of children (Table 6.5).

Older children under the age of 16 years were less likely than younger children to be living with both natural parents. For example, Table 6.5 shows that in 1991, the most recent year for which these data are available, 78 per cent of children aged 4 or younger were living with both natural parents compared with 72 per cent of those aged 5–15 years. The younger a child, however, the more likely its parents

Table 6.5: Distribution of children according to living arrangements by age-group of child (1991 figures include premarital cohabitation information)

Children aged 0–18 of women aged 18–49*   **Great Britain**

Current living arrangements of child	Age of Child							
	0–4		5–9		10–15		16–18	
	1981	1991	1981	1991	1981	1991	1981	1991
Living in the Household with:	%	%	%	%	%	%	%	%
Both natural parents** currently:								
• married	86	71	81	70	76	71	68	63
• cohabiting	1	7	x	2	x	1	x	x
Subtotal	87	78	82	72	76	72	68	63
Natural mother and 'stepfather'⁺ currently married:								
• mother married at time of birth**	x	1	3	2	5	4	6	4
• mother not married at time of birth	3	1	3	2	4	2	2	2
Subtotal	3	2	6	5	9	6	8	7
Currently cohabiting:								
• mother married at time of birth**	1	1	1	2	1	3	1	2
• mother not married at time of birth	1	1	x	1	1	1	x	x
Subtotal	1	2	2	3	2	4	1	2
Lone mother currently:								
• separated	3	4	3	5	2	4	4	3
• divorced	2	4	4	7	5	8	6	8
• widowed	x	x	x	1	2	1	1	3
• single	3	10	2	5	1	2	x	1
Subtotal	8	17	9	19	10	15	9	14
Not Living with Mother	x	1	2	2	4	2	14	14
Base = 100%	1980	1782	2232	1618	2936	1785	1284	810

Source: Derived from the General Household Survey, 1981 and 1991.

Notes: * Includes children of small number of women aged 16 or 17.

     ⁺ Some of these stepfathers may be the child's natural father. In 1981, he was not married to the mother at the child's birth and, in 1991 he was not married to her nor living with her in premarital cohabitation.

     ** In 1991 'married' includes child born in premarital cohabitation.

were to be cohabiting. In 1991, 7 per cent of children aged 0–4 years were living with both natural parents who were cohabiting compared with 1 per cent of children aged 10–15 years. This suggests substantial recent changes in childbearing behaviour.

It is difficult to ascertain from these cross-sectional data to what extent the greater proportion of younger children living with cohabiting parents reflects the increase in births outside marriage and to what extent these unions will be converted into marriages or break up as children get older. The increase in the proportion of children living with parents who are cohabiting since 1981 suggests that this is the result of extra-marital childbearing within cohabiting relationships but the proportions do not tally with those suggested by co-resident, joint birth registration. The registration figures show that between 11 and 16 per cent of all births from 1987 to 1991 were jointly registered by parents living at the same address (Table 6.3). The GHS data on the living arrangements of children 0–4 years show only 7 per cent living with cohabiting natural parents. What has happened to the other 4 to 9 per cent of children who were jointly registered by co-resident parents? Their parents have either married or parted. This suggests some movement out of cohabitation early in a child's life. If the transformation is to becoming a married-couple family then little will change for the children concerned. There is some evidence that this is happening in the reclassification of the 1991 data to include children born in pre-marital cohabitation, shown in Table 6.4, as discussed earlier. There was more effect of this reclassification for the youngest children who are also most likely to have cohabiting, natural parents. If, however, cohabiting unions have a high breakdown rate, as has been shown in other countries, then the children's prospects may not look so promising, given the evidence on the increased likelihood of economic hardship among lone parent families apart from any emotional distress.

Children Living with Lone Mothers

Most children under 16 years of age who are not living with both natural parents live with a lone mother. This is the family type that has shown the greatest change in the 1980s in Britain for children of all ages. The proportion of children living in lone-mother families more than doubled between 1981 and 1991 for children aged 4 or under and 5–9 years of age; from 8 per cent to 17 per cent and from 9 to 19 per cent respectively; and it increased by 50 per cent for children aged 10–15 years (Table 6.5, Figure 6.1). The proportions of families that have lone parents will differ from the proportion of children living in such families because the number of children in a family varies in different types of families (Figure 6.1). This is one reason why international comparisons of the proportion of children living in lone parent families are not easy. We know that lone parents with children are most frequently found in Denmark and Britain, with Germany and Belgium following close behind (Family Policy Studies Centre, 1994). The lowest proportions are found in Greece, Italy and Spain. How these data on families convert to children

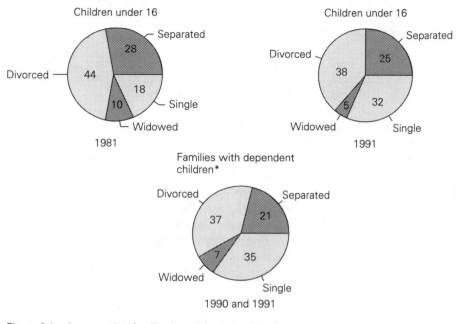

Figure 6.1: *Lone mother families by mother's marital status*
Note: *Under 16 or 16–18 and in full-time education
Source: Data on children derived by author from GHS. Data on families from GHS, 1991 Report

is not clear but we do know that the proportion of children living in lone mother families in the US is even higher than in Britain (Hernandez, 1995).

The proportion of children living in lone-parent families arising from marital breakdown increased substantially in the 1970s (Clarke, 1992) and the proportion of children living in divorced or separated lone–mother families was still growing in the 1980s. In 1991, 6 per cent of children under 16 years lived with a divorced lone mother and 4 per cent with a separated lone mother. Older children were more likely than younger children to live in divorced lone-mother families; for example, 4 per cent of children under age 5 in 1991 compared with 8 per cent of children aged 10–15 (Table 6.5).

The largest growth for children in lone-parent families during the 1980s was for those where the mother had not been legally married. The increases are particularly noticeable for the youngest age-group of children, increasing from 3 per cent to 10 per cent of children aged 4 or under between 1981 and 1991. As mentioned earlier, it is impossible to speculate from these cross-sectional data on living arrangements how much of this increase reflects the growing tendency for cohabiting couples to have children outside marriage whose relationships break down after the birth, or how much it reflects a growing tendency for mothers to have children without being in a co-resident relationship. The quandary will remain until we have evidence on the stability of cohabiting relationships and changes in children's living arrangements.

Children Living in Stepfamilies

There has been a small increase in the proportion of children living in stepfamilies during the 1980s; from 8 per cent of children under 16 years in 1981 to 10 per cent (Table 6.4). It should be remembered that these figures are not really directly comparable since we have corrected the 1991 figures for premarital cohabitation. This means that the 1981 estimate for children in 'stepfamilies' was an overestimate. It was known only that the mother of a child was not married at the time of the child's birth. Some of the men classified as stepfathers were the natural fathers of the child and were living with the woman at the time of the child's birth. We can identify such cohabitations that developed into marriage for the GHS since 1989 and the 1991 figures include such information. The four subcategories of stepfamily in 1991 are, therefore, that the mother and stepfather are currently either married or cohabiting, cross-classified by the mother's marital status at the child's birth. Basically, this decides whether the stepfamily is a result of marital breakdown or not. This category of 'marital breakdown' includes children born outside marriage to cohabiting partners who married at some point after the birth but eventually separated. Alternatively, if the child was born outside marriage but not to co-resident parents who married at some later date the stepfamily would not have followed a marital breakdown. These families may have been co-resident at the birth of the child but as a marriage did not ensue we would not know about its existence. We have no way of knowing the exact family relationships of these children. Also, we do not know how many children were born to mothers who never lived with the father, who started to live with the father after the child's birth or who did not cohabit at the child's birth but married the father eventually. Children in these last two scenarios would be misclassified as being in a stepfamily, unless the natural parents had since separated. It is only if children's circumstances at birth and their relationship to each household member were asked that we could arrive at precise estimates of their family circumstances.

The most recent GHS in 1991 asked both men and women for the first time about the presence of stepchildren, which has produced the estimate that 8 per cent of families with dependent children were stepfamilies (OPCS, 1993). It would not be easy, however, to link this information from fathers to the mothers' birth and marital histories in order to check the validity of an assumption of stepfatherhood.

Older children are more likely than the younger ones to live in stepfamilies; in 1991, 6 per cent of children aged 10–15 years were living in a married couple stepfamily (*de jure*) and a further 4 per cent in a cohabiting stepfamily (*de facto*) compared with 2 per cent of children aged 0–4 years in both types of stepfamily (Table 6.5). From this sparse evidence it would appear that the majority of these older children in stepfamilies were born in a previous marriage (including premarital cohabitation) rather than outside marriage. The likelihood of a child living in a stepfamily increases with the age of the child as does the likelihood of such a child being born in a previous marriage.

Does Family Change Matter for Children?

Recent changes in patterns of family formation and dissolution, notably increases in birth outside marriage and divorce, can be seen to have led to changes in both the composition of families into which children are born and the likelihood of transit from one family type to another during the course of their childhood years (Clarke, 1992). The proportion of children experiencing the conventional life cycle (parents married at the time the children are born and continuing married until they are adult) could fall as low as 50 per cent (Clarke, 1992). Increasing marital dissolution and childbearing outside marriage have resulted in a growing proportion of children experiencing life with a single parent, generally their mother, at some point in their lives. Increasing cohabitation and remarriage mean that more children will be experiencing living in stepfamilies. A reconstituted two-parent family is likely to have complex social, material and emotional ties which may have an adverse impact on children.

Does it matter that a minority of children are increasingly experiencing a variety of family settings as they pass through childhood and adolescence? Most people have an opinion in this matter and it continues to receive widespread attention. Could it be that the gains for adults are at the expense of their children and also, possibly, fathers, many of whom lose co-residence if not total contact with their children when relationships break up? The jury are still out for the final verdict on this matter but the research evidence has been accumulating. The problems of drawing overall conclusions have been summarized recently in an extensive review of the British evidence to date on the outcomes for children who have experienced lone parenthood or family disruption or both (Burghes, 1994).

Apart from any adverse psycho–social effects, most concern about the increase in lone parenthood is usually because there is a large differential in the economic well-being of two-parent families and female-headed, lone-parent families. In 1990/1991 nearly 60 per cent of lone-parent families were living in poverty, as defined by having under half of the average income after housing costs, compared with 23 per cent of couple families (Kumar, 1993). The plight of so many lone mothers reflects the disadvantages they face in the labour market (Joshi, 1987) and the social security system (Bradshaw, 1989; Burghes, 1993). Lone parenthood is the second highest risk factor for children being in poverty, being lower than only unemployed families (Kumar, 1993).

The 1991 GHS showed that stepfamilies were, also, more likely to be disadvantaged in terms of housing and income compared with couple households. The survey identified differences between stepfamilies and other families with dependent children headed by a married couple, most notably that stepfamilies were more likely than other families to live in local authority housing, probably partly a result of their greater likelihood of having a weekly household income in the lowest category tabulated (£200 or less) (OPCS, 1993).

It would appear that the children of parents who do not follow the traditional family norm are being disadvantaged in these respects. Why, then, do parents risk their children's, and possibly their own, well-being by adopting demographic behaviour that makes this more likely? Regardless of what has happened in the past or what may happen in the future, families in Britain are in a transition from adapting to a society with a single norm of family life to a society in which a plurality of norms is acceptable. The structures and dynamics of the modern family should be seen as a continuation of this long-term adaptation to longer life expectancy and economic development. How children will fare in this process only time will tell.

Conclusion

The demographic projection is for continued changes in children's family circumstances. It could be that there will be a change towards a more stable family life for children, defined in demographic terms, but this looks very unlikely. At the present time, the majority of children are living with their parents who are married or who are cohabiting, some of whom will marry at a later date. There is a growing minority, however, that are living with a lone mother or living in a reconstituted family and the proportion of children experiencing these alternative family forms over their childhood will be much higher.

Further work is needed if a more sensitive demography of children's family lives is to be achieved. Longitudinal data are available from cohort studies, panel data and linked data but children's circumstances will be evident only in relation to the adults they are with at the time of interview. Only if children are followed in a longitudinal survey or retrospective questions are asked about their living arrangements and family relationships will we be able to give exact estimates of children's family circumstances and their likelihood of experiencing family change. These are essential first steps in assessing children's family lives which will enable the development of responsible policies to safeguard their wellbeing in the future.

References

ANDERSON, M. (1983) 'What is new about the modern family: An historical perspective', in *The Family*, British Society for Population Studies Conference Papers, Occasional Paper 31, London, Office of Population, Censuses and Surveys.

ANDERSON, M. (1994) 'Today's family in historical context', *Family and Parenthood Seminar Papers*, York, Joseph Rowntree Foundation.

BABB, P. (1955) 'Birth statistics 1993', *Population Trends*, **79**, London, HMSO.

BRADSHAW, J. (1989) *Lone Parents: Policy in the Doldrums*, London, Family Policy Studies Centre.

BROWN, A. (1986) 'Family circumstances of young children', *Population Trends*, **43**, London, HMSO.

BUCK, N., GERSHUNY, J., ROSE, D. and SCOTT, J. (1994) *Changing Households: The British Household Panel Study 1990–1992*, ESRC Research Centre on Micro-Social Change, University of Essex.

BUMPASS, L.L. (1984) 'Children and marital disruption: A replication and update', *Demography*, **21**, pp. 71–82.

BUMPASS, L.L. (1990) 'What's happening to the family?: Interactions between demographic and institutional change', *Demography*, **27**, p. 4.

BURGHES, L. (1993) *One-Parent Families: Policy Options for the 1990s*, London, Family Policy Studies Centre.

BURGHES, L. (1994) *Lone Parenthood and Family Disruption: The Outcomes for Children*, London, Family Policy Studies Centre.

CENTRAL STATISTICAL OFFICE (1995) *Social Trends*, **25**, London, HMSO.

CLARKE, L. (1992) 'Children's family circumstances: Recent trends in Great Britain', *European Journal of Population*, **8**, pp. 309–40.

COUNCIL OF EUROPE (1994) *Recent Demographic Developments in Europe 1993*, Strasbourg, Council of Europe Press.

ELDRIDGE, S. and KIERNAN, K. (1985) 'Declining first marriage rates in England and Wales: A change in timing or a rejection of marriage?', *European Journal of Population*, **1**, 4, pp. 327–45.

ERMISCH, J. (1990) *Fewer Babies, Longer Lives: Policy Implications of Current Demographic Trends*, York, Joseph Rowntree Foundation.

EUROSTAT (1993) *Demographic Statistics*, Office for Official Publications of the European Communities, Luxembourg.

FAMILY POLICY STUDIES CENTRE (1994) *Families in the European Union*, London, FPSC.

FERRI, E. (1994) 'Family research using cohort data', Plenary session at Seminar on Researching Families, Social Research Association/Family Policy Studies Institute, 24 March, Regents College, London.

FURSTENBERG, F.F., NORD, C.W., PETERSON, J.L. and ZILL, N. (1983) 'The life course of children of divorce: Marital disruption and parental contact', *American Sociological Review*, **48**, pp. 656–68.

HALSEY, A.H. (1993) 'Changes in the family', *Children and Society*, **7**, 2, pp. 125–36.

HASKEY, J. (1983) 'Children of divorcing couples', *Population Trends*, **31**, London, HMSO, pp. 20–6.

HASKEY, J. (1988) 'Trends in marriage and divorce, and cohort analyses of the proportions of marriages ending in divorce', *Population Trends*, **54**, London, HMSO, pp. 21–8.

HASKEY, J. (1989) 'Current prospects for the proportion of marriages ending in divorce', *Population Trends*, **55**, London, HMSO, pp. 34–7.

HASKEY, J. (1990) 'Children in families broken by divorce', *Population Trends*, **61**, London, HMSO, pp. 34–42.

HASKEY, J. (1993a) 'Trends in the numbers of one-parent families in Great Britain', *Population Trends*, **71**, London, HMSO, pp. 26–33.

HASKEY, J. (1993b) 'First marriage, divorce, and remarriage: Birth cohort analysis', *Population Trends*, **72**, London, HMSO, pp. 24–33.

HASKEY, J. (1993c) 'Lone parents and married parents with dependent children in Great Britain: A comparison of their occupations and social class profiles', *Population Trends*, **72**, London, HMSO, pp. 34–44.

HASKEY, J. (1994) 'Stepfamilies and stepchildren in Great Britain', *Population Trends*, **76**, London, HMSO, pp. 17–28.

HERNANDEZ, D.J. (1995) *America's Children: Resources from Family, Government, and the Economy*, New York, Russell Sage Foundation.

HOEM, B. and HOEM, J.M. (1992) 'The disruption of marital and non-marital unions in contemporary Sweden', in TRUSSEL, J., HANKINSON, R. and TILTON, J. (Eds) *Demographic Applications of Event History Analysis*, Oxford, Clarendon Press, pp. 61–93.

HOFFERTH, S.L. (1988) 'Recent trends in the living arrangements of children: A cohort life table analysis', in BOGAARTS, J., BURCH, T.K. and WACHTER, K.W. (Eds) *Family Demography*, Cornell, Oxford University Press.

INGLEHART, R. (1977) *The Silent Revolution: Changing Values and Political Styles among Western Publics*, Princeton, Princeton University Press.

JENSEN, A.-M. (1994) 'Fathers and children: The missing link', in Brannen, J. and O'Brien, M. (Eds) *Childhood and Parenthood: Proceedings of the International Sociological Association Conference*, London, Institute of Education.

JONES, C. (1992) 'Fertility of the over thirties', *Population Trends*, **67**, London, HMSO, pp. 11–17.

JOSHI, H. (1987) *Obstacles and Opportunities for Lone Parents as Breadwinners in Great Britain*, Paper 8, OECD Conference of National Experts on 'Lone Parents: The Economic Challenge of Changing Family Structures', Paris, December.

KIERNAN, K. (1989) 'The family: Formation or fission', in JOSHI, H. (Ed) *The Changing Population of Britain*, Oxford, Basil Blackwell.

KIERNAN, K. (1992) 'The impact of family disruption childhood on transitions made in young adult life', *Population Studies*, **46**, pp. 213–24.

KIERNAN, K. and ELDRIDGE, S. (1987) 'Inter and intra cohort variation in the timing of first marriage', *British Journal of Sociology*, **38**, 1, pp. 44–65.

KIERNAN, K.E. and ESTAUGH, V. (1993) *Cohabitation: Extra-marital childbearing and Social Policy*, Occasional Paper 17, London, Family Policy Studies Centre.

KIERNAN, K. and WICKS, M. (1990) *Family Change and Future Policy*, London, Family Policy Studies Centre/York, Joseph Rowntree Memorial Trust.

KUMAR, V. (1993) *Poverty and Inequality in the UK: The Effects on Children*, London, National Children's Bureau.

LERIDON, H. (1990) 'Cohabitation, marriage, separation: An analysis of life histories of French cohorts from 1968 to 1985', *Population Studies*, **44**, pp. 127–44.

LESTAEGHE, R. (1991) 'The second demographic transition in western countries: An interpretation', IPD- working Paper 1991–2, Interuniversity Programme in Demography, Vrije University, Brussels.

MANSFIELD, P. and COLLARD, J. (1988) *The Beginning of the Rest of Your Life?*, London, Macmillan.

McLANAHAN, G. and BUMPASS, L. (1988) 'Intergenerational consequences of family disruption', *American Journal of Sociology*, **94**, pp. 130–52.

McRAE, S. (1993) *Cohabiting Mothers: Changing Marriage and Motherhood?*, London, Policy Studies Institute.

MURPHY, M. (1995) 'Are cohabiting unions more likely to break down than marriages?', *Changing Britain*, **2**, Swindon, Economic and Social Research Council.

NI BROHLCHRAIN, M., CHAPPELL, R. and DIAMOND, I. (1994) 'Educational and socio-demographic outcomes among the children of disrupted and intact marriages', *Population*, **49**, 6, pp. 1585–612.

OPCS (1992a) *Marriage and Divorce Statistics, England and Wales, 1990*, OPCS Series FM2 No. 18, London, HMSO.

OPCS (1993) *General Household Survey 1991*, Series GHS no. 22, London, HMSO.

OPCS (1993a) *Birth Statistics*, Series FM1 no. 20, London, HMSO.

OPCS (1994) *Marriage and Divorce Statistics, England and Wales, 1991*, OPCS Series FM2 no. 19, HMSO, London.

RAPOPORT, R.N., FOGARTY, M.P. and RAPOPORT, R. (Eds) (1982) *Families in Britain*, London, Routledge and Kegan Paul.

RENDALL, M. (1994) 'The household demography of adolescent single mothers over their parenting lifetimes', Paper presented to the Population Association of America Conference, Cornell University.

ROLL, J. (1993) *Lone Parent Families in Europe*, London, Family Policy Studies Centre.

SIMONS, J. (1994) 'The cultural significance of western fertility trends in the 1980s', Paper presented at the IUSSP Seminar on Values and Fertility Change, February 16–19, Sion, Switzerland.

THORNES, B. and COLLARD, J. (1979) *Who Divorces?*, London, Routledge and Kegan Paul.

YOUNG, M. and WILLMOTT, P. (1973) *The Symmetrical Family*, London, Routledge and Kegan Paul.

UK COUNCIL FOR UN INTERNATIONAL YEAR OF THE FAMILY (1994) *Family Agenda For Action.*

UNITED NATIONS (1994) *United Nations Convention on the Rights of the Child*, UNICEF.

UTTING, D. (1995) *Family and Parenthood: Supporting Families, Preventing Breakdown*, York, Joseph Rowntree Foundation.

WHITE, L. and BOOTH, A. (1985) 'The quality and stability of remarriages: The role of step-children', *American Sociological Review*, **50**, 5.

Chapter 7

Children's Constructions of Family and Kinship

Margaret O'Brien, Pam Alldred and Deborah Jones

Although most adults may have a common-sense understanding of 'the family' there is much debate in social science about the meaning and indeed usefulness of the term itself (Bernardes, 1985; Trost, 1990). Radical changes in how adults live together and raise children have shaken received wisdom concerning definitions of the family. Humpty Dumpty has fallen off the wall and his fragments cannot be reassembled in quite the same way (Laslett, 1991). In the latter part of the twentieth century new words have been created to describe the diversity of families that are emerging — one-parent family, bi-nuclear family, network family, reconstituted family, blended family — leading some to call for more precision in the use of 'family words'.

Typically the word family is used to refer to a heterosexual married couple and their dependent children who reside in one household sharing resources. In the 1980s family sociologists in particular, notably Bernardes (1985), began to re-appraise the term family, to disentangle its various meanings. Most writers about the family now make a clear distinction between household and family pointing out that the two are not always coincidental. Families exist within and between households and not all households contain families. Demographic analysis shows that in the UK the proportion of households containing a married couple with dependent children has declined from 38 per cent in 1961 to 24 per cent in 1991 (Utting, 1995). There is an increasing number of households containing individuals living alone and an expansion of households with lone parents and their children. At an individual level it is clear that the experience of family life is complex and fluid. Over the life course individuals enter into, exit from, and redefine a range of relationships although, for many, a significant amount of time is spent in nuclear family households. Culturally too family life is represented by a wider range of signifiers: for instance media images of dyads in locations outside of the home (mother and child alone, father and child on the move in cars or in aeroplanes) coexist alongside the more conventional static home-based group images of two parents and two children eating together around a table. The word family prefixes many hitherto stand-alone objects and activities: the family car, the family disco, the family holiday. Not surprisingly therefore research shows that adults hold contradictory beliefs or 'multiple personal realities' about the family (Morgan, 1985; Trost, 1990).

What is still relatively unexplored is how children make sense of discourses and patterns of family life. Recent estimates suggest that only just over one half (53 per cent) of current UK children can expect to spend their whole childhood living with their married, biological parents (Clarke, 1992). Clarke (this volume) predicts that there will be increasing diversity in children's life-time family experiences. She suggests that, in comparison to previous cohorts, UK children born from the 1980s onwards will experience less time in their life span with two natural parents and more movements into and out of household types. Over relatively brief periods of time more children will experience significant restructuring of kin networks and household circumstances: transition from a two-parent household to a one-parent household and back again is now a common pathway for a growing proportion of children. Such transitions involve simultaneous expansion and contraction of kin networks, typically the loss of a co-resident natural father but the gain of a step-father, half-sibling and a further set of grandparents. Increasingly, the narratives of stories for children are grappling with fluidity and change in family and kinship ties (Cox, 1995).

The main academic discipline to examine children's experience of family life has been developmental psychology although the research has had a rather narrow focus (e.g., Gilby and Pederson, 1982). Typically developmental psychologists have traced an age-related sequence in children's acquisition of the concept family and have shown that as children enter their second decade they are more likely to dem-onstrate understanding of complex kinship arrangements (for instance, that consan-guinity continues between biologically related individuals irrespective of changes in the emotional and legal aspect of their relationship). Psychologists traditionally locate maturation in cognitive processes as the explanatory mechanism for this age pattern-ing although some have suggested that personal experience plays a part since, for example, children from divorced families tend to have more sophisticated understand-ing at all age levels (McGurk and Glachan, 1987). Unfortunately, the developmental paradigm has often rested on the assumption that there is one, correct definition of the family, typically the nuclear family, against which children's knowledge is judged, and so tends to exclude detailed exploration of non–nuclear family forms.

The adequacy of cognitivist explanations has been contested by those psycho-logists and sociologists concerned to move beyond a view of children as being only adults in the making (e.g., Richards and Light, 1986; Dunn, 1988; Alanen, 1990; James and Prout, 1990). These writers have begun the process of setting children's relationships and development within the context of the social institution of child-hood. As James and Prout have argued:

> the social institution of childhood [is] an actively negotiated set of social relationships within which the early years of human life are constituted. (James and Prout, 1990, p. 7)

It appears that the early years of human life, at least in western societies, are increasingly taking place in a familial context of flux and change, created in recent generations by parental separation and not parental death. In order to understand how children make sense of contemporary family and kin relationships we argue in this chapter that it is important to give space to their own experiences, representations and language. As James and Prout suggest in this volume 'the family represents a social context within which children discover their identities as 'children' and 'selves'. Giving voice to children's perspectives and conceptualizing them as active in the making of their own lives is implicit in the emergent paradigm of childhood studies. Research data collected within this frame of reference can allow comparisons to begin to be made between adult and child accounts and experiences of family life.

Studying Children's Constructions of Family Life

In this chapter we will draw on two empirical studies of children living in East London. Project 1 was designed to examine young children's accounts of their own families and to elicit their beliefs about 'the family'. Seventy-nine children from one inner East London borough were investigated. Our intention was to focus on children in their first five years at school; when UK children are for the first time spending significant amounts of time with other children and non-kin carers in institutional contexts. The average age of the children was 9 years, but the group consisted of three different school classes: 7-year-olds, 9-year-olds and 10-year-olds. Since age grading has been such a central concern of previous research on children's views of family life the research was designed to allow variation by age to be explored although not to govern fieldwork and interpretation.

Project 2 was conducted with older children (average age 14 years) and was also designed to give a profile of their views on, and constructions of, contemporary family life, as well as capture accounts of their daily lives at home, at school, at work and in leisure. The children lived in an outer East London locality and are part of a larger investigation of inter-generational perceptions of family life in East London. 600 children in six of the eight state secondary schools in the borough were surveyed.

Whilst the two studies were carried out in schools, research strategies were very different. In Project 1 a more ethnographic style was adopted with one of the investigators spending at least two weeks in each class group, getting to know the children before involving them more explicitly in the concerns of the research. Fieldwork was carried out over a three month period in each class group. As well as examining children's views on family life through participant observation and interviews, the research was set up to cover the naturally occurring daily activities of children in school contexts: writing, drawing, and conversation about topics introduced by adults. Data from the older children in Project 2 was collected through a more brief encounter of about one hour where children completed a questionnaire in the classroom and then took away a diary to complete at home over the subsequent week.[1] Project 2 was designed in this way so that specific subsamples of children living in differing household types could be identified and followed up to be investigated in the context of their own families. In both projects consent to participate in the research was requested of each individual child as well as the head teachers. A minority of children were withdrawn from Project 1 because of teachers' concerns

Table 7.1: Children's households by school class (Project 1)

Type of Household	School Class		
	7 Yrs	9 Yrs	10 Yrs
n=	(21)	(28)	(30)
Two parents and children only	76	68	63
Two parents, children and other	10	14	7
One parent and children only	14	11	13
One parent, children and other	0	4	13
Grandparent and children only	0	0	4
Grandparent, children and others	0	4	0

about the children's personal difficulties at home. In addition a number of the children in Project 1 did not consent to having their interview tape-recorded. Whilst this chapter describes children's constructions of family and kinship through a mix of methodologies, it must be remembered that the research setting was the public forum of a school and variations in representation across setting, for instance between the school and the home, have not yet been explored (Mayall, 1995).

As the children in our studies went to school each morning they left a range of families behind (Table 7.1). Significant proportions of the children in both samples no longer lived with both birth parents. For instance 37 per cent of children from the oldest class group in Project 1 had experienced parental separation or divorce and were living with only one of their parents. Children in the youngest class group in Project 1 were more likely to be still living with their natural parents. In the second Project many of the children had also personally experienced changes in household and family structures in their first fourteen years of life. Whilst a majority currently lived with both birth parents (68 per cent), 14 per cent lived in stepfamily households (12 per cent with their mothers and step-fathers, 2 per cent with their fathers and step-mothers) and 14 per cent in lone parent households (10 per cent lone mothers, 4 per cent lone fathers). 4 per cent co-resided with just grandparents, other kin or foster parents.[2]

'A Proper Family'

Fieldwork in Project 1 indicated that children often had considerable knowledge of each other's background and family circumstances. It was not uncommon for children to make asides to each other in the classroom about another child's father 'running away' or the arrival of a mother's 'new boyfriend'. Their accounts suggested that school records were often out-of-date. Children's own personal experiences, both from school and home, were drawn on when they were explicitly asked about their views on family life.

A vignette methodology was adopted to examine children's beliefs about the family. This method has been used with adults and has provided an illuminating window on their normative views of family life (Finch and Mason, 1993). Our research vignettes, or short stories, were developed to include a range of contemporary lifestyles (adapted from Trost, 1990). The stories were skeletal in content and acted as prompts for children to elaborate their views. Whilst ostensibly about the different ways adults and children live together, the vignettes also covered the gendered positions of parents, the permanence of marriage, the legitimacy of non-marital child-rearing, single parenthood, the nuclear family; all important issues in debates about contemporary family life. As Finch and Mason (1993, p. 12) show, hypothetical questions about third parties enable individuals to articulate publicly expressed norms about what is 'right and proper' for others:

> This type of research can tap beliefs at one level — the level at which people acknowledge publicly what is right and proper for third parties. But it does not tell us whether or how such beliefs get translated into relationships within families, or how far they are reflected in the responsibilities which people acknowledge for their own relatives.

The five vignettes were:

1 Married couple without child
  Bill and Betty are a married couple without any children. Are they a family?
2 Married couple with child
  Jenny and Dave are a married couple with a 6-year-old son called Ben. Are they a family?
3 Cohabiting couple with child
  Jim and Sue live together with their 6-year-old son called Paul. They are not married. Are they a family?
4 Lone mother with child
  Sally is divorced with a 10-year-old daughter Karin. Karin lives with Sally. Are these two a family?
5 Non-residential divorced father and child
  Karin's father, Tom, lives at the other end of the city. Are Karin and Tom a family?

Project 1 children were asked, in the context of an individual interview, whether they felt the people in the story were a family or not and then to give justifications for their opinion (for Project 2 the vignettes were included in the survey questionnaire). Children were left to use their understanding about what a family might be and were told that there was no right or wrong response.[3] A summary of children's views on whether each scenario constituted a family are outlined in Table 7.2.

Of all the lifestyles presented a married couple with a child was the most frequently affirmed by children as being a family. Nearly all children in both projects clearly felt that this way of living constituted a family. Presence of a child was cited as the major justification for a married couple with a child being a family ('because they've got a child'). Children were described as 'holding' and 'keeping' a couple

Table 7.2: Children defining a vignette as a family, by age of child (Project 1 and 2): percentages

		Vignette				
		1	**2**	**3**	**4**	**5**
7-year-olds n=21	Yes	33	86	20	33	38
	No/ Unsure	67	14	80	67	62
9-year-olds n=25	Yes	52	96	35	64	52
	No/ Unsure	48	4	65	36	48
10-year-olds n=30	Yes	27	100	40	40	33
	No/ Unsure	73	0	60	60	67
Project 1 Total n=76	Yes	37	95	33	46	41
	No/ Unsure	63	5	67	54	59
Project 2 Total n=384	Yes	52	98	74	72	47
	No	48	2	26	28	53

together. Some felt that adults would be miserable if they did not have children to live with. A smaller number of children invoked close emotional feelings between the adults and child in the story as making the group a family: 'They like each other and get on together. They are a good family' (10-year-old). Clearly for children, couples without children, even married couples without children, are not a family. 63 per cent of children in Project 1 and 48 per cent of those in Project 2 thought that a married couple did not constitute a family: the main reason being the absence of children 'you need children to make a family' (9-year-old). Irrespective of age, children as a group appeared concerned about household size when discussing the nature of families. No vignette included more than one child, which often provoked responses such as 'it's half a family' (10-year-old); 'just the two of them' (10-year-old), not a 'full-up family' (7-year-old discussing a divorced mother and daughter), 'a teeny, weeny family' (7-year-old talking about a divorced mother and child). Despite the growth of dyadic family images in popular culture these results show the continuing importance of the nuclear four person family grouping and residual potency of cultural norms about ideal numbers of children in families. For children families are meant to be groups of people and should not be 'too small'.[4]

However, when responses to the vignettes were taken as a whole it appeared that the principle of the presence of children 'making' a family came into conflict with another principle, voiced particularly by younger respondents, that parents living with children should be married. 54 per cent of children in Project 1 and 26 per cent of children in Project 2 felt that a cohabiting couple with a child was not a family, mainly because the parents were not married. Younger children seemed most unsure about the nature of cohabitation as one child put it 'that's a complicated one' (9-year-old); 'you need to be married if you're going to be a family' (7-year-old); 'before you have a child you should get married' (9-year-old); 'it's not a proper family yet' (9-year-old). Some children were unsure of the child's status or permanence of the living arrangement, for others it appeared to provoke feelings of vulnerability: 'It's not really a family because they are not married . . . being married is more secure. She could run off with another man.' (10-year-old); 'what would happen if they love each other but don't look after the child?' (7-year-old).

The minority of younger children who described a cohabiting couple and child as a family justified their decision on the grounds of co-residence 'they live together' (7-year-old) or emotional closeness 'you don't need a piece of paper to show you love somebody' (9-year-old). As can be seen from Table 7.2 a majority of the older children were more accepting of cohabitational lifestyles, also invoking the principle of love and emotional closeness.

In many of these responses children were showing awareness of the continued higher status and legitimacy of marriage in British culture and perhaps the real structural fragility of living with parents who are not married. Recent research indicates that relationship breakdown is higher amongst cohabiting couples with children than for married couples with children (Kiernan and Estaugh, 1993). Moreover, despite the dramatic recent increase in births outside marriage, living in cohabitational households is not yet legally affirmed, celebrated or socially sanctioned in the same way as marriage. Currently the language used to describe non-married emotional relationships is clumsy and vague; the most common adult term to describe the couple is 'partner', a loan from the world of employment and business. A further indication of the marginality of the lifestyle is the formal legal nature of cohabiting child–father relationships. Under English law if a cohabiting couple separate a child has no immediate right of access to the father (under *The Children Act 1989*, unmarried fathers have no formal parental reponsibilities, either during their relationship or after a separation, unless special application is made).[5]

Responses to vignettes of lifestyles including parental divorce showed that lone mother and child households were generally endorsed as being a legitimate family form, particularly by older children: 72 per cent of the 14-year-olds felt lone mother and child households were families, as did 46 per cent of the younger children. The main reason offered by children in both projects was a view that a divorce did not alter the continuity of the mother–child tie, 'They're still a family, even if mum and dad split up, whatever' (10-year-old). Biological and emotional closeness between mothers and children were referred to by children 'they have the same blood' (9-year-old). The fact that mother and daughter still lived together was the second most commonly mentioned reason.

Those that felt a lone mother and child household was not a familial lifestyle generally invoked the absence of a father figure: It's only got a mum, hasn't got a dad' (10-year-old). 'You need mother, father and children to make a family'

(10-year-old). The tenuous nature of relationships between fathers and children after divorce is shown by the relatively low proportion of children, in both projects, who felt that non-residential fathers and their children constituted a family: less than half the children in both samples responded positively to this idea. The majority of children thought that because the two no longer co-resided they were no longer a family. These children appeared to assume that when fathers lived apart from children they had little contact with them: 'Not really no, because she couldn't see him very often, because they are not living together' (10-year-old). A minority of children implied that divorced fathers had committed some misdemeanour: 'he's naughty' (7-year-old) or that families needed mothers 'it's not complete without mum' (9-year-old). Those that felt otherwise stressed the continuity of biological and emotional closeness 'he's still Karin's Dad' (9-year-old), 'she might still love him, and him her' (10-year-old).

There was a complex association between expressed beliefs about vignettes and the actual family circumstances of children. For instance, in the 14-year-old sample, when compared to children who had always lived with their birth parents, those who had experienced parental separation in their lives were more likely to say that non-residential fathers and children did not constitute a family. This was especially the case for children living in stepfather households, a significant proportion of whom had irregular contact with their biological fathers.

The material suggests that with respect to the fifth vignette children, like adults, are drawing on lived experience and cultural discourses concerning the peripherality of divorced fathers. A majority of children still live with their mothers after marital separation and the decline in contact between non-residential divorced fathers and their children has been well documented (e.g., Bertaux and Delcroix, 1992). In this context it is understandable that for some children a father is central to family life only when he is co-resident. However, further research is needed to clarify the relative importance of parental gender and co-residence in shaping children's perceptions of the stability of family relationships after divorce, for it may well be that children have similar perceptions of non-residential mothers.

Children Talking Together about Family Life

In order to explore the negotiation of norms about family life small group discussions were held with some of the children in Project 1. These took place after they had been individually interviewed. Children were selected from a range of family backgrounds and cultures and were asked to discuss the vignettes again and if possible come to a group consensus. The purpose of this agenda was to encourage an exchange of views in the group. Group composition was carefully discussed with class teachers to ensure that it did not include children who had unharmonious relationships with each other, so as not to upset a particular child. The discussions took place in a quiet room away from the classroom, lasted on average three-quarters of an hour and were tape-recorded. We found that the children were very keen to participate in group discussion. An extract from one of the discussions is presented in some detail below to examine some of the issues in more depth. All the children were 9 years old. The children's names are self-chosen pseudonyms.

Veronica: Girl. Lives with mother and father and two older brothers. Youngest child in family. White British. Non-religious.

James: Boy. Lives with grandparents, aunt and his cousin aged 6. His mother and stepfather live nearby, with younger stepbrother. Parents separated when he was 6 years. No regular contact with father (although has had phone calls). White British. Non-religious.

Zain: Boy. Lives with mother and younger brother. Born in Poland. Parents separated. Father from Pakistan, mother from Poland. Catholic.

Thahera: Girl. Lives with mother, father, two brothers and two sisters (she is the second child). Born in UK, parents from India. Muslim.

Alan: Boy. Lives with mother, her new boyfriend and sister. Another older sister lives nearby. Mother white British. Parents separated when he was 5/6 years old. No contact with father, born in the West Indies. Non-religious.

In this group most of the discussion centred around the vignettes about lifestyles after parental divorce. A predominant dynamic was an attempt by the two girls who lived in nuclear family households, Veronica and Thahera, to convince the others that both lone mother and child households and non-residential fathers and children were legitimate family forms. The children who had experienced some form of parental separation in their lives argued that parents, particularly fathers, needed to show caring contact with children before they could be considered part of a family. It was notable that each of these children had little or no contact with their own non-residential father, which clearly influenced their feelings about this issue. Both Veronica and Thahera initially invoked the principle of consanguinity in their argument:

Thahera: Miss, I think that Sally and Karin are family and Sally and her father are family because they've all got the same flesh of blood, but I don't think Sally and her husband [Karin's father] are family because they've got nothing to do with each other anymore and they haven't got the same blood of flesh.

(Interchange follows with Veronica supporting Thahera's position)

Alan: I don't think all three of them are a family, because the little girl, I don't think she's a family with him because she don't live with him or nothing and he might have forgotten everything about her and might even have gone and had another child or something.

Veronica:	But, Alan, her dad's still got the same flesh of blood.
Alan:	Yes, but I don't think it counts, right. I think it counts on what he does, like. She might not even know where he is. My mum and dad split up three or four years ago. I don't know where he is. He ain't sent us no money or nothing. I don't know where he is.
Researcher:	So what you feel is, the contact or whatever is more important than the actual blood relation?
Alan:	Yes.

(Discussion continues for some time mainly between Veronica and Alan, without much change in position. Alan offers more examples of negligent paternal behaviour 'just say if he started nicking your money, taking things, getting you into trouble you wouldn't count him as family would you?')

Researcher:	Right. It sounds as if you two have got as far as you're going to get. There's two distinct positions on that and James and Thahera are desperate to talk. Which one of you wants to go first?
James:	Thahera can go first.
Thahera:	Miss, but . . .
Researcher:	Go on, Thahera.
Thahera:	But just say that you knew where your father was, right.
James:	I don't.
Thahera:	Just say that your mum was very ill. She was really badly sick, she was critical and you knew where your father was. Who would you phone? You'd, I would phone my father.
Veronica:	Would you phone your uncle or would you phone your aunt or would you phone your . . .
Thahera:	Yes, but you don't always know your aunt's phone number.
Zain:	I would phone for an ambulance.

(The children start talking simultaneously and Thahera and Veronica attempt to ascertain who James would phone if his mother was seriously ill, and then if his mother and father died. He eventually says he would phone for an ambulance and go to his big sister's house. After this is established Thahera introduces a further traumatic scenario for Alan to consider.)

Thahera:	If your mother and father were both dead you'd probably go to an orphanage or you'd probably just live on the street or something.
Alan:	Yes, I didn't want to go to an orphanage.
Thahera:	You'd probably go to your grandmother's uncle.

> *Alan:* All my grandmothers and my great-grandmothers are dead.
> *Zaid:* Alright, you'd probably live on the street.

(Thahera then turns her attention to James and asks)

> *Thahera:* Do you meet your dad?

(James relates that he does not see his father, although he has phoned and he knows where he lives. He points out that his father does not send him cards 'or nothing', a point which is taken up later by Alan).

> *James:* I don't want to see my dad. I want to see my mum.
> *Alan:* I don't want to see my dad either. He knows our address, he knows my birthday, he cannot forget my birthday, it's Christmas day [event changed by authors], right and they're just getting a divorce through sort of thing . . . she (mother) phoned and said you can send the kids birthday cards, I'll let 'em have 'em. Right. And she said like, sometime, right, would you like to have the children, for half-term? And he said yes. And you know what? He never turned up for months. And we found out he's hired a car and he's gone to Brighton for a holiday like.

(After further elaboration by Alan, Veronica and Thahera announce to the group that they have changed their positions).

> *Veronica:* I just want to say that . . . Alan's convinced me . . . about Karin and his dad aren't family with Karin.
> *Researcher:* Right I see.
> *Thahera:* I think Alan's convinced me, miss, because, oh God, what he said because I just think he convinced me.

These discussions show that individual opinions were not totally fixed. Children could persuade each other to change position, particularly after listening to accounts where others had relevant experience and had been upset by parents. The discussions enabled more specific conditional aspects of family life to be unpicked and explored in depth by the children. For these children talking about divorce spontaneously generated consideration of parental departure, abandonment and even death. Children used the group to examine the boundaries of acceptable parenting for them as children and particularly the deserving and undeserving father after divorce. A father who forgot his child's birthday did not deserve to be included in a family grouping. It appeared that children, like adults, can hold contradictory principles of what makes a family: whilst being aware of the formal relevance of consanguinity in defining a family this principle becomes a secondary one in the face of parental disregard.

In addition, the dialogue shows that opinions expressed about the vignettes were not just the products of individual children's understandings and emotional coping strategies but were also themselves social products constructed in this particular research context. When Alan had been interviewed on his own before the group discussion he had endorsed both post-divorce lifestyles as legitimate family groups, as did all the other children, except Zain. It may well be that children test out their own positions about a topic through constructing different accounts or what Hallden (1995, p. 78) calls 'narrative fictions' in response to different research contexts.

Children's Drawings of Their Families

Whilst children's accounts of their own family lives emerged when they talked about other children's families, in both projects attempts were made to focus more directly on respondents' own families through diaries, stories, drawings as well as interviews (because of length constraints only drawings are discussed here).

Drawing is an important everyday activity in which younger children engage. We wanted to explore what children came up with when they were asked to draw their own family (see Issacs and Levin, 1984) (Project 1). A further motivation for using drawings came from a comment in Young and Willmott's introduction to *Family and Kinship in East London*. One of the authors lived in the area during fieldwork and described his child returning from school and saying:

> The teacher asked us to draw pictures of our family. I did one of you and Mummy and Mikey and me, but isn't it funny, the others were putting in their Nannas and aunties and uncles and all sorts of people like that. (Young and Willmott, 1962, p. 14)

On the basis of previous research we anticipated that children would draw those who were emotionally significant to them and wondered how this might vary across different family types (Klepsh and Logie, 1982). Children were asked to draw a picture of their whole family and then write a story about their drawing. After receiving this somewhat general request several asked for more guidance on what exactly they should draw. Here are fieldnotes of classroom interaction in the first minutes after a class of 10-year-olds was asked to draw their family (Project 1):

> First question: 'all your family or just your house?' Talking amongst themselves, showing each other, reluctance, 'cos not good drawer' — 'This is rubbish' etc — 'All my cousins?' 'cos I've got eighteen cousins and I'm just going to draw my mum and dad and me' — 'Do you draw yourself?' — 'Do you draw your mum and dad?' — 'Miss, can I draw my pets?' — 'Miss can you draw your grandparents, nan and granddad?' . . . — It's up to you. [said many times]

In a very short period children articulated the key issue: whether or not their representation should go beyond the co-residential unit. Our response was to convey to the children that their drawing could be of whatever they wanted. In general it appeared that the 7- and 9-year-olds felt more at ease with drawing in a classroom setting, whilst the 10-year-olds were more self-conscious and concerned about creating realistic images 'I wish I could draw.' (10-year-old) 'I can't do my dad [right]'

(10-year-old). We wondered whether this pattern was an indicator of how children themselves age-graded their own activities; for 10-year-olds this sort of drawing may be perceived as a 'childish' activity.

The largest group of children (40 per cent of the total sample of Project 1), eventually drew the individuals they lived with, indicating that in this particular context a family was the household unit. For the remaining children there was not a direct match between the co-residential unit and the number and composition of human figures in their family drawing. Some did not include all the members of their household (27 per cent), whilst others added individuals outside the household (29 per cent). In 4 per cent of cases it was not clear who was depicted in the drawing. There were no significant age differences to this general patterning which contests a traditional psychological prediction that younger children would produce a less accurate or household-matched drawing.

Those who drew their co-residential group adopted a conventional style: parents to the left of the paper (usually indicating that they were drawn first), often father before mother, then the children, biggest to smallest (Figure 7.1). This drawing was created by Adress, a 9-year-old boy who lives with his parents and three siblings — two older brothers and younger sister. He was born in the UK, of Pakistani parents. Dad is drawn to the left followed by mum and an age-graded set of children. All the male figures have hats and there are brand names printed on some of the hats and shoes; it was not uncommon for boys particularly to indicate brand names on clothes.

Children's accounts about why they included the people they did in their drawings indicated that several principles guided the activity. All the human figures had a consanguineal, affinal or adoptive relationship to the child (no child included a friend or an unrelated adult in their drawing although several included a household pet). In the main children included those with whom they lived, but not always everyone in the house. Non-co-resident kin appeared to be included either when they were seen regularly or if they were emotionally and/ or practically important to the respondent.

Moreover, household type rather than age emerged as significant in trying to make sense of the way children drew their families. As Table 7.3 shows, children living in non-nuclear households were more likely to produce family drawings which did not match the household membership. The most common pattern was to include in the family drawing individuals who were not co-resident (in addition to drawing either the whole or part of the co-residential unit). 60 per cent of children living in one-parent households drew in this way in comparison to 18 per cent of children living in two-parent households. These additional figures drawn were not in the main biological fathers but were primary and secondary kin (grandparents, cousins, older siblings, aunts and uncles and so on). This finding suggests that markers in addition to co-residence are especially important when some children in one-parent households depict their family; extended kin networks may be particularly significant.[6]

In turn, it is possible that for children in conventional nuclear families more significant and emotionally important figures are those with whom they live. It must

Figure 7.1: Drawing of the family by 'Adress'

Table 7.3: Composition of children's family drawing by household type (percentages)

| | Type of household | | |
	Two parent n=60	One parent n=15	Other n=2
Identical composition to household	48	13	0
Fewer figures than in household	32	13	0
More figures than in household	18	60	100
Unclear	2	13	0

be remembered also that children's representations are part of a social world where the nuclear family model is strongly valued, indeed as seen in previous sections the respondents themselves adhered to the view that the nuclear family was the 'proper family'. Accordingly, in the context of this research, children in nuclear families may have been trying 'to get it right' (in relation to wider cultural norms) and children in lone mother families may have drawn more figures in order to achieve a representation that resembled a two-parent family in size.

Figure 7.2: Drawing of the family by 'Alan'

Figure 7.2 is a drawing produced by Alan, one of the children who took part in the group discussion described above. His family drawing consists of four figures: mother, self and two sisters. His mother is surrounded by her children. Alan is on one side and two sisters on the other.

The non-residential sister who is included in the family drawing is 18 years old and has only recently left home. During the small group discussion Alan talks about his sister's house as a place he would go to if his mother was ill. In his story he writes of his father 'I don't count him as family because he can't even remember our birthdays.' He also mentions this issue in the group discussion. Whilst drawing Alan asked whether he could include his mother's new boyfriend (a 'nice' man who had made him a go-cart) but decided not to although it was indicated he could. In the individual interview the mother's boyfriend was cited as a main source of instrumental support (for instance, helping to fix toys) and his mother as the main provider of emotional support (the person he would go to when he felt sad). Alan's biological father, with whom he had no contact, was not included in the drawing.

Conclusion

These studies suggest that, as with adults, children's concepts of family are complex, fluid and sometimes contradictory. What counts as family for young children is not straightforward although consanguinity, co-residence, consistent care, size, the presence of married parents and other children are important. Whilst a diversity of family models are available for children in their conceptualizations of family life, the nuclear family remains a potent image. When children examined contemporary lifestyles the vignette they most strongly endorsed as being a proper family was the married couple and child living together. Several children, notably the younger respondents were especially uncertain about the status of cohabiting parents and of post-divorce lifestyles. Perhaps this uncertainty reflects the continuing structural fragility of these household forms and the lack of clarity of children's position within them. Whilst there has been a growth in cohabitation and one parent households through the 1980s in the UK many children in these research projects continued to place great significance on marriage and the nuclear family. For some children, particularly those who had experienced parental separation, the idea of family went beyond the household or conjugal pair. Such children drew on primary and second-ary kin as important figures and resources in their lives, but excluded non-resident fathers. This finding gives some support to Boyden's (1990, p. 201) suggestion that 'new alliances and innovative survival strategies' may be adopted by children and adults in the wake of breakdown in traditional networks.

Notes

1 We would like to thank Julia Brannen for her help with the design of the questionnaire.
2 Whilst over 90 per cent of the children in both projects were born in the UK, children in Project 1 were much more likely to have had parents who had been born outside of the UK particularly from the Asian subcontinent. Inner East London is much more eth-nically diverse than outer East London, which has an ethnically homogeneous profile dominated by those whose parents originate in the UK. Both localities are traditionally working class, which was reflected in the project samples (O'Brien and Jones, in press, 1996). Older children were more likely to have had mothers who worked outside the home (48 per cent of 7-year-olds' mothers worked in contrast to 62 per cent of the mothers of 14-year-olds).
3 As Solberg argues elsewhere in this volume, in a school environment it is important to emphasize to children that a research procedure is not some sort of test. But inevitably such a view must have been present, for instance, the children in Project 1 despite pro-testations to the contrary called the researcher 'Miss' (an English child's description of a female teacher).
4 Any future researcher using this methodology would be advised to construct vignettes including more than one child. The proportion of one-child families was low in both project samples (less than 10 per cent in both projects) and even rarer for ethnic minority children.
5 However, under the UN Convention on the Rights of the Child, all children have a right of access to both parents.
6 The relationship of children to their non-residential biological father is complex: whilst he may not be drawn as a separate figure there may be other references to him. For instance, one child who had not seen her father, who was living in the USA, for over five years had USA written on her drawn T-shirt. Further research needs to be carried out with children of divorce who have regular contact with the non-residential parent. In Project 1 most of the children in lone mother households had little or no contact with their fathers.

References

ALANEN, L. (1990) 'Rethinking socialization, the family and childhood', in ADLER, P., ADLER, P., MANDELL, N. and CAHILL, S. (Eds) *Sociological Studies of Child Development: A Research Annual*, **3**, Greenwich, CT.

BERNARDES, J. (1985) 'Do we really know what "the family" is?', in CLOSE, P. and COLLINS, R. (Eds) *Family and Economy*, London, Macmillan.

BERTAUX, D. and DELCROIX, C. (1992) 'Where have all the daddies gone?', in BJORNBERG, U. (Ed) *European Parents in the 1990s: Contradictions and Comparisons*, New York, Transaction Books.

BOYDEN, J. (1990) 'Childhood and the policy makers: A comparative perspective on the globalization of childhood', in JAMES, A. and PROUT, A. (Eds) *Constructing and Reconstructing Childhood*, London, Falmer Press.

CLARKE, L. (1992) 'Children's family circumstances: Recent trends in Great Britain', *European Journal of Population*, **8**, pp. 309–40.

COX, R. (1995) 'Reading about the family in contemporary children's fiction: Modes of representation', in BRANNEN, J. and O'BRIEN, M. (Eds) *Childhood and Parenthood*, London, Institute of Education.

DUNN, J. (1988) *The Beginnings of Social Understanding*, Oxford, Basil Blackwell.

FINCH, J. and MASON, J. (1993) *Negotiating Family Responsibilities*, London, Routledge.

GILBY, R. and PEDERSON, D. (1982) 'The development of the child's concept of the family', *Canadian Journal of Behaviourial Sciences*, **14**, 2, pp. 110–21.

HALLDEN, G. (1995) 'The family — A refuge from demands or an arena for the exercise of power and control — children's fictions on their future families', in MAYALL, B. (Ed) *Children's Worlds Observed and Experienced*, London, Falmer Press.

ISSACS, M. and LEVIN, I. (1984) 'Who's in my family?: A longitudinal study of drawings of children of divorce', *Journal of Divorce*, **7**, 4, pp. 1–21.

JAMES, A. and PROUT, A. (1990) (Eds) *Constructing and Reconstructing Childhood: Contemporary Issues in the Sociological Study of Childhood*, London, Falmer Press.

KIERNAN, K. and ESTAUGH, V. (1993) 'Cohabitation: Extra marital child-bearing and social policy', Occasional Paper 17, London, Family Policy Studies Centre.

KLEPSH, M. and LOGIE, L. (1982) *Children Draw and Tell: An Introduction to the Projective Uses of Children's Human Figure Drawings*, New York, Bruner Mazel.

LASLETT, P. (1991) 'Opening address', *Child, Family and Society*, European Commission Conference, Luxembourg.

MAYALL, B. (1995) 'Children in action at home and school', in MAYALL, B. (Ed) *Children's Childhoods Observed and Experienced*, London, Falmer Press.

McGURK, H. and GLACHAN, M. (1987) 'Children's conception of parenthood following divorce', *Journal of Child Psychology and Psychiatry*, **28**, 3, pp. 427–35.

MORGAN, D. (1985) *The Family, Politics and Social Theory*, London, Routledge and Kegan Paul.

O'BRIEN, M. and JONES, D. (in press, 1996) 'Family and kinship in an outer London borough: Continuity and change', in RUSTIN, M., BUTLER, T. and CHAMBERLAYNE, P. (Eds) *The Regeneration of East London*, London, Lawrence and Wishart.

RICHARDS, M.P.M. and LIGHT, P. (1986) *Children of Social Worlds: Development in a Social Context*, Cambridge, Polity.

TROST, J. (1990) 'Do we mean the same by the concept of family?', *Communication Research*, **17**, 4, pp. 431–43.

UTTING, D. (1995) *Family and Parenthood: Supporting Families, Preventing Breakdown*, York, Joseph Rowntree Foundation.

YOUNG, M. and WILLMOTT, P. (1962) *Family and Kinship in East London*, Middlesex, Penguin Books.

Chapter 8

'Helping Out': Children's Labour Participation in Chinese Take-away Businesses in Britain

Miri Song

Introduction

Recent sociological studies of ethnic businesses have tended to depict ethnic migrant groups' concentration in the small business sector in quite positive terms, particularly in light of high levels of unemployment in most western societies. Committed family labour has been said to be a key 'ethnic resource' for the viability and competitiveness of these businesses, many of which would not survive without the help of family members (Ward and Jenkins, 1984; Waldinger, Aldrich and Ward, 1990). Feminists have rightly pointed out that analysts' references to family labour obscure the fact that it is often women's (usually wives') unpaid labours which sustain ethnic businesses (Phizacklea, 1988).

However, children's labour participation has been even more neglected in studies of ethnic businesses. Although there has been a growing body of literature on 'the second generation' of ethnic migrant children in the UK, most of this literature has not focused upon the work roles of children in ethnic businesses. Rather, this literature has emphasized ethnic migrant children's cultural identities, educational performance, and inter-generational relationships (e.g., Watson, 1977; Saifullah-Khan, 1979; Ghodsian and Essen, 1980; Parker, 1995).

Chinese take-away businesses in Britain are a good example of small, family-run ethnic business, in which children can contribute substantial amounts of labour and assistance. There are approximately 157,500 Chinese in the UK, according to the 1991 Census (Owen, 1992). The majority of the Chinese in Britain are from the New Territories, the rural part of Hong Kong (Runnymede Trust, 1986). They are heavily concentrated in various aspects of the Chinese catering trade, given the limited labour market opportunities that many Chinese people face (Baxter, 1988). Although various Chinese communities have long been established throughout many parts of Britain, they have been quite under-studied in comparison with Asians (people originating from the Indian subcontinent) and Afro-Caribbeans in Britain.

In a typical study of Chinese children in Britain in the 1970s, Jackson and Garvey (1974) argued, not surprisingly, that Chinese children's school performance was negatively influenced by their work in their parents' take-away businesses. However, the authors also reported that Chinese children were often not registered for school: 'If there are any questions, there is always the switch routine. Children are moved onto another area and another business, until the inquiries peter out' (1974, p. 12). Although not wholly unsympathetic to the difficulties faced by Chinese parents, Garvey and Jackson's overall depiction of Chinese families was that Chinese parents were rather ruthless and hard-hearted in their manipulation of children's labours, and that Chinese children's lives were filled with dirty work and misery — end of story.

In contrast, the Chinese young people I interviewed spoke a great deal about their parents' concerns that their children obtain a good education. Although twenty years have passed since Jackson and Garvey's study, very little has been written about Chinese families in Britain which challenges such a reductive view of their family and work lives. As a result, Chinese children's labour participation in their family businesses (and that of other ethnic migrant children) has tended to be seen in quite a negative and disapproving light, in spite of the fact that there have been very few empirical studies which have documented the lives of Chinese families in Britain.

In most advanced capitalist western societies, it is not the norm for children to contribute 'productively' to their family economies, although children may perform household chores or childcare.[1] In contrast, it is not unusual for children in poor families in 'Third World' societies to contribute to their family economies, through industrial waged work, agricultural work, or work in informal sectors (Rodgers and Standing, 1981; Lai, 1982; Ennew, 1982). For instance, children from poor families in Hong Kong, particularly daughters, may leave school early in search of waged work (Easey, 1979; Salaff, 1981).

Much research on child labour has focused upon debates around its legal and moral legitimacy (Standing, 1982; Morrow, 1992), and the European Union's 1994 directive on the protection of young people at work has highlighted this issue. Within Britain, which has opted out of a number of the EU directive stipulations, jobs such as babysitting, running errands, or helping with charities are not covered by child labour legislation, but the same rules and regulations apply to children working in family businesses as to children in other forms of employment (Pond and Searle, 1990).[2] However, in comparison with industrial employment, children's labours performed within the confines of a family business have traditionally been regarded as more benign: 'Prohibiting children who are under the legal age from helping out on the family farm or in the shop while under the watchful eye of parents is seen as an unreasonable interference by the state in family life' (MacLennan, 1985, p. 31).

In fact, not all children's labours performed within the 'family' sphere are regarded equally in Britain, or in many other western societies. Researchers conducting the National Child Employment Study in Britain investigated 'the stereotype of child labour as a phenomenon associated with Asian family business'. The study found that it was a 'myth that children's employment is mainly concerned with Asian family businesses', given that white and Afro-Caribbean children were proportionately slightly more likely to work in their sample (Pond and Searle, 1990,

p. 12). One reason why children's work in ethnic businesses may be negatively singled out in Britain, as in other western societies, is that children's work in Chinese take-aways, for instance, is performed in a racialized work niche associated with derogatory notions of being Chinese; work in a take-away business does not evoke the wholesome images of children helping out on the family farm.

While I do not dispute that children's labour participation in family businesses can have educationally and developmentally detrimental effects upon children, or that parents have a great deal of authority and control over their children's labours, I would argue that we need to reassess and broaden the way we think about children's work in small family-run ethnic businesses. Children in these families tend to be depicted too simplistically as victims, rather than as agents, who are active in shaping their work roles and who attribute meanings to their labour participation (Qvortrup, 1985; Leonard, 1990; Morrow, 1992).

It is all too easy to conceptualize children's labour participation in Chinese take-aways in terms of stark oppositions, as being voluntary or coerced. Some culturally based explanations of Chinese family members' work commitments have tended to assume that children unproblematically want to help out, pointing to the strong filial bonds which are central to Confucian principles (e.g., Benedict, 1979). Without discounting cultural norms, such essentializing arguments fail to consider how such commitments may arise in response to families' situations, as ethnic migrant families engaged in a family strategy (Glenn, 1983). Conversely, patriarchal authority and power has been central in explaining how women's and children's labours may be 'incorporated' into family economies (Finch, 1983; Delphy and Leonard, 1992). Patriarchal authority is legitimized by means of tradition and personal loyalty, which is not 'rational', but personal and affective (Newby, 1977; Hood-Williams, 1990). However, there are also limits to what patriarchal authority and control can explain. For instance, in their study of young people in family farms, Wallace *et al.* (1994) observed that, '. . . [family] roles had to be negotiated and there was scope for young people to resist or to comply with the dominant authority within the family' (p. 524). A sole reliance upon arguments about Chinese culture or about patriarchal control is inadequate to explain children's own commitments to working for their families, even though such commitments often entail both positive and negative experiences.

Therefore, in addition to cultural norms and patriarchal authority, children's labour participation in Chinese take-aways must include the normative and affective dimensions of working for one's family. Furthermore, Chinese children's labour participation must be studied in the context of families' experiences of migration and ethnic migrant status in Britain, including families' experiences of racism and social marginalization. This article is derived from my small-sample doctoral research on young peoples' (mostly in their early–mid 20s) family and work experiences in twenty-five Chinese families running take-aways predominantly in the Greater London area. Like Jones (1992), I use the term 'children' to refer to a family relationship and 'young people' to refer to the interviewees in this study. Young peoples' accounts provided complex understandings of how family relationships both shaped, and were shaped by, working together.[3]

Chinese Parents' Reliance upon Their Children

Chinese parents relied upon their children in a number of ways. Firstly, Chinese children provided valuable labour in their take-away businesses. Young people usually worked at the counter, where they took orders from customers, and often went back and forth between 'the front' (the counter area) and 'the back' (the kitchen), to expedite the whole process; they also helped to clean up after the shop closed. While it was predominantly their parents' responsibility, some young people also helped with food preparation and cooking. In addition to shop work, mothers and daughters in these families performed most of the domestic housework (see Song, 1995).

Many Chinese parents also relied upon their children for English language mediation and/or business skills which they did not possess. Typically, parents in these families had had little or no formal education. Many Chinese young people reported attending meetings with solicitors and accountants, in order to translate for their parents. Furthermore, young people often accompanied their parents to doctors' appointments or to teachers' meetings for younger siblings. In these families, children often played a central role in not only running the take-away business, but also in aiding their parents in most facets of their lives.

One of the most striking and persistent themes raised in interviews with these young people was that they grew up with a great deal of responsibility (see Brannen this volume). According to Wong, whose parents relied upon him and his brother for 'everything', 'we are our parents' guide-dogs to the world'.[4] Wong and his brother, Fai, as the two eldest children, grew up helping out in the shop almost every night. Their parents had no formal education, spoke no English, and did not drive. Not only did Wong and Fai accompany their parents to most appointments and places, but Fai was responsible for the bookkeeping and business management of the shop by the time he was 15 years old. Furthermore, the two brothers knew how to cook and how to do counter-work; in this respect, they were much more flexible workers than their parents, who were confined to the 'back' of the shop — the kitchen.

However, there was some diversity in terms of how much parents relied upon their children. In contrast with Wong's and Fai's experience, above, the children in three of the twenty-five families had relatively minor work roles. For instance, Theresa's and her brothers' labour participation in their take-away was much more limited; most significantly, Theresa and her brothers did not need to perform any work as mediators for their parents. Theresa's parents spoke fluent English, and her mother had worked as a nurse in Britain before she married. Theresa's labour participation was only occasional, and when she did work, she was confined to counter-work, for she did not know how to cook any dishes. Furthermore, her parents employed kitchen staff, leaving their children relatively free of helping out.

Undoubtedly some Chinese parents did rely upon their children's labours in take-aways, either because they could not afford to hire employees, or because they wished to save money. But I found parents' reliance upon their children to be much more complex than has been suggested thus far.

The hiring of employees (to replace children) was seen by a number of young people as problematic. In addition to issues of affordability, high turn-over, especially with part-time staff, was a common problem; children in these families were a much more reliable labour source. More importantly, running a family business was an intensely private affair for these families. Full-time employees in take-aways (who were almost always Chinese) expected to get free room and board, in addition to pay, and if the family lived above the shop, this often meant that they must live together with their employees. Many interviewees reported concerns about being able to trust employees, particularly if an employee worked at the counter, handling cash transactions as well as customer relations. Furthermore, much of the mediating and 'caring' work that young people performed could not be performed by employees; much of this work was a 'labour of love' that was not restricted to set shop hours or tasks.

Keeping a take-away business family-only was a way in which Chinese parents were able to preserve their sense of autonomy and control, so much of which was compromised by their status as ethnic migrants in Britain. Parents' reliance upon children's labour participation in the take-away was also understood by some young people as a way of keeping children safe at home. According to Wong, his parents were concerned about keeping them protected in a foreign environment, which they found hostile and unfamiliar:

> At the time, I just thought that it was her [mother] forcing us to work in the shop and everything else, but it wasn't that . . . But it was purely because she was such a protective person, my mother looks at the world from the worst possible angle, and she expects life to be full of badness. It was more the protective feeling because my parents are always saying, 'Yes, you have to remember that you are in someone else's country', which I think is crap, basically. If there were any problems with neighbours being out of order, they'd say, well, we won't complain, we're in someone else's country.

Also, working together as a family was inextricable from most young peoples' understandings and experiences of 'family'. In most western family economies based upon waged work, there are some identifiable demarcations between 'public' and 'private' spheres. In Chinese take-away businesses, like other family businesses, the interests of these families are often seen to be very closely tied to those of the business (Rosenblatt *et al.*, 1985; Wheelock, 1991).

'Helping Out' in the 'Family Work Contract'

Most of the young people in this study grew up working in their families' take-aways, and experienced their work as 'part and parcel' of their daily lives. Young people in a minority of families started working in their shops when they were older, typically in their mid-late teens; this was usually due to the fact that these families had been running their shops for a much shorter period, at the time of interview, than families where young people had started working from a young age.

For instance, Wong and Fai were 10 and 8 years old, respectively, when their take-away shop was started. They started helping out in the kitchen, as soon as the shop opened, doing 'simple' things like peeling prawns and washing up. The incorporation of their labour was gradual — rather similar to the process in which daughters 'drifted' into caring for their elderly mothers (Lewis and Meredith, 1988). As the two brothers got older, and more experienced, their work roles expanded and diversified as well.

Wong amd Fai could not report any specific moment at which they were told to work by their parents. For these brothers, their parents' expectations that the children would help out had always been implicit and unquestioned. In other words, nothing had been explicitly 'negotiated' (Finch and Mason, 1993) between the parents and children, regarding children's labour participation. In most families, there was very little discussion between parents and children about children's labour participation. Rather, growing up in the take-away and working for the family seemed to be 'natural' and 'second nature' to most young people.

In these families, young people seemed to share a number of common views and meanings attributed to their labour participation, which were embodied in what I call a 'family work contract' (FWC). In contrast with most 'public' employer–employee contracts, which are formalized and explicit, 'family work contracts', as they were understood by these young people, were viewed as implicit understandings upheld collectively by family members. These young people spoke of their labour participation in ways which recognized that their families' relations of production differed from those in employer–employee relationships. For example, young people often made the distinction between 'helping out' and 'work,' in which 'helping out' involved work which was meaningful in itself, and which was normatively pre-scribed, while 'work' was seen in terms of delimited work roles in an impersonal context.

The meanings Chinese young people attributed to helping out were central to their understandings of their 'family work contracts': Both moral and material meanings and pressures were seen to underly the act of helping out (Rapp *et al.*, 1979). Not only did helping out contribute directly to the survival and success of the family business, but it also was a 'duty' which affirmed family membership (Chan, 1986, p. 9).

Firstly, helping out was seen to be necessitated by family survival. All the young people in the sample seemed to have a heightened awareness of the precariousness of survival. Most young people, like Paul, grew up with the knowledge that the survival of their family's livelihood depended upon their own labour participation:

> We did accept the fact that this is how Chinese families cope if they were to immigrate to England. It was the only way. Like my mum and dad can't speak English. What can they do? The best way is to open a restaurant or take-away. I don't see any other way, to be honest, to survive. I accepted it completely.

For ethnic migrant families such as the Chinese in Britain, experiences of racism, discrimination, and social marginalization could intensify feelings of family solidarity (Saifullah-Khan, 1979). Helping out represented a collective act of family survival and strength, in the face of racist hostility and marginalization, and many young people were evidently proud of the hard work they had contributed to their family businesses.

In addition to survival pressures, many young people also felt 'invested' in their family businesses, and noted that their own well-being and futures were integrally dependent upon their shops:

MS: Do you think you should help out?

WC: Yes. I'm just as responsible as my parents really, cause it's a family business, we have it, it's not like oh, I'm just doing my job, and that is it, and I don't care about anything else. I care for it, and we really feel that it's our own business.

Secondly, 'helping out', as opposed to 'work', implied good will and a willingness to contribute one's labour. This willingness to help out was seen to derive from the fact that family relationships were 'special', as opposed to employer–employee relationships (Finch, 1989). As Sue noted, 'With your family, you have to work extra hard, because it's your family, whereas if you're in 9 to 5, you don't kill yourself over it'. Sue is articulating the fact that there are no clear boundaries or limits to what one *should* do in a FWC, in contrast with employment, where one's 'job' is clearly delineated.

There was a striking normative consensus amongst young people that they should, in principle, help out in their family businesses, and that willingness to do so should not be attached to remuneration. As Ming put it, 'They [parents] say that there's no price tag to family obligations.' In fact, some respondents such as Likmun were very uncomfortable about accepting any money from their parents:

It's because being a family business, it's part of our lives, and you don't think, it's doesn't feel like real work, you know? It felt awkward, the idea of receiving a wage.

Getting paid for helping out seemed to contradict many young peoples' understandings of the FWC: Accepting payment for helping out was not always easy for children who knew that the acceptance of payment diminished collective family resources. On the other hand, some children noted that *their* getting paid, as opposed to an employee, was acceptable, since it all 'stayed in the family'. Also, young people who received payment reported that it was difficult *not* to accept money, because money was one of the only things that their parents could give to them — most parents had little time and energy to take their children on holidays and family outings. These young people understood that receiving money from their parents helped to assuage their parents' guilt about relying upon them.

For young people who felt ambivalent or negative about helping out, although they believed they should, payment could be seen to legitimize, and to regulate labour participation, which was supposed to be impervious to commodification. According to a few young people, payment was seen as a 'bribe' to help out: 'It was a tie. We provide a service, and my mother paid us off, and it's OK.' In practice, FWC's could not be completely disassociated with money: Helping out saved families money in their businesses. Nevertheless, most young people attributed positive meanings onto helping out, by emphasizing their contributions to family survival, and by contrasting helping out in a FWC with employer–employee relations in waged work.

Ambivalence and Contradictory Experiences Associated with Helping Out

Although most young people believed in helping out, children's experiences of working with their families tended to be ambivalent and multi-layered — helping out could be oppressive or have negative associations, as well as be empowering and affirming, simultaneously. Working for their families can be contradictory for ethnic minority children because, in addition to both moral and material pressures to help out, they can also derive considerable support from their families, in the context of racism (Hood–Williams, 1990, p. 158).

A commonly reported difficulty with helping out, particularly if parents relied upon their children for language mediation, was not so much the shop work, which was often reported to be monotonous, but the pressure to help out:

MS: How do you feel about being so heavily relied upon?
KM: Survival. They can't survive, I mean, without me. It's obligation really. Part of the family. You're meant to do this for the family. I mean, *it's not like on a friendship basis.* Yeah, that's no choice. I mean, if they ask you to do something, it's not as if you could say no, isn't it [laughs]. You can't say no. . . . (my emphasis).

Many young people spoke about the strength of 'family' and 'family obligations' in ways which suggested the double-edged nature of family ties. While 'family' provided support and membership, *vis-à-vis* the larger society, it was also associated with powerful norms about family obligations. According to Colin:

It's family ties that come up, you know. We'd all be quite happy not to do this. It's like a magnet; it just draws you. In a way, it isn't that bad. You do make some money, and it's fairly safe, but the emotion factor can be vindictive.

The 'sting' which most young people associated with helping out was guilt. If young people didn't want to help out, or felt resentful about helping out, they inevitably felt guilty. Most parents worked extremely long hours, and it was very difficult for most young people *not* to help out. In addition to feeling guilty, not helping out could endanger the family livelihood and one's reputation in the family. As with most young people, parental approval and a positive moral identity in the family was important to them. According to Sui,

> In that sense [working hard], I had quite a lot of respect, because I was able to help out and they can't say, 'Oh, my daughter's no good'. Because I did help out and everything, in the ways they wanted.

Thus young people in these families tended to experience a constant tension between feeling that they wanted to help out and feeling that they *had* to help out.

Another key way in which young people experienced ambivalence and contradictory feelings about helping out stemmed from the fact that they had to reconcile two polarized notions of 'family' — Chinese and British. While cognizant of the mythologizing of traditional Chinese families, Chinese families were characterized by interviewees in terms of children helping their parents, and with the notion of collective, rather than individual interests, which were associated with being 'western' (see also Brannen this volume). Helping out was recognized by all the young people as a Chinese norm in Britain — it was a positive emblem of Chinese cultural identity in Britain. Every young person remarked that 'everyone else does it' (helped out).

Although helping out could be a source of ethnic pride, many young people in this study were also acutely aware of how their own families diverged from the (white) British family ideal, which was characterized by one or both parents as breadwinners in a 9 to 5 lifestyle, and leisure time spent together as a family. This was perhaps most keenly felt by young people whose parents had relied upon them as mediators with the 'outside' world; in fact, some young people were uncomfortably aware of role-reversals, in which children looked after their parents in various ways. Even young people who were understanding about their parents' reliance upon them sometimes felt resentful toward their parents for not being like 'other' parents. According to Anna,

> It was difficult coming to terms with the fact that they were not like other parents: talk to them, get advice, take you on holiday, etc. But they always had your best interests at heart. You had to realize their constraints, and that they didn't fit the ideal of parents.

Some young people also expressed that they had mourned a loss of a 'real childhood', which was conceived of as carefree. Many young people had restricted social lives, especially during the weekends, when business was busiest.

Furthermore, some young people were very self-conscious about degrading racialized stereotypes which linked Chinese people to the take-away trade — a trade which entailed Chinese people 'serving' their (predominantly) white public (Parker, 1995). For instance, when Lisa went away to university, she constantly encountered other students who seemed to be surprised to see her there:

Like, you know, people will always see you as Chinese. It was because they really hadn't seen an Oriental person from behind the counter walking out, freely, as it were.

Although Lisa, like others, felt there was nothing intrinsically objectionable to running a take-away business, she felt that it was incumbent upon young people to leave the catering trade, so that they did not contribute to the perpetuation of such stereotypes.

One factor which helped young people to reconcile Chinese and British ideals of 'family' and to mitigate resentment toward their parents was the fact that many white British people were seen to be unsympathetic, and lacking in understanding of their families' situations. This lack of understanding could be very alienating for Chinese young people. According to Sue,

Quite a few friends had birthday parties, always on Saturday evenings. We could never go because we had to help out in the shop. Some of my friends just couldn't understand it; they thought it was quite barbarous, actually. They don't understand how my family operates, that we were from a different world from them. Our fathers do not have 9 to 5 jobs, we don't have evenings and weekends free, or holidays.

Another way in which Chinese young people coped with their ambivalence about helping out was by looking to their parents' experiences as a reference point for their own. Many Chinese parents grew up working as children from a young age, often having foregone schooling; for many parents, children helping out was completely 'normal', even in the British context. Furthermore, Chinese young people tended to have an acute awareness of how hard their parents had worked all their lives; young people told stories about their parents' childhoods, which were often poverty-ridden. In comparison with their parents, most young people felt extremely privileged, particularly in terms of the educational opportunities they had in Britain.

Young people born and raised in Hong Kong were especially aware of being privileged, in relation to their parents. Individuals raised in Hong Kong tended to experience much less tension between the two ideals of 'family' than those young people born and raised in Britain. Most of those raised in Hong Kong expressed that they did 'not mind' working, and that they had expected to work, given that many of them had experienced poverty in the New Territories. For example, when asked how she felt about helping out, Yee Ling replied:

It was what you had to do to survive, if you're poor. It's not a matter of liking it or disliking it. Put it this way. If you're poor, you just have to learn [a new trade] . . . We worked every night. You had to.

Therefore, children raised in Hong Kong tended to be extremely fatalistic and pragmatic in their views about helping out; like their parents, it was regarded as an integral and necessary part of their family lives.

In fact, most young people evidenced great empathy for their parents. For instance, they were aware that their parents' reliance upon them could be difficult for the parents themselves, and they were anxious not to make it any harder for their parents to ask for their help. According to Annie, who reported that she 'hated' working in the shop: 'I know that my mother is very proud. And for her to ask me to help her was really like, coming down, on a different level'. Thus young peoples' sensitivity to their parents not having to ask them for help suggests a complex dynamic in the ways in which children may perceive parental authority and their own agency.

Conclusion

We need more complex approaches to the study of children's labour participation in ethnic businesses, in which children's own views and experiences of helping out are investigated. Firstly, children 'helping out' must be seen in terms of their upholding a 'family work contract': Helping out must be examined in terms of both parents' reliance upon their children's labours, as well as children's own commitments to their parents and family livelihoods. Secondly, Chinese children's work experiences are much less unitary than has been suggested in existing research. In spite of the fact that most young people believed, in principle, that they should help out in their family businesses, doing so entailed tension and ambivalent feelings and experiences.

Much of this ambivalence stemmed from the fact that Chinese young people had to come to terms with their 'productive' roles, *vis-à-vis* their parents, who often relied upon them both as workers and as mediators. Such parent–child relationships call into question paradigms of the 'dependent' child and the parent as breadwinner and provider, and point to the need for more diverse conceptualizations of parent–child relationships and more processual analyses of inter-generational 'give and take' over time (Jones, 1992).

The issue of children's labour participation in ethnic businesses has wider implications for groups other than the Chinese in Britain. Children's labour participation in ethnic businesses is of continuing importance in the 1990s because a) many ethnic migrant families, including Asian and Cypriot families, continue to rely upon ethnic businesses as a viable family livelihood; b) second generation children of many ethnic migrant groups are themselves seeking employment in the larger labour market, and may rely upon these businesses as a safety net against unemployment. As long as various ethnic migrant groups rely so heavily upon the small business sector, a fuller understanding of children's labour participation in ethnic businesses is necessary for informed social research on the family and work lives and family relationships of ethnic migrant groups.

Notes

1   However, recent research on young people in Britain suggests that they may make financial contributions to their parents, especially in working class families (Jones, 1992).

Also, young people in Britain increasingly constitute a key workforce in certain sectors, especially in retail (Hutson and Cheung, 1992).

2 The legal limits of employing children (those under school leaving age, usually 16) in the UK are as follows: No child under 13 can be employed, except young farmers at least 10 years old, as well as young actors. Children cannot work before 7 am or after 7 pm, or during school hours on any school day. Nor can children work more than two hours on any school day or on a Sunday. Since these regulations cover any child who works in a trade carried out for profit, whether or not the child is paid, these regulations clearly also apply to family businesses (Pond and Searle, 1990).

3 I had great difficulty in recruiting Chinese parents for interviews. This difficulty was partly due to the fact that I conducted the interviews in English (speaking no Cantonese or Hakka), and many parents did not speak English. However, I was able to interview six mothers from the sample families.

4 The names of interviewees have been changed.

References

BAXTER, S. (1988) 'A political economy of the ethnic Chinese catering industry', Unpublished PhD thesis, Aston University.

BENEDICT, B. (1979) 'Family firms and firms families: A comparison of Indian, Chinese, and Creole firms in the Seychelles', in GREENFIELD, S.M., STRICKON, A. and AUBREY, R. (Eds) *Entrepreneurs in Cultural Context*, Albuquerque, U. of New Mexico Press.

CHAN, A. (1986) 'Employment prospects of Chinese youth in Britain', London, Commission for Racial Equality.

DELPHY, C. and LEONARD, D. (1992) *Familiar Exploitation*, Cambridge, Polity.

EASEY, W. (1979) 'Child labour in Hong Kong', London, Anti-Slavery Society.

ENNEW, J. (1982) 'Family structure, unemployment and child labour in Jamaica', *Development and Change*, **13**, 4.

FINCH, J. (1983) *Married to the Job*, London, Allen and Unwin.

FINCH, J. (1989) *Family Obligations and Social Change*, Cambridge, Polity Press.

FINCH, J. and MASON, J. (1993) *Negotiating Family Responsibilities*, London, Routledge.

GARVEY, A. and JACKSON, B. (1975) *Chinese Children*, National Education Research and Development Trust.

GHODSIAN, M. and ESSEN, J. (1980) 'The children of immigrants: Social and home circumstances', *New Community*, **8**.

GLENN, E.N. (1983) 'Split household, small producer and dual wage earner: An analysis of Chinese-American family strategies', *Journal of Marriage and the Family*, February, pp. 35–46.

HOOD-WILLIAMS, J. (1990) 'Patriarchy for children: On the stability of power relations in children's lives', in CHISHOLM, L., BÜCHNER, P., KRÜGER, H. and BROWN, P. (Eds) *Childhood, Youth, and Social Change*, Basingstoke, Falmer Press.

HUTSON, S. and CHEUNG, W. (1992) 'Saturday jobs: Sixth-formers in the labour market and the family', in MARSH, C. and ARBER, S. (Eds) *Families and Households*, London, Macmillan.

JACKSON, B. and GARVEY, A. (1974) 'The Chinese children of Britain', *New Society*, 3 October.

JONES, G. (1992) 'Short-term reciprocity in parent–child economic exchanges', in MARSH, C. and ARBER, S. (Eds) *Families and Households*, London, Macmillan.

LAI, A, (1982) 'The little workers: A study of child labour in the small-scale industries of Penang', *Development and Change*, **13**.

LEONARD, D. (1990) 'Persons in their own right: Children and sociology in the UK', in CHISHOLM, L., BÜCHNER, P., KRÜGER, H. and BROWN, P. (Eds) *Childhood, Youth, and Social Change*, Basingstoke, Falmer Press.

LEWIS, J. and MEREDITH, B. (1988) *Daughters Who Care*, London, Routledge.

MACLENNAN, E. (1985) 'Working children', London, Low Pay Unit.

MORROW, V. (1992) 'A sociological study of the economic roles of children, with particular reference to Birmingham and Cambridgeshire', unpublished PhD thesis, Faculty of Social and Political Sciences, U. of Cambridge.

NEWBY, H. (1977) 'Paternalism and capitalism', in SCASE, R. (Ed) *Industrial Society: Class Cleavage and Control*, London, Allen and Unwin.

OWEN, D. (1992) 'Ethnic minorities in Britain: Settlement patterns', National Ethnic Minority Data Archive 1991 Census Statistical Paper 1, Centre for Research in Ethnic Relations, U. of Warwick.

PARKER, D. (1995) *Through Different Eyes: The Cultural Identities of Young Chinese People in Britain*, Aldershot, Avebury Press.

PHIZACKLEA, A. (1988) 'Entrepreneurship, ethnicity, and gender', in WESTWOOD, S. and BHACHU, P. (Eds) *Enterprising Women*, London, Routledge.

POND, C. and SEARLE, A. (1990) *The Hidden Army*, London, The Low Pay Unit.

QVORTRUP, J. (1985) 'Placing children in the division of labour', in CLOSE, P. and COLLINS, R. (Eds) *Family and Economy in Modern Society*, London, Macmillan.

RAPP, E., ROSS, E. and BRIDENTHAL, R. (1979) 'Examining family history', *Feminist Studies*, **5**, 1.

RODGERS, G. and STANDING, G. (Eds) (1981) *Child Work, Poverty and Underdevelopment*, Geneva, ILO.

ROSENBLATT, P., DE MIK, L., ANDERSON, R. and JOHNSON, P. (1985) *The Family in Business*, San Francisco, Jossey-Bass.

THE RUNNYMEDE TRUST (1986) 'The Chinese community in Britain: The Home Affairs Committee Report in context', London, The Runnymede Trust.

SAIFULLAH-KHAN, V. (Ed) (1979) *Minority Families in Britain*, London, Macmillan.

SALAFF, J. (1981) *Working Daughters of Hong Kong*, Cambridge, Cambridge University Press.

SONG, M. (1995) 'Between "the front" and "the back": Chinese women's work in family businesses', *Women's Studies International Forum*, **18**, 3.

STANDING, G. (1982) 'State policy and child labour: Accumulation versus legitimation?', *Development and Change*, **13**, 4.

WALDINGER, R., ALDRICH, H. and WARD, R. (Eds) (1990) *Ethnic Entrepreneurs*, Newbury Park, Sage.

WALLACE, C., DUNKERLEY, D., CHEAL, B. and WARREN, M. (Eds) (1994) 'Young people and the division of labour in farming families', *The Sociological Review*, pp. 501–30.

WARD, R. and JENKINS, R. (Eds) (1984) *Ethnic Communities in Business*, Cambridge, Cambridge University Press.

WATSON, J. (Ed) (1977) *Between Two Cultures*, Oxford, Oxford University Press.

WHEELOCK, J. (1991) 'Small businesses, "flexibility" and family work strategies', Sunderland Polytechnic Business School Research Paper.

Chapter 9

Discourses of Adolescence: Young People's Independence and Autonomy within Families[1]

Julia Brannen

This chapter is concerned with the significance of young people's transitions from childhood to adulthood within British society. It starts with a brief overview of public and official discourses concerning the definition of boundaries between adolescence and adulthood. Next, drawing upon a London-based study of the parenting and health of young people (Brannen, Dodd, Oakley and Storey, 1994), it considers different social constructions of adolescence as defined by parents and their 16-year-old children, the impact of these constructions upon the ways in which parents and children negotiate their relationships with one another, and the implications of these patterns of negotiation for young people's independence and autonomy within their families of origin.

Public Policy Discourses of Adolescence

The essence of being a young person is not in being but in *becoming*. That is, adult society values young people primarily because they are adults in the making (Frankenberg, 1993). Public discourses are much occupied, though not necessarily very consciously or coherently, with defining the boundaries between childhood and adulthood, the points at which young people acquire rights and responsibilities which pertain to adult status. However, the age of majority varies across different areas of social and economic life. For example, the voting age for UK young people was reduced in 1969 from 21 to 18 years and recent changes in family law give young people a greater say in matters which affect them (Roll, 1990). The raising of the school leaving age from 15 to 16 which occurred in 1972–3 is a counter example. More recently, changes in the UK Social Security legislation have abolished young people's right to unemployment benefit in the 16–18 age group and lowered benefit levels for the single unemployed in the 18–25 age group. The transition implies no ordered progression of increased rights and responsibilities.

The ambiguities surrounding the age of majority is a reflection of the heterogeneity and unevenness of cultural, social and economic change. Not surprisingly, public discourses concerning young people are themselves often contradictory. On the one hand, young people are constructed as having rights and considerable autonomy through their status as consumers. On the other hand, adolescence is being extended and parental responsibility prolonged as high levels of youth unemployment have led to a severe contraction in the numbers of (mainly working class) young people joining the labour market following the end of compulsory schooling. Norms have been restructured which emphasize training and education for young people despite the continuing decline in job opportunities (Jones and Wallace, 1992). Old discourses of parental responsibility have acquired a renewed emphasis with parents expected to continue being responsible for their young people's material well-being and for their development as citizens. This discourse is legitimated on moral rather than practical grounds. Underpinning public discourses is the construction of young people as threatening the moral and social order but in the context of the retraction of the Welfare State. Yet despite the importance policy makers place on parents as agents of socialization and social control, there is virtually no support for them. This neglect of the parents of young people is reflected in the failure of academic research to consider young people as part of households and families (Jones and Wallace, 1992; Allatt and Yeandle, 1992).

Professional and Academic Discourses

Whilst professional and academic discourses are part of the public discourse, each constructs young people in particular ways. Until recently sociologists have studied youth as a social category within the wider society in contrast to the way that they have studied children namely within the close confines of family. Generational relations within families have been neglected and young people have been studied within the public domain — in schools, peer groups, lifestyles and private markets. The household domain, which is a key arena in which the transition to adulthood takes place, has been ignored. Young people's transitions to adulthood from their own perspectives have been less evident.[2] The theoretical focus has been the issue of the social control of, rather than the extension of rights and responsibilities to, young people in the transition to adulthood. Moreover, the concentration upon youth within the public arena has led, until recently, to the neglect of young women.[3]

By contrast psychologists have focused directly upon young people's transitions to adulthood from the perspective of young people as individuals and within the context of the private sphere of family life. Through the prism of developmentalism, focusing on biologically based change and its consequences for psychological development, the transition is structured as a scheduled passage characterized by emotional turmoil and a process of identity formation (see Coleman, 1990 and Rutter, Tizard and Whitmore, 1976, for a discussion). Adolescence is normatively portrayed in terms of a process of separation from parents and the development of ambivalent feelings towards them. The assumption that young people should strive for independence and that parents should be facilitative of their attempts is not questioned.

Like sociology, the psychological model of adolescence has paid little attention to gender.

Health educators regard young people as a prominent target for their messages although teenagers are one of the healthiest groups in the population, judged by any standards. Health education models assume that biological development in adolescence is accompanied by an increase in personal responsibility for health (see Graham, 1979 for a critique). Drawing (implicitly) upon developmental psychology for a model of adolescence, health education conceptualizes young people as free individuals who in their normative passage to independence make autonomous decisions about health and lifestyles quite independently of their families. Insofar as health educators take account of social relations, they focus on the inculcation of life skills and the consequent enhancement of young people's self-esteem, assertiveness and problem solving (Tones, 1983; Collins, 1984; Nutbeam, Hagland, Farley and Tillgren, 1991). The growth of self-esteem is supposed to equip young people to resist peer group pressures and to conform to messages delivered by schools and other health educationists. With the focus on the individual, the family context is ignored.

Academic and professional discourses and, in some cases, public policy discourses premise their ideas on western cultural values concerning the rights of the individual. This perspective, as Gilligan (1982) has pointed out, is also implicitly gendered — that is it is based on a male model of development. Gilligan argues that a female model of development lies in the continuing importance of attachment of young women to their families and more generally of their responsibilities and obligations to others.

The individual rights discourse is culturally as well as gender blind. It takes little or no account of the fact that cultural values concerning the regulation of young people by parents, kin, and communities and their transitions to adulthood may differ from those presumed by academics and professionals. For example, parents born and brought up for example in non-western societies may have different expectations concerning the rights of elder versus younger household members. Different norms may operate with respect to the significance of the household as a collectivity as distinct from the notion of the individual household member (see also Song in this volume). Thus adolescence may not necessarily be defined in individualistic terms as entailing an increase in young people's rights to autonomy and independence.

Parents and Young People's Constructions of Adolescence

In the Adolescent Health and Parenting Study, the aim was to explore the transfer of responsibility from parent to young person, particularly around health issues. The study included a mix of families of different ethnic/cultural origins and social class groups which enabled us to investigate whether adolescence was constructed differently by different groups of parents and young people.[4] While we did find that adolescence was constructed in a variety of ways by parents, we of course found that these different social constructions did not necessarily translate neatly into different patterns in terms of young people's actions. Young people as social actors develop their own agendas, and are subject to, and act upon, a variety of influences deriving from a number of different contexts. However, ethnic origin was still the factor most likely to discriminate between young people in our study with respect to health and risk-taking behaviours (Brannen, Dodd, Oakley and Storey, 1994).

The following discussion highlights the variety of ways in which parents define adolescence and its consequences in terms of the negotiation of relationships between parents and their 16-year-olds. These data are based upon both mothers' and fathers' accounts and those of the young people concerning their relationships. In the first discourse of adolescence, parents construct their obligations and young people's transition to adulthood from an individual rights perspective; young people are ideally freed from parental interference in their move to *achieving* independent adult status. In the second construction, parents' management of, and young people's active participation in, the transition to adulthood is prescribed according to institutional rather than personal rules. The change in young people's status at this point is an *ascribed* rather than an achieved passage.

The conceptual distinction between parents in terms of their expectations of young people's status transitions translates into different approaches to the regulation, or control, of young people which have consequences for young people's independence and autonomy. Parents' strategies of control are conceptualized as follows: (a) 'institutional' modes of control whereby parents enforce prescribed forms of behaviour with respect to young people's status within the household; (b) 'personal' modes of control in which parents assume that young people control their own destinies, that is they create their own passage through adolescence as autonomous household members with minimal overt interference from parents (Bernstein, 1971, 1975). Personal modes of control rely heavily on strategies of covert parental influence especially through communicative means while institutional modes assume direct rule enforcement if norms are infringed. While in practice there is likely to be a mix of different control modes within households, nonetheless distinctive characterizations can be read from parents' and young people's accounts.

These discourses of adolescence are structured by social class, culture and gender. Ideas and expectations concerning ascribed status changes — notably the prescribed age at which working class young people were (once) supposed to enter the labour market — are class-related and originate from the time when there were plenty of low status jobs available for 16-year-olds. Expectations of achieved status changes are also class-related and occur mainly in professional middle class households. Transitions to adulthood are governed by culture as well as class, with some groups placing greater importance upon continuing attachment of young people to their families and kin and other groups emphasizing the importance of individuals' right to separate from them. Discourses are also differentiated according to the sex of the parent and the young person.

As suggested above, the cases in our study can be grouped conceptually according to a typology composed of two dimensions. One dimension relates to dominant constructions of adolescence within families and households: young people's pathways to adulthood as individualistic, individualized and developmental versus collectivist status

Parents' view: adolescence as achieved status

| Young people high autonomy | A B | D C | Young people low autonomy |

Parents' view: adolescence as ascribed status

Figure 9.1:   A model of parental discourses of adolescence by young people's autonomy

changes in the context of generational attachment — hierarchical as well as horizontal. These different constructions imply different modes of control by parents of young people and lead to the negotiation of different types of relationship. The study households can be grouped according to these constructions as determined by parents and according to the outcomes as brought to bear by young people themselves. The two dimensions can be considered in relation to one another and, as the following grid suggests, there are four possible patterns (Figure 9.1). In practice the households distribute themselves between three of the cells: (A) those where the transition to adulthood is an achieved status and in which young people have relatively high autonomy; (B) those in which the transition is ascribed and young people acquired high autonomy; (C) those in which the transition is ascribed and the young people have low autonomy but high responsibility. We found no cases in cell D where the transition is achieved with young people having relatively little autonomy.

The Transition to Adulthood: Achieved Status and High Autonomy

These parents and, to a lesser extent, their young people subscribe to an individual rights model of the transition to adulthood. Young people are ideally expected to free themselves from parental control and interference as they move towards adult status. Expectations shift from the role of the parent as the overt agent of social control to a greater emphasis on *internal* self-control exerted by young people (Bernstein, 1971, 1975). In this group, parents adopt covert control strategies through modes of communication while allowing young people a considerable degree of autonomy. However it is important to note as the cases will suggest in practice mothers are those who engage in communicative strategies with young people.

Concepts of 'child-centredness' and 'person-centredness' apply to some households in this group and, as others have shown (Walkerdine and Lucey, 1989), this approach may also typify early child rearing practices. The discourse is shaped by professional ideologies but also by popular discourses around the self. Self-development and the successful negotiation of intimate relationships are defined as central goals. Intimate relationships are voluntaristic and commitment is founded on choice. Relationships are constantly renegotiated as couples decide to stay together only as long as they like or love one another and are in receipt of reflexive rewards (Giddens, 1991).

Within this group of households, young people renegotiate, with parental legitimation, their relations with their parents. Thus the young person pushes for independence and the parent creates new conditions which allow this to occur and which at the same time provide a new basis for the relationship. In this process, norms governing relations between parents and young people are renegotiated and rules as such disappear; the goal is for the relationship to develop into an 'adult-like' relationship based on equality, reciprocal liking, trust and understanding. Thus parents endeavour to become friends and confidants to their children: 'It's very open. It's a very trusting relationship . . . It's a friendship.' (Mother talking about her relationship with her daughter.)

In behaving like a friend or confidant, the parent must still exercise some control in order to fulfil the requirement of a 'responsible parent'. This dilemma is solved in terms of the employment of a new kind of communication pattern whereby communication becomes the mechanism of control enabling parents to monitor young people outside face to face relationships. Young people are thus required to inform parents of the activities in which they engage outside the home. This surveillance involves a shift from visible to invisible forms of control (Bernstein, 1975).

Communication also sets up an arena in which bargaining can take place between young people and parents. Thus if young people perceive parental communication as too intrusive, they may develop counter strategies to fend off parents and to create boundaries around their presumed autonomy. A crucial strategy available to young people is to withhold information about their external activities or to threaten to do so, thereby testing parents and exposing the invisible power upon which the relationship rests.

In this group, parents were concerned not to appear prescriptive and controlling. For parents and 16-year-olds the most contentious issue at this point concerned going out and about or staying in. Thus parents sought information from young people concerning their whereabouts. The grounds whereby parents justified this requirement are various and suggestive of weak rather than strong rule enforcement. For example, in the following example, a UK born father claims that communication is a matter of 'common politeness' and implies that the 'rule' is applicable to all household members:

> Letting everyone know what the hell is happening which is a rule . . . and having friends in, the rule is 'you tell us'. Again, it's a rule of what-you-call-it — common sense, politeness, manners rather than a rule.

Some parents simply say that they *like* to know, rather than require to know, where their young people are or when they are coming home. This language, too, is suggestive of weak rather than strong rules:

> No hard and fast rules. I just *like* to be told when they are coming in, where they are going and they all know they can ring if they need a lift. (Mother)

In this last remark, the mother suggests that the way is also open for the young man to make demands upon his parents for their help and protection — namely the invitation to telephone her for a lift. Knowledge is represented as reciprocal: just as the parent knows the whereabouts of the young person, so too the young person knows about the availability of the parent to help out.

In addition to preference and common politeness, some parents — notably mothers — give a further justification for knowing about their children's where-abouts, namely that knowledge alleviates worry. (The extent to which worry emerged as a maternal rather than a paternal issue is remarkable.[5] While we might expect more non-UK born parents to express worry about their young people because of racism in the society, worry was an 'excuse' articulated more commonly among the UK born mothers. Thus, a mother said that she worried if her son did not notify her in advance when he stayed out in the evening. Moreover, she presented her tend-ency to worry as a personal failing rather than a result of real external dangers:

> I always like them to phone up if they're not coming straight home because I have a dinner waiting . . . I would worry if they didn't . . . Worry is one of my downfalls. I do see dangers.

In accordance with her failure to see her own feelings as legitimate, she remarks that it is her son's dinner which is the main reason for his coming home on time.

For mothers worry had markedly less legitimacy than other reasons for try-ing to restrict young people; worry was seen as a female weakness to which only mothers were 'prone'. The fact that worry is a likely consequence of bearing a life-long responsibility for children from their birth onwards was insufficient justification for exerting control over them. Similarly, no recognition was given to the fact that worry is also a product of the contradiction between norms of parental responsibil-ity and of young people's supposed autonomy.

In controlling young people's comings and goings mothers in this group used the interrogative mode: 'Where are you going? Who are you going with?' rather than the imperative mode — 'You can go out' or 'You can't'. For these parents the *form* of communication was the form of control. The following case concerns a middle class household in which the mother operates a communicative strategy vis-à-vis her oldest daughter, Sandra. The family is comfortably off; it is also white, British and middle class with liberal values. Sandra's father is a middle manager in a public relations company, and her mother is a teacher. Both parents have struggled financially to send Sandra and her siblings to private schools. Sandra is not restricted by her parents and at weekends often frequents clubs in central London returning home in the early hours. She describes her relationship with her mother as both 'close' — in affect terms —, and 'open' — meaning that she mostly tells them about her whereabouts. Her mother's portrayal is one of parental licence in response to her daughter's bid for greater freedom:

> We don't clamp down rigidly. We gradually got to that stage without too many major upsets . . . It's letting them do these things they want to . . . I

still get worried, but you've got to allow them to do certain things. You just can't say no all the time.

Sandra describes herself as a discloser: 'I can speak to people, the people I'm closest to — friends, my mum, my cousin,' while her mother claims, 'She'd certainly talk to me about it. I wouldn't say everything, but she certainly talks to me about most things.'

Both mother and daughter appear to have discussed a number of key issues both in the present and the past. For example, they discussed the start of Sandra's periods, and a number of other matters relating to sex and sex education. Sandra's mother says Sandra talks to her about her boyfriend, though somewhat superficially. According to Sandra, her parents know that she has had sex, though information was relayed through the discovery of her diary. Quite how this happened was not revealed, but Sandra did not make any complaint in the interview about 'prying parents': 'It was through a diary. It was very stupid. It caused quite a lot of tension . . . But they got over it.' Where such a discovery was made by parents who adopt more overt (institutionally based) strategies of control, they would probably have responded much more severely. Certainly young people in those households in which different cultural values operated with respect to young people's independence went to great lengths to keep their 'illicit' activities secret from their parents.

In accordance with the communicative strategy of control adopted by her mother, Sandra is expected to say where she is going, with whom and for how long. As Sandra says, her parents are fairly free and easy about her going out, but, 'My mum likes to know where I am and, er, what time I'll be back . . . They do try to let me be as independent as possible.' In return for being open about her activities, Sandra has a high degree of autonomy. Through the acquisition of information from her daughter, Sandra's mother alleviates her own anxiety about her welfare, and her sense of maternal responsibility is discharged. Thus, though she lacks the power to constrain her daughter, she feels that at least she knows where she is.

These parents drew upon the discourse of 'individual rights', the right of young person to create his/her own trajectory to adulthood. Thus adulthood constitutes an achievement of the individual young person while parents' role is not to obstruct or contradict the normative notion of the young person's rights. The new status of young person as adult is not conferred mechanistically in the sense that the young person steps into a new status with clearly defined responsibilities and duties. Rather it is a person-centred passage which the young person is expected to construct for herself and in which she exerts control over herself. These ideas resonate with the sociological concept of individualization which is used to refer to a new social process in which young people as social actors construct their economic and social pathways in terms of jobs and leisure activities.[6]

Transition to Adulthood: Ascribed Status and High Autonomy

In these households parents confer autonomy upon young people in response to a scheduled status change which is governed by class norms and the structure of the labour market. The study provides some variability in the extent to which young people stayed on at school or entered the labour market at 16.[7] Until the 1970s entry to the labour market for working class young people was expected to take place at the end of compulsory schooling; it was not a matter of individual negotiation but was socially scheduled. In contrast to the mainly middle class, group (a) households, working class parents in group (b) marked young people's entry into the labour market as a moment in *time* and as an event having practical and symbolic significance by giving them greater individual freedom. In this group parents move from a situation whereby they overtly control young people according to a set of explicit norms which proscribe certain activities and put limits around their freedom to a situation in which when their young people enter the labour market they expect them to become masters and mistresses of their own destinies. These young people assumed adult status as workers; they were not simply treated differently according to age criteria.

Sally Rimmer had recently left school and found a job in an optician's. She was living with her mother, a single parent who had two (low status) part-time jobs, and her elder sister who was also at work. Both mother and daughter describe having a 'close' relationship, which, they said, was based on 'trust' and 'friendship'. Her mother noted, somewhat hopefully: 'Deep down, she thinks we can sit and talk about anything.' Even before Sally left school, her mother allowed her some freedom but expected to have some say about her daughter's whereabouts. Looking back to this time, she admits to some lack of success in controlling her daughter: 'I think you do worry, but, basically, you've got to put your trust in them to a certain extent. You can only guide them.' Since leaving school, Sally acquired a new boyfriend who was much older than her. However despite being 'close' to her mother, Sally was not forthcoming about her relationship, which annoyed her mother:

> She didn't tell me. He's five years older than her . . . I think she's been out with him a few times before she told me. I was a bit annoyed . . . I said I'd sooner *know* than not know.

Like the mothers who deployed communicative strategies, Sally's mother wanted her daughter to talk to her about her new relationship, but since her daughter's new status as a worker gave her the right to be independent, she found it impossible and unjustifiable to insist on having a say about her daughter's relationships.

Working-class fathers also expected their sons to be significantly more independent at the point when their sons joined the labour market. Unlike the fathers in group (a) who did not describe themselves as ever having been strong disciplinarians, these fathers saw themselves as much less strict when their children left school. A father described a change in his uncompromising attitude to bringing up his son: 'My philosophy is if a kid's done wrong, beat him' — when his son started work. However these fathers justified this change in attitude in a variety of ways and not always in terms of young people's changed status. Some fathers said they had also vacated the authoritarian role with their youngest children. One of these fathers, whose prowess as a sportsman was failing, said that, at 55, he felt generally 'past it', and that he could no longer compete with his sporty son. Also, he believed that the disciplinarian role he once played with respect to his older children was 'rather out of date'.

> Once they've left school, you can only take so much responsibility. Once they are over 18 or they're out earning money, they've got to be responsible for their own actions. They are expected to be semi-adult. When they're kids at school, yes, parents should be responsible. They should expect to know where their kids are. (Father)

Like other fathers in the study, these UK born, working-class fathers did not describe themselves as particularly 'close' to their young people who, they said, were closer to their mothers. Few shared interests with their young people. (Sport and going to the pub constituted the main interests shared with sons). Communication over personal matters was rare whatever the sex of the young person. Insofar as any sons disclosed their feelings (not a manly thing to do), they did so via their mothers who were also the main channels of information between young people and fathers. It is interesting to note that the son who had the best relationship with his father described it in terms of being able to talk and joke, and have an equal relationship. But he also referred to their former hierarchical relationship before he started work and more generally underlined the difficulty men have in displaying affection towards one other:

> Yeah, we have [a good relationship]. Like we talk more now. We sort of understand each other. We joke now and that . . . We go bowling [and drinking] and have a good laugh . . . I care for my Dad, as well as Mum, but it's harder for a bloke to say it's — like that . . . It's mainly my Dad's more in charge 'cos he's like . . . He's the man of the house . . . But we're mainly sort of equal now, like since we've all left school. (Son now at work)

Transition to Adulthood: Ascribed Status and Low Autonomy but High Responsibility

In this group, parents conferred greater responsibility upon young people as they got older — for example, expecting them to take care of others, to contribute to household chores, and to pay due attention to their studies. However these parents did not grant them or see them as having a right to greater individual autonomy based on ideas of self-development and individual rights. The approach of adulthood signified greater responsibility for *others* notably to household members or the wider kin group (see also Song in this volume). New duties were part and parcel of explicit or understood cultural expectations concerning age-appropriate behaviour rather than adolescence as a distinctive phase of the life course. These norms were clearly understood by parents and young people even if the latter did not always abide by them. The idea that parents should no longer attempt to regulate their young people or that young people were exempt from normative regulation by virtue of becoming 16 was significantly absent.

This group of households includes a substantial number of parents born and brought up outside the UK, most in India or via East Africa while a few came from the Middle East. Their expectations of 16-year-olds and their concepts of adolescence differed significantly from those of UK born parents. For example, psychological notions of adolescence as a time of emotional turmoil were notably absent. Signs of rebelliousness in young people and conflict with parents were construed as abnormal, individual characteristics rather than a necessary part of adolescence. Where parents reported young people as being emotional, they sometimes described it as a pathological response to being 'torn between two cultures'.

These parents, moreover, regarded the notion of young people 'leaving home' as a typical facet of British lifestyles and as undesirable and often highly problematic. They said that their young people 'never leave home', by which they meant that they stayed part of the kin or family group. Several said that the notion of encouraging young people to leave home had directly resulted in the current UK social phenomenon of widespread homelessness among young people. Compared with UK born parents, the non-UK born parents were more likely to favour continuing ties of material support and obligation, especially the idea of giving significant financial help to children at the point when they set up house. They were also more likely to favour their children giving them support in old age.

Parents of Asian and Middle Eastern origin clearly did not expect their young people, especially girls, to engage in leisure activities outside the home: to go out at night with friends; to mix with peers; to have opposite sex relationships (sex was automatically ruled out); to smoke; to take alcohol; or to engage with drugs. These issues were not negotiable. Parents did not define non-engagement in terms of health prevention. Parents aimed to protect their children by keeping them safe at home regarding these activities as emanating from western culture and threatening the moral character of young people. Especially with respect to young women, they put at risk their reputations and hence their marriageability. These parents did not speak the language of personal responsibility nor did they articulate the idea of taking risks in moderation. This is not to say however that young people in these households never engaged in these activities. However, they were significantly less likely to do so compared with young people of UK born parents. Moreover, those who did engage kept their activities secret from their parents. Young people did not overtly flout institutional norms and thus acted in accordance with norms of 'respect' for parents but might act on quite different beliefs in other social contexts.

Parental expectations of these young people were not necessarily couched simply in terms of prohibition. Positive emphasis was placed upon respect for elders. Young people as they grew older were expected to take on additional responsibilities especially *vis à vis* adults, notably entertaining guests to the house. As well as the addition of responsibilities, young people gained exemption from other duties such as household tasks on the grounds of their status as students. In many of these households, considerable emphasis was placed upon the value of studying and not simply upon education as a means to an end.

Aznive's parents, who came from a country bordering the Persian Gulf and were members of a Christian religion, did not expect their daughter to be independent at 16. Aznive was also the eldest child with a younger brother and sister who were still at school. They live over her father's shop (a chain grocer's) in which mother and daughter work unpaid. In this household the father rather than the mother appeared to set the rules. Aznive described her father as 'very strict' while her father's account makes it clear that he was in practice very concerned about the kind of people with whom his daughter mixes, fearing that, in associating with young men, she might lose her (sexual) 'respectability': 'I'm very strict on that. If I lose my temper, they know it.' Paternal authority appeared to have become especially marked in Aznive's adolescence. Aznive said that she and her father were closer during her childhood: 'We've grown apart just a bit.' Asked how she thought her father felt about her, she responded 'He tends to hide his feelings, and doesn't like to express himself too much. But I know he cares about me.' Caring was thus expressed not through affect but through paternal strictness. In his interview, her father did not put into words what he felt for his daughter, and said he did not know his daughter's view of their relationship. One reason for the father's silence might be that he felt uncomfortable with a female interviewer, though the alternative argument is persuasive — that his failure to articulate care in affect terms means that it cannot be divorced from his paternal role.

According to Aznive, her teenage years brought increased domestic responsibility. She was expected to help her father unpaid in the family business. She shouldered most of the housework, including taking care of her younger siblings during her GCSE examinations, because her mother had to go away to recover from a severe attack of rheumatoid arthritis. Aznive had largely conformed to parental expectations, but also displayed some resistance to the restrictive regime. Thus, despite acknowledging that her upbringing had made her more responsible — in accordance with her parents' view of what her new status should be, she was also making a bid for more autonomy. In her account, she describes the emergence of a 'freer' side to her character, an identity which she conceals within the grumpy demeanour she adopts in the private sphere of her family:

> I went through a stage where I was rude to my parents. I don't know why. I just snapped at them all the time . . . I went through a stage when I wanted to be myself — to have my own space type of thing . . . They say girls mature quicker than boys. I must have had it hard in my early teens . . . [Parents] were very strict . . . 'cos at home I have quite a lot of responsibilities, and, like, I've taken these responsibilities seriously . . . Like when I go out with my parents — 'cos there's a lot of social activities . . . I know how to handle myself. I'm a very kind of mature person. But when I'm with my own friends I'm totally different. I can relax and be myself.

Unsurprisingly, Aznive did not discuss sexual matters with her father, and did not expect to: 'With my Dad, I can only tell him certain things that he needs to know.'

Nor did they talk about educational decisions at the end of the fifth year. Her mother's recent serious illness was also not discussed. With her mother she described herself as 'more open'. Her father also states that, 'She can talk to her mother.' Asked about discussing boyfriends and sex education, he replied curtly, '(My children) know my opinion very well.'

Relationships in this group are qualitatively different with respect to sons compared with daughters, with sons having more autonomy than daughters but significantly less than sons in other groups. The following case concerns a father and son of Chinese origin. Again, it was the father who set limits upon his son's autonomy. Interestingly, the father but not the mother proffered himself for interview, albeit with some reluctance. Chenglie Wang's father was a mild-mannered man whose son described him as 'easygoing' and 'unselfish' — 'Whatever he does, he does for us, like. When he works so hard he's working for us.' His manner and style belied his rather authoritarian orientation to parenting. Of peasant roots, he grew up in Malaysia and moved continents twice in order to pursue his studies, finally completing his architectural training in the UK. His main aim was that his children should 'do well at school', and he was no less strict with his youngest child, his only son, Chenglie. He restricted his son's activities and vetted his friends, wanting to know 'what type of family . . . how they study.'

Chenglie was generally in agreement with his father's educational aspirations, and was aiming to go to university. He accepted and conformed to the house rules:

> I wouldn't say there are strict rules. But all the children [his sisters are grown up but live at home] know what they should be doing, what's expected of them. No one says . . . It's like a mental compromise between all of us. We all know where we can go and where we can't. (*How do you feel?*) I think it's good. I mean we can know, learn about rules that are always there. (*Like?*) Like you always have to study . . . You can't always go out everyday — stay out to a really late time. There are set rules. Everyone knows them.

While Chenglie abided by the rules, describing himself as a 'young adult . . . still under the guidance of parents', he was slightly resentful that his parents saw no place for 'fun' in his life. Moreover, as already indicated, he respected his father for his 'provider role'.

Neither party described the relationship as 'close'. Significantly, Chenglie mentioned a connection which belonged to the past rather than the present — the way his father used to help him with his maths homework. He excuses his father now on the grounds that, 'He's so busy', and also makes some interesting comments concerning the different caring styles of his two parents. While Chenglie says that his mother expresses her concern for him by worrying, the fact of fatherhood and his status as the only son are sufficient indication that his father cares for him. However, Chenglie was initially somewhat hesitant in his reply to the question whether his father cared for him:

I think so . . . My Dad's not a worrier. If you know someone's worrying a lot, then they obviously care for you. If he does, he doesn't show it that much. (*You mean physical affection?*) Not that much . . . But I think he does care, 'cos I'm the only boy in the family and fathers always like to have sons. So if I do well, he's happy.

Worry is seen as a form of weakness here and thereby the antithesis of fatherhood.

Communication between father and son was limited; neither saw it an important issue. Indeed, since Chenglie conformed to the rules, there was little to tell that his parents did not already know. Chenglie described his attitude to disclosure as 'mainly keeping things to myself', while his father's only reference to, and concern about, communication with his son was to do with which subjects he proposed to study. His father assumed that his son was staying on at school. Discussion of sexual matters was taboo, and both Chenglie and his father considered that he was too young to have a girlfriend.

In this household, normative rules governing fatherhood and age relations precluded father and son being close in an affective sense. The son's progress through the education system was their main point of connection. Thus caring was embodied in the shared activity rather than the *expression* of concern. Since the son largely conformed to the household rules, he had little personal autonomy, and had no need to confide or confess private matters. For the same reason, there was no conflict in the father–son relationship. As another son of Asian origin parents put it: respect demands distance in a relationship:

(*What do you mean by respect?*) They're older than you. You can't treat them as if they're your age. I can't treat my dad like my best mate, or I'm in trouble. Some things I can say to my friends. I can mess around, joke around. I can't say that to my Dad. (Sandeep Kumar)

While Chenglie was closer to his mother, there was not a great deal of communication there either. In this respect, Chenglie's remarks about the importance of having a girlfriend (he did not have one) are significant. Asked whether he approved of young men of his age having girlfriends, he commented, 'It's good to have someone to talk to openly.' Paradoxically, the desired goal of openness was undermined by the lack of boundaries between his own world and that of the household.

Conclusion

The discourses which govern young people's transitions to adulthood define not only the amount of independence which young people have but the basis upon which rights and responsibilities are extended to them. I have indicated that the individual rights discourse which is so evident in psychologists' and health educationists' definitions is not necessarily prevalent in all parents' constructions of adolescence and their treatment of their young people. Parental definitions of adolescence, the ways in which parents exert control over young people, the relationships which parents and young people develop with one another and the degree to which young people gain or assume independence are differentiated by social class, culture and gender. Moreover these structural factors interact with one another with different outcomes. The current public policy emphasis upon the responsibility of parents and the de-emphasis upon the rights of young people as citizens of the society is likely to impact differently upon different groups within our society. For non-UK origin parents, especially those from the Indian subcontinent, greater emphasis upon parental responsibility reinforces their own cultural values and practice and may lead to even greater restriction of their young people, especially girls. By contrast, UK born parents will have to reshape their parenting strategies in ways which may go against their own experience of growing up and contravene their young people's expectations. While we did not focus upon young people's beliefs and actions outside the context of the family, their own accounts testify that at 16 parents' values and modes of control are still salient influences upon them.

Notes

1   This chapter is based upon a chapter written in Spanish: 'Proximidicali y apertura: derectios y responsabilides de los hovenes', in Musito, G. and Allatt, P. (Eds) (1994) *Psicosiologia de la Familia*, Valencia, Albertros Education, pp. 147–65.
2   The exception is a major programme of research called the 16–19 Initiative funded by the Economic and Social Research Council.
3   The work of McRobbie (1991) and Griffin (1985) represent a new departure.
4   The self-selected ethnic origins of the questionnaire sample of young people are as follows: 64 per cent who said they were of white UK origin, including 'other European', 18 per cent who classed themselves as of Asian origins, 11 per cent who ticked the Afro-Caribbean origin category or identified themselves as black British, and 8 per cent who were placed in a miscellaneous group consisting of those of African, Arab, Chinese or different origin including 'mixed ethnicity'. The household study under-represented the black group but over-represented the miscellaneous group.
5   48 per cent of mothers say they worry 'a lot' about their young people compared with 7 per cent of fathers.
6   This is said to produce growing differentiation within social classes (See Chisholm *et al.*, 1990).
7   In the questionnaire survey and the household study, there was a roughly equal split between those young people with fathers in high status jobs and those with fathers in low status jobs. With respect to education and employment intentions, over half expected to stay on in the sixth form with a further 10 per cent going to Sixth Form college and 15 per cent into a further education college. 11 per cent expected to go into employment and only 3 per cent into a youth training scheme. By the time of the interview, fifteen of the young people (from sixty-four households) had left full time education.

References

ALLATT, P. and YEANDLE, S. (1992) *Youth Unemployment and the Family: Voices of Disordered Times*, London, Routledge.

BERNSTEIN, B. (1971) *Class, Codes and Control, Vol. I: Theoretical Studies Towards a Sociology of Language*, London, Routledge and Kegan Paul.

BERNSTEIN, B. (1975) *Class Codes and Control, Vol. 3: Towards a Theory of Educational Transmissions*, London, Routledge and Kegan Paul.

BRANNEN, J., DODD, K., OAKLEY, A. and STOREY, P. (1994) *Young People, Health and Family Life*, Buckingham, Open University Press.

CHISHOLM, L., BUCHNER, P., KRUGER, H. and BROWN, P. (Eds) (1990) *Childhood, Youth and Social Change: A Comparable Perspective*, Basingstoke, Falmer Press.

COLEMAN, J. (1990) *The Nature of Adolescence*, 2nd ed., London, Routledge.

COLLINS, L. (1984) 'Concepts of health education: A study of four professional groups', *Journal of Institute of Health Education*, **22**, 3, pp. 81–8.

FRANKENBERG, R. (1993) 'Trust, culture, language and time', Consent Conference No. 2, Young People's Psychiatric Treatment and Consent, London, Institute of Education, Social Science Research Unit.

GIDDENS, A. (1991) *Modernity and Self-identity: Self and Society in the Late Modern Age*, Cambridge, Polity.

GILLIGAN, C. (1982) *In a Different Voice: Psychological Theory and Women's Development*, Cambridge, MA, Harvard University Press.

GRAHAM, H. (1979) 'Prevention and health; every mother's business: A comment on child health policies in the 1970s', in HARRIS, C.C. (Ed) *The Sociology of the Family: New Directions for Britain*, Sociological Review Monograph 28, University of Keele.

GRIFFIN, C. (1985) *Typical Girls?*, London, Routledge and Kegan Paul.

JONES, G. and WALLACE, C. (1992) *Youth, Family and Citizenship*, Buckingham, Open University Press.

McROBBIE, A. (1991) 'The politics of feminist research: Between talk, test and action', in McROBBIE, A. (Ed) *Feminism and Youth Culture: From Jackie to Just Seventeen*, London, Macmillan.

NUTBEAM, D., HAGLAND, B., FARLEY, P. and TILLGREN, P. (1991) *Youth Health Promotions*, London, Forbes Publications.

ROLL, J. (1990) *Young People: Growing up in the Welfare State*, Occasional Paper No. 10, London, Family Policy Studies Centre.

RUTTER, M., TIZARD, J. and WHITMORE, K. (1976) *Educational Health and Behaviour*, London, Longman.

TONES, B.K. (1983) 'Education and health promotion: New directions', *Journal of the Institute of Health Education*, **21**, pp. 121–31.

WALKERDINE, V. and LUCEY, H. (1989) *Democracy in the Kitchen: Regulating Mothers and Socialising Daughters*, London, Virago.

Chapter 10

Conceptualizing Parenting from the Standpoint of Children: Relationship and Transition in the Life Course

Pat Allatt

This chapter explores the concept of parenting as voiced by children and adolescents. Using a life course analysis it charts their constructions, revealing in these early representations the beginnings of continuities in parent–child relations which span individuals lives. In so doing it challenges assumptions which, despite accumulating evidence, still tend to see the young as spinning off from the parental home into independence and adulthood, and gives place to a neglected field — the parenting of the older adolescent (Oakley, 1987; Brannen *et al.*, 1994). It illuminates social processes and sentiments already at work in these early years, laying the foundations of the subsequent histories of parent–child relations.

Two theoretical themes run through the chapter. First, a focus on the life course directs attention to the concept of the child as a relationship. For whilst individual biography is a process of change and becoming, in diverse ways we remain children, held throughout life, willingly or reluctantly, in the web of parent–child relations. A configuration of many dimensions, the embrace may be symbolic, lodged, for example, in the idea of home; cemented over the life course by flows of resources, material and non-material; bonded by normative expectations, rights, obligations and affectivities; or anchored in memory. These strands both invade emotional interiors and influence performance, and hence are shot with tensions which might combine the ambiguities of welcome, resentment and rejection.

Aspects of this configuration are found, albeit unevenly, in the literature addressing parent–child relations at different points in the life course. For example, referring to the steady help parents provided for an unemployed couple, Wallace noted that 'children were tied to parents through the life cycle in different ways at different periods . . . transition to adulthood involved a change in relationships with parents, but it did not involve severing links' (Wallace, 1987, p. 178). Much earlier Bell (1968) described the flows of resources from middle class parents to their married children (see also Harris, 1983 citing Pitts, 1964). And more recently de Vaus (1994) uncovered continuities in the relations and exchanges between adults and their still independent parents, before the latter become frail and reliant.

Second, a life course approach directs attention to transitions, for continuity in these relations is neither an automatic nor a natural phenomenon but the outcome of social processes, some more overt than others. The components of the situation are not static. Confining the focus to childhood and adolescence, change is inherent in the physical, psychological and social development of the young, and heightened if set within a culture which values individualism and independence with the ensuant shifts in power between the generations.

Much of the focus on children's and young people's transitions has been on those between the private domain of the family and the public domain of school and labour market. This early phase of the life course, however, is patterned by multiple transitions, both macro and micro. And many of the latter, although carrying significance for the world beyond the family, take place within it. Thus age-related statuses are enhanced as children encounter and move through the publicly determined life events of starting school, changing schools, and entry into the labour market. Frequently, however, these movements are accompanied by normatively expected domestic transitions. Examples abound in the familial regulation of children's money and time — from incremental 'pocket money', through allowances to board money, and from temporal rules about coming in and staying out, to temporal guidelines and trust.

However, as Douglas (1966, p. 96) notes, persons in states of transition are dangers to the system, 'simply because transition is neither one state nor the next'. Hence these transitions, embedded in the routines and values of the everyday workings of parent–child relations, are closely monitored by both parents and children. It is children's perceptions of these relationships and transitions as they inform their representations of parenting that are described in this chapter.

The Young People and the Studies

The young people's accounts in the chapter are mainly drawn from a qualitative study of eight families of young people and their parents, conducted in Teesside in the north-east of England in 1989 and 1990.[1] The families were middle- and upper-working class as defined by parental occupations and family histories, and each contained a 15/16-year-old and an 18/19-year-old. Of the sixteen young people eleven were still at school, preparing for public examinations or awaiting the results, and expected to continue into the sixth form or college or proceed to university. Three of the five who had left school were 18/19 years of age and all were in trainee posts; of the two younger leavers, one was on a (then) YTS programme and the other a clerical assistant following the firm's YTS scheme. Additional data are from an earlier, related study (Allatt and Yeandle, 1992). Based in Newcastle upon Tyne in the mid-1980s, the study was of forty working class families of parents and children in their late teens and early 20s still living in the parental home. All the young people had completed their full-time education, and had variously experienced government training schemes, employment and unemployment.

In the chapter the analysis of young people's representations of parenting is in three parts. The first examines the symbolic mechanisms of placement and attachment as these are found in the concept of home, parental worry and auto/biography. The second looks at children's constructions of parents and parenting — parents as an entity and as individuals, what they do, and what they have achieved. Finally, the chapter examines transformations in parenting style over the years of childhood and adolescence. Although aware of their importance, no systematic comparisons are made between age groups, gender or social class, but they are noted where they are relevant to a theme.

Symbols of Placement and Attachment

In the young people's accounts of parenting were three symbolic representations which served to place them: the concept of home, signifying a geographical place or group where you belong; parental worry, signifying the site of unconditional concern; and auto/biography, signifying historical and genetic place in the lineage — who you take after, what you were like when little, what they were like when they were little. I now examine each of these in turn.

Home

I've always sort of got a *home* here. (Charles Jackson)[2]

The concept of home is complex and pervasive. Both subjective and objective, it concerns feelings of belonging, of moral claims to be there, as well as material and emotional support and physical place. To be homeless connotes a deep sense of loss and lack of place in a society. In both senses the idea of home underpins both lay understandings and current social policy, especially with regard to the reduced state entitlements and lesser claim to citizenship of young people couched in the rhetoric of parental responsibilities. Thus to quote Julie Burchill (1995) writing on friendship, 'Friendship like home is where you turn to when no-one else will have you.'

Several studies suggest how these perceptions colour young people's lives (Kiernan, 1985; Wallace, 1987). For the ragged process of leaving home — children leaving and returning due to entry into higher education, periods of employment away from home, experimental independence, or trial partnerships or marriages which break down — is only possible against a backdrop of home, a parental household to which return. Thus, as Colin Roberts said, 'I'd go away [to university] but I'd still live here.' And Christina Green, a junior commercial trainee, who had rejected a university place because of her boyfriend, explained that she 'wouldn't like to move too far away from home'. 'She's a home bird, really', said her mother. Whilst, Sally Taylor, a trainee pharmacist, reflecting on the substantial material subsidies provided by parents, observed, 'It's *cheap*, isn't it, living at home?'

The idea of home, however, is not an amorphous all absorbant entity. At the extreme, studies of the young homeless reveal parental homes both ejecting and rejecting their young (Jones, 1994). But, importantly, even welcoming homes have norms, boundaries and rules of acceptance which must be recognized and negotiated despite the young's moral claim to be there. To retain its significance and continuity within the culture, children must be sensitized to the subtleties which infuse the meaning of 'home' and which they might unwittingly transgress.

Such threats to the parental, and indeed societal, meanings of home appear most forcibly at those transitional points of the life course when the older adolescent hovers between dependence and independence. Marginal states are dangerous to the system and 'marginal individuals are both in danger and emanate danger' (Douglas, 1966, p. 96).

In the Teesside study, most of the young people displayed a sense of home as somewhere that accepted you as you were. Arguably, despite the tensions which might surround such issues as household help or timekeeping these were largely unproblematic because the pattern of daily life, shaped by schooling and the total parental dependency of most of the group, controlled threats to the parental concept of home. In the older children's accounts and in those who had left full-time education, however, hitherto unspecified understandings were more likely to be exposed. For these children were not only in that dangerous interstice between dependence and independence; but the danger was compounded by the collision of the concept of home with the culturally expected freedoms of growing up — the dangerous social pollution of internal contradiction 'when some of the basic postulates are denied by other basic postulates, so that at certain points the system seems to be at war with itself' (Douglas, 1966, p. 122).

Thus whilst understandings of home are embedded in the relations of property, property signifies the sacred.[3] This was illuminated by the Taylor family as they grappled with the tension between the concepts of lodger and home. Sally, resented her parents strictness over the time to be in at night, pointing out that at 19, 'being how old I am, I should be able to come in what time I want'. She explained, however, that arguments with her parents, especially her mother, 'come down to my being the lodger', unwittingly articulating the paradox of home and independence. She found her parents' strictures a mystery, 'You try to do your own thing and then get into trouble for not *being* there, sort of. You can't win.'[4] But to treat the parental home as a lodging, with the instrumental, tenuous relationships that this implies, transgresses the idea of home which by its essence is rich in affective bonds. It is to treat home as mere accommodation, as a utility devoid of obligation to other occupants, where it is acceptable to come and go as one pleases, to be out all the time apart from eating and sleeping, and to take others for granted.

This illuminates the norms surrounding parental ownership and goods willingly given to children. Thus Jenny, an unemployed 17-year-old in Wallace's study who had left home, trod cautiously, consciously or unconsciously negotiating the pitfalls:

> Well, I can just go up me mum's any time, and just sort of open the fridge and eat anything I want to and, I mean, I do that, I don't feel guilty about doing that, 'cause I know me mum won't mind at all. If I go into her and say, 'Is it all right if I have such and such?' she says, 'Yer silly cow, you

can have what you bloody well like. Just take it', sort of thing. (Wallace, 1987, p. 96)

The caution, however, is not without foundation. The comments of Jones' (1994) Scottish homeless respondent, desperate to return home, show not just pride. They also recognize home as lying within the parental gift, the paradox of their own moral claim to a place in it, but yet the difficulty of re-entry. 'I didn't want to ask to come home. I wanted them to ask me!' Again drawing upon Douglas (1966, p. 123), 'The most dangerous pollution is for anything which has once emerged gaining re-entry.'

Thus whilst certain domestic rules, such as times to come in, shade into guidelines as children move towards a greater independence, those surrounding the treatment of home may retain the harder edge of enforceable rules of exclusion, admittance and comportment. The moral claim to a place, and parental willingness or eagerness to provide support in its various forms, has to be accompanied by a recognition, through appropriate behaviour, of home's sacred qualities. It is not to be sullied by money and independence — the ability to pay for, or contribute to, one's keep, to afford to go out, or the status of age. And as there are no formal rituals, it must be made overt in other ways, one of which is through talk, whether discussion or argument.

Worry and Reciprocity

It just shows they *care*. (Paula Green)

Whilst home symbolizes physical location and place in the social structure of domestic relationships, so worry symbolizes a place in people's affections. Running through young people's accounts of home, and echoing the findings of Brannen (this volume), was the motif of parental, largely maternal, worry. It was portrayed in several ways — nagging, interfering, fussing, insisting on times to come in, helping with homework. 'I think mum worried herself *sick* about it — making a mountain out of a molehill *again*', said Charles Jackson, when describing how, because they lived on a remote farm, he had stayed with friends the last few times he had gone out, returning the next morning. Yet although irritating, young people saw parental worry as part and parcel of being a proper parent, symbolizing concern. As Paula Green said, when talking about how her parents worried when she spent 'all at once' the allowance she had just started getting, 'it just shows they *care* and that they're *bothered*.' It echoed 15 year-old Chenglie Wang, 'If you know someone's worrying a lot then you know they care for you' (Brannen this volume).

Parental care and worry, however, was bound within a system of reciprocities. Not only did young people recognize parental worry as a signifier of care, but they knew, or sensed, that to make their parents happy was part of this system. They might, for example, try to alleviate the worry. Keeping to the rules or understood times for coming in, telephoning if they are going to be late or letting parents know if plans for the evening had changed were major features in the pattern. Thus Colin Roberts pointed out that there was 'no *set* rule *time*, because I'm usually in by a good time. But generally I think it's around half ten, eleven. My mam would be *worried* if I got in a lot later . . . If I'm going to be later, if I'm watching a film or something, I always ring them, and tell them. 'Cos I know our mam does worry.' Similarly, Andrea Taylor felt she should telephone if she was going to be late 'because she worries about me.' Christina Green, asked about what sort of things she and her parents agreed upon, said, '. . . I agree on the types of rules that my parents set over the household, such as what times we should come in or to tell them where we are, because I know they will worry. So I do try and agree with the things that . . . that pleases them, yeah.' Others circumvent parental worry by not telling them anything that might raise their concern.

Additionally children might purposely forgo a right, like 18-year-old Kathleen McGuiness, in the Newcastle study, who had just obtained work after a distressing spell of unemployment (Allatt and Yeandle, 1992). Two contrasting decisions illustrate how she tempered her claim to independence. 'As I say, I now tend to stop at Suzanne's overnight though I know Mam doesn't like it. She said it was my decision so I did . . .' In contrast, on another occasion with this new friend she said:

> No. I'm going straight home. She says, 'What's the matter?' ('cos I normally go in for a cup of coffee). I says, 'Oh . . .', 'cos me mam had said, you know, 'Are you going to be late?' [mimics]. So I says to her, 'I'm going straight home to keep mummy's face happy.' (Allatt and Yeandle, 1992, p. 73)

Similarly, the Teesside young people were aware that with regard to school work and parental concern about their futures 'doing your best' would make parents happy.

Auto/Biography and Identity

> I look like me mam, and I take after me dad. (Andrea Taylor)

The third locating symbol of continuity lies in the construction of those aspects of identity which hook the individual into their genetic and domestic histories. Children use parents to provide them with their past, linking them to their babyhood and infancy before memory is established, and to their genetic heritage, family lineage and the historical pasts of parental childhoods. It is against this that the young can eventually assess their own historical predicament.[5]

Parents are the archivists of identity. Remaining unknown to the individual unless re-constructed and transmitted, the early foundations of identity — who you are and how you came to be here — are largely handed over by parents. Four aspects of this parental archive, and children's engagement with it, appeared in the Teesside families — what you were like when you were little, who you take after, what your parents were like at your age, and, attached to the latter, family histories, particularly that of grandparents.

The following briefly illustrate these themes and their locating properties. Colin Roberts, searched both narrative and photographs for his early identity. When asked what he liked to talk to his parents about when he was younger, he replied, 'I . . . dunno. I used to like to talk about when I was little. What, what it was like, what *I* was like, and *get* the photos down and I'd look at them. And, um, generally looking through photo albums, I used to like doing.' The importance of this search and ultimate ownership of identity was illustrated by a 4-year-old outside the study, explaining his refusal to disclose the details of his day at nursery school, 'No. You know more about me than I do.'

The young people were always able to say something about the extent to which they were like their parents, alluding to similarities with their parents 'at their age'. Paula Green, when asked who she was like, said, 'Dad tells me I'm like him, not liking homework.' And Andrea Taylor, when asked if she felt like her parents, responded,

> Not really. Well . . . most people say that I'm like, I look like me mam and I take after me dad . . . 'cos he's more outgoing and he's always out at the pub . . . Me mam's not *shy* but she'll stop in every night.

Whilst her elder sister, Sally, produced a reversed and contested observation — that her parents 'always say that I look like my dad and act like my mam when they were our age, and everybody else says the opposite, so I don't know.'

Transmitted through parental narratives, the young people knew of their parents' early lives and opportunities. Peter Gregson, for example, was able to locate himself within a configuration of different parental class backgrounds, whilst Sally Taylor could recount her mother's advice on factory work, ' "I had one of those when I was your age," sort of thing, y'know. "It's long hours for little pay." '

Representations of Parents

This section looks at how parents are perceived by children. It deals with the idea of the parental entity, cooperation and difference, achievements, what parents do for you and want for you and their guardianship of the moral order.

The Parental Entity

They used to be like one, like one person to *me*. (Colin Roberts)

Ronald Fraser (1985, p. 105) recollecting his childhood image of his parents writes: 'There was no unity of love between them for me. In fact, I have no sense of them as a couple, as parents, as lovers . . .' This contrasts with images held by the Teesside young people. Colin Roberts articulated this most clearly:

(So who did you talk to the most?)

> Well my mum and dad always used to be together. So I would talk to them as one person really. I didn't . . . they never . . . I never used to hardly go to them separately at all. Unless it was something like Christmas presents, or birthday presents. You know they used to be like one, like one person to *me*.

Mr Roberts was now working away from home for most of the week. But when asked who gave him his pocket money Colin said: 'Mum gives me it but . . . it doesn't really matter who it's off. It's from them.' Similarly, Christina Green, talking about the 35 pounds monthly allowance she moved onto on entering the sixth form explained that 'dad' always gave her the money, 'But it was from *both* of them, but it was always my dad who gave me it.'

There were other images of joint parental endeavour, some accompanied by normative prescriptions on the part of young people, both in decision-making and parenting itself. Thus Paula Green felt her parents made joint decisions about money and, moreover, that they should, 'I don't think it *should* be one person'; Jayne Bentley expressed similar sentiments. Joint parental effort frequently focused on schooling. Sally Taylor, when asked if her parents thought education important replied, 'My dad did. I mean we had to be almost dying before we could stay off, and mam backed my dad up in anything about school.'

Within this unity, however, young people saw parents as having distinct roles, household maintenance by fathers and housekeeping by mothers. They also drew upon distinct attributes of each parent. The Brayshaws, for example, had a clear division of parental labour, Mr Brayshaw taking care of the sporting activities whilst Mrs Brayshaw provided support with homework. Children, might also draw differently upon each parent to suit their own purposes. As Andrea Taylor said: 'I get on better with me dad in one way and me mam the other way. Me dad's more lenient on time and going out, but I can talk to me mam better . . . Dad'll cover for me a lot . . . they both cover for me in different ways.' And Christina Green, noting that while 'she got on' with both parents, observed, 'Sometimes I think I get on with one better than the other, but [it's] if we disagree over something.' She talked to her mother. 'Mum always knew how to get things out of me when I was troubled; it was always mum I went to.'

Parental Achievements

> They've got *us* haven't they, really [laughter]. (Sally Taylor)

Within this conception of parents, the young people located themselves at the heart of parental achievement. Their views of their parents' greatest achievements centred on home, job, and, said with some amusement, 'having them'. The following gives the flavour of the responses: 'Dunno. Having *me* (laughs). I dunno. Getting the shop. Getting the home' (Andrea Taylor); 'Bought a house. My mam's got a newish car. They've got *us* haven't they, really' (laughter) (Sally Taylor); 'Bringing Chris and I up. An' getting the jobs and having the home that they've got' (Paula Green); 'Having good jobs and being able to afford the things they can afford, looking after their money properly . . . bringing us up properly. I'm not really *sure*' (Christina Green); 'Maybe . . . getting this *home* and *us* . . . just the family' (Colin Roberts).

This centrality was reflected in perceptions of both parental tasks and parental happiness. For when asked what their parents did for them several had difficulty in articulating it. The background of support and services were so taken for granted, so obvious, that they could not easily be brought to mind. 'Loads of things, everything', said Paula Green. 'Wash and cook and everything, really' replied Colin Roberts. Parents were also seen as going 'out of their way' to help their children, providing a welcome background of support; although, as Christina Green observed, 'They like to help as much as they can — but they've got to give you some *freedom* as well.' Parents were also seen as wanting to see them happy. Christina Green, asked what she thought parents would want for her in five years time, felt that it would be 'just whatever . . . makes me happy'. Moreover, a child's happiness was seen to underpin parental happiness, as John Brayshaw observed, making them happy when they were old as they watched their happy adult children.

Guardians of the Social and Moral Order

In several ways parents were seen as the guardians of social order, both in the family context and in relation to the outside world. They 'kept you on the right road, seeing you kept the right times and that' (Allatt and Yeandle, 1992); 'brought you up properly'. Such steering was perceived as a legitimate task; for although Paula Green did not like her parents 'telling her what to do and when to come in', she added, 'But I suppose they have a right to, really.' In this endeavour, as Jayne Bentley observed of the learning aspect of board money contributions, they were 'helping you towards your future'.

Payment of board money marks a major transition into the public domain, as children leave full-time education and enter the labour market; some of the reverberations upon the domestic sphere have been discussed under the concept of home. As noted, however, childhood and adolescence is also replete with micro-transitions within the domestic domain itself, for example, in the use of time, access to money, allocation of space and the transfer of responsibilities.

These smaller domestic transitions also carry the polluting dangers noted by Douglas (1966), threatening the moral and social order of family life — its values and its hierarchies. Consequently, not only do parents take pains to control the danger, but children, recognizing this as a parental task which deeply affects them, closely monitor it. One example is the maintenance of the principle of fairness at the transitional points in a child's money career. Although interpreted by families in different ways, resulting in different familial systems for the allocation of tasks and resources (Allatt and Yeandle, 1992), fairness is widely acknowledged as a tenet of family life (Backett, 1982) — 'We have a policy of doing the same for both children', said Mrs Phillips. Within these familial systems a child's money career passes through age-graded transitions — from the parent–child transfers of pennies 'for sweeties', through the more formally institutionalized 'pocket money' and clothes allowance years, to the child–parent transfer of board money. Some of these transitions are signified by the amount received as 'pocket money'. Colin Roberts described the gradations.

> I think it was about 25 pence a week every Friday or something. (*At what age was that?*)
> Pretty young. About . . . I'm not sure, about 5 upwards till . . . And then every couple of years it went up to, like, 50 pence, then a pound, one twenty-five. One twenty-five. *Now* it's on two pound fifty a week.

These financial increments, however, not only symbolize parental recognition of the sequential stages in the progression to adulthood, but also demarcate the age-graded sibling hierarchy located in the concept of equity. The value of fairness is jealously guarded by children, and parental dispensation of it is closely monitored since it intimately reflects a child's relative status. Monitoring is witnessed in the transgression of norms; there was an outcry, for example, from the two Bentley sisters when their younger brother was seen to leapfrog one of these stages, 'A pound at his age!'

In terms of equity between siblings young people see parents as courts of appeal. This was vividly illustrated in the Newcastle study when Hugh Clark, unemployed, was in dispute with his employed sister over the choice of television programme. His mother described the incident, feeling powerless to intervene because of the moral superiority paid employment continues to endow.

> She [her daughter] says, 'I've just come in from work', and all that. 'You've got your telly upstairs', a black and white . . . and he wanted to watch snooker. Well what can you do, I mean, she's going out to work . . . So he just gives in . . . reluctantly like. (Allatt and Yeandle, 1992, p. 76)

Because of this underpinning of equity, young people are not only aware of differences between siblings but recognize that, in some instances, parents might legitimately treat them differently. Paula Green, for example, anticipating lower grades in her examination results than those achieved by her sister, felt that, whilst her sister's reward had been a leather coat, she might only 'get an anorak or something'. This thought had not even crossed her parents' minds; as her mother separately related, she would receive the same as her sister whatever the outcome.

Parents were seen as the maintainers of a moral order in another sense. They sustained a bounded system of monitored reciprocal trust. This lay in the inculcation in their children of appropriate trust — whom to trust, how far to trust and when to trust (Baier, 1985). Thus the Teesside young people saw parents as the first people to turn to if they were in trouble, and felt parents would be upset should they first approach others. Moreover certain practices were contained within the family, and the boundaries patrolled by parents. Such practices were those which, if out of control, carried potential material and moral repercussions, bringing both young person and family into disrepute. The money transactions of borrowing and lending were central, and the practices and expectations surrounding them defined safe territory as lying within the family palisade. Consequently, borrowing was confined to members of the family household. As Andrea and Sally Taylor observed of their parents attitude, each choosing identical words though interviewed separately, 'They wouldn't like it if I borrowed outside the family.' Andrea Taylor described a childhood incident, 'I remember once when I was little and I borrowed fifty pence off someone and I got (*****!) done for it.' For as Sally explained, 'If it's the family it doesn't *matter* so much, because they know they're going to get it back.' Christina Green described the internal loan system — how she might buy something on her mother's Barclaycard or borrow a few pounds from her if she 'didn't have cash on her', but always paid it back and was never late. 'There was nothing like *that* . . . I used to pay it back. I don't borrow money and then forget about it . . . I don't like debts hanging over my shoulder.' She felt her parents trusted her. Mr Hughes, in the Newcastle study, also described a familial system of trust; here the children left 'I owe you's' in his wallet for money borrowed (Allatt and Yeandle, 1986). Yet such trust seemed to be built out of, or indeed accompanied by, a system of controls. Sally Taylor clearly recognized those adopted in her household. When asked if she always repaid her borrowings she replied, 'I wouldn't forget about it [laughter]. There's a running total if you borrow more than once.' And whilst Mr Taylor always lent Andrea money when she asked, nonetheless, as she pointed out, the gesture was accompanied by the comment, 'When am I going to get it back?'

The strength of such monitored trust, however, whereby familial boundaries were constantly reaffirmed, was heightened by its reciprocal nature, the practice and moralities of borrowing operating across the generations. Thus, parents borrowed from their children, for petty cash for school dinner money, for example, or the price of a drink if they had run out of change. And in families where the handing over of 'pocket money' was not a weekly ritual, running totals of what parents owed children were pinned up in the kitchen. Against this moral patterning it is not surprising that lending and borrowing amongst friends seemed to be confined to the price of the odd mars bar.

Transformations in Parenting Style

They don't shout now (Colin Roberts)

This final section turns to children's and young people's perceptions of parenting styles. As Brannen notes (this volume), parents do not stop worrying nor do they relinquish control as children approach adulthood, but bring other mechanisms into play. Within different family cultures, however, the transition to adulthood is not necessarily based upon the same premise. Julia Brannan suggests in chapter 9 two models. In one, the transition was to ascribed statuses of increased responsibility, especially domestic responsibility for young women. Whilst this model was particularly prevalent amongst the Asian origin families, it echoes Bates' (Bates, 1990) observations concerning white working class girls. The second, stemming from an individual rights perspective, was of transition to an achieved status of independent adulthood. Here attempts to retain control were made through changes in parents' modes of communication, particularly evident around issues of how and where young people spend their time. Parents, especially mothers, talked, discussed and queried, as they laboured to exert an indirect control over their young.

Young people are aware, to different degrees, of these transformations in parenting style. Deborah Jackson, for example, recounted minor changes of strategy when asked if there was anything she did not like about her parents:

> Not really apart from when mum gets really *cross* about little things. She has little notices at the moment. And she realizes that writing a little *notice* and sticking it somewhere has more effect than *shouting* at us . . . It's usually the shower room, and, 'Brush shaving bits out of basin after use' (laughs). 'Please put toothbrushes in the *green* mug', or something like that.

Some young people, however, were more keenly aware of how the transformation in parental styles signalled the gradual transfer from parent to child of responsibity for self. In the Teesside study this was displayed in the issue of homework. Colin Roberts described the change. 'They don't really *make* me [do my homework]. They just help me. They just, you know . . . They *used* to shout at me but not now. Now I get it done myself. But I didn't used to.' Mike Phillips was able to elucidate, in his case, the underpinning processes:

> Well not so much now they don't force me [to do homework] . . . but they just remind me that . . . They say, 'Well, if you don't do it then it's your problem. It's going to affect you in the long run.' . . . Which is not actually forcing me to do it, 'it's making me think about it, so in the end I will do it.

That 'the person who must pass from one [state] to another is himself in danger' (Douglas, 1966, p. 96) resonates in the Phillips' message to their son.

Conclusion

This chapter has selected certain representations of parents and parenting held by young people, and hence the patterns and images revealed are necessarily partial. A more extensive analysis of these data and the extension to young people with different experiences are likely to produce more and different images. Nonetheless, concepts drawn from a life course perspective have higlighted processes through which imagery is filtered. The first theme, the concept of the child as an enduring relationship, illuminated the early foundations of continuities in parent–child relations which extend over time. The second, life course transitions, brought together not only the macro- but also the micro-transitions of these early years, which, by the very fact of being transitions, threaten the system, in this case the familiar order — although the household practices within which transitions are embedded resonate with the wider culture.

Symbolic continuities, evidenced in young people's accounts of their relations with their parents, were lodged in the concepts of home, parental worry and its reciprocities, and auto/biography. Within this configuration, the parenting which young people described offered them a niche and identity in relationships, affectivities and domestic history. It provided them with a sense of attachment which reached back into the past and held the potential for extension into the future. That such continuities can be shattered, and that competing norms and values are subject to negotiation at transitional points in the life course, was illustrated from a range of sources and centred on the concept of home.

In their representation of parenting, these young people saw themselves as central to their parents' lives, as constituting a major parental achievement. Parents were perceived not only as a single entity but as also having distinguishing attributes upon which children could draw and use to their own ends. They were seen as the guardians of the social and moral order, who, at times of threatening transitions would ensure the maintenance of such key familial values as equity and the statuses embedded in sibling hierarchies. Children keenly monitored parental performance in these tasks. Parents were also seen as those to turn to first when in trouble or in need of support, who would be upset if children turned elsewhere. In this parents were defining the boundaries and territories of appropriate trust upon which not only family life but the wider society is founded. It was especially evident with regard to money, lending and borrowing embedded in a system of monitored and reciprocal trust. Finally, the young were aware that parental styles were not fixed, but changed as parents shaped them in response to their children's progress through the multi-faceted transitions to adulthood.

Notes

1   The data in the chapter are drawn largely from an associated study of the *ESRC 16–19 Initiative: Family Processes and Transfers in the Transition to Adulthood* (Grant No. XC05250019), and referred to here as the Teesside study. Further data are taken from a related study (the Newcastle study), also based in the north-east, funded by the Leverhulme Trust and entitled, *Family Structure and Youth Unemployment in an Area of Persistent Decline*. Other data are drawn from studies by Brannen *et al.* (1994), Brannen (this volume), Jones (1994), and Wallace (1987).
2   All emphasis in the quotations is that of the respondents.

3 The sacred quality of home is a theme deeply embedded in popular culture (Allatt in press).

4 Despite her confusion over her own behaviour, Sally Taylor could recognize the sacredness of home when she felt others violated it. When asked if she disapproved of anything about her parents she said, 'I hate it if [my dad's] been out to the pub and he'll come in and if he has a drink when he's at *home* after he's been *out*, well that annoys me. But no, otherwise.'

5 Amidon (1995) introduced a review of a book depicting America's 'Victory Culture' which turns the invader into the invaded with a 'priceless' childhood photograph of 1967, capturing himself and his brother playing soldiers, kitted in second world war gear and awaiting 'the kraut'. Ironically, he notes, at the time America was 'fighting a bloody war in Vietnam'. He concludes the review by wondering 'if the boys in my neighbourhood had tried to locate our games in Mekong, then America's current efforts to return to bellicose insularity might be seen as the disastrous folly they are.'

References

ALLATT, P. (1996) 'The political economy of romance: Popular culture, social divisions and social reconstruction in wartime', in HOLLAND, J. and WEEKS, J. (Eds) *Women and Sexuality*, London, Macmillan.

ALLATT, P. and YEANDLE, S.M. (1986) '"It's not fair, is it?": Youth unemployment, family relations and the social contract', in ALLEN, S., WATON, A., PURCELL, K. and WOOD, S. (Eds) *The Experience of Unemployment*, London, Macmillan.

ALLATT, P. and YEANDLE, S.M. (1992) *Youth Unemployment and the Family: Voices of Disordered Times*, London, Routledge.

AMIDON, S. (1995) 'Review of *The End of Victory* by Tom Englhardt', *Sunday Times Books*, 26 March, p. 3.

BACKETT, K. (1982) *Mothers and Fathers*, New York, St Martin's Press.

BAIER, A.C. (1985) 'What do women want in a moral philosophy?', *Nous*, **XIX**, 1, pp. 53–63.

BATES, I. (1990) 'No bleeding whining minnies: The role of YTS in class and gender reproduction', *British Journal of Education and Work*, **3**, pp. 91–110.

BELL, C. (1968) *Middle Class Families*, London, Routledge and Kegan Paul.

BURCHILL, J. (1995) *The Sunday Times*.

BRANNEN, J., DODD, K., OAKLEY, A. and STOREY, P. (1994) *Young People, Health and Family Life*, Buckingham, Open University Press.

DOUGLAS, M. (1966) *Purity and Danger: An Analysis of the Concepts of Pollution and Taboo*, London, Routledge and Kegan Paul.

FRASER, R. (1985) *In Search of a Past: The Manor House at Amnersfield 1933–1945*, London, Verso.

HARRIS, C.C. (1983) *The Family in Industrial Society*, London, George Allen and Unwin.

JONES, G. (1994) *Family Support for Young People*, Edinburgh, Centre for Educational Sociology, University of Edinburgh.

KIERNAN, K.E. (1985) 'Leaving home: Questions and queries from statistics', Paper presented at Workshop 5: Problems in Methodology in Family and Household Research, University of Manchester, 22 November.

OAKLEY, A. (1987) 'Gender and generation: The life and times of Adam and Eve', in ALLATT, P., KEIL, T., BRYMAN, A. and BYTHEWAY, B. (Eds) *Women and the Life Cycle: Transitions and Turning Points*, London, Macmillan Press, pp. 13–32.

PITTS, J.R. (1964) 'The structural–functional approach', Cited by Harris (1983) in CHRISTENSEN, H.T. (Ed) *Handbook of Marriage and the Family*, Chicago, Rand McNally.

VAUS DE D. (1994) 'Relations between adults and their parents: The role of gender, life stage and social mobility', Paper presented at the British Sociological Association Annual Conference: Sexualities in Context, University of Central Lancashire, 30 March.

WALLACE, C. (1987) *For Richer for Poorer: Growing Up In and Out of Work*, London, Tavistock Publications.

Chapter 11

The Economic Circumstances of Children in Ten Countries

Steven Kennedy, Peter Whiteford and Jonathan Bradshaw

State Parties recognise the right of every child to a standard of living adequate for the child's physical, mental, spiritual, moral and social development. (Article 27 United Nations Convention on the Rights of a Child)

. . . children must come first because children are our most sacred trust. They also hold the key to our future in a very practical sense. It will be their ideas and their resourcefulness which will help solve such problems as disease, famine and the threats to the environment and it is their ideas and their values which will shape the future character and culture of our nation. We need to do all we can to ensure that children enjoy their childhood against a background of secure and loving family life. That way, they can develop their full potential, grow up into responsible adults and become, in their turn, good parents. (Margaret Thatcher, George Thomas Society, Inaugural Lecture, 17 January 1990)

Introduction

The last decade has seen an increasing number of expressions of concern about the relative economic status of children in developed societies. For example, in the past the United Nations Children's Fund concentrated its attention on the status of children in Third World countries. However, in the late 1980s it became alarmed that 'changes in labour markets, environmental conditions, in family structure, in internal and international migration, in the organisation of society and in other aspects of life . . . (may have caused) new and subtler forms of deprivation' (cited in Bradshaw, 1990, p. 1) in industrial societies and launched an enquiry into child poverty and deprivation in industrialized countries including the UK.

Similar concerns have been expressed elsewhere — but particularly in the English-speaking countries. The report for the UN Children's Fund carried out in the UK (Bradshaw, 1990) and its follow-up (Kumar, 1993) revealed that British children, contrary to political rhetoric, did not come first during the 1980s. In fact between 1979 and 1991/92 the proportion of children living in families with incomes below 50 per cent of the average (after housing costs) increased from 10 per cent to 32 per cent while average living standards increased by 36 per cent (Department of Social Security, 1994). In the United States, Preston (1984) argued in a well-known article that private and public choices had dramatically altered the age-profile of well-being, so that conditions had deteriorated for children and improved for the elderly. Preston referred to official estimates that poverty increased for those under 13 years of age from 16 per cent in 1970 to over 20 per cent in 1982, while among those aged 65 years and over it decreased from 25 to 15 per cent. More recently, Haveman and Wolfe state that 'the nation's concern for the well-being, education, and development of its children is again on the rise, reaching a level not seen at least since the 1950s' (1993, p. 153).

In Australia, Saunders and Whiteford (1987) estimate that financial poverty among dependent children increased from 6 per cent in 1966 to around 20 per cent in 1986 (although subsequently alleviated by the Government's child poverty reforms). In Ireland, the Survey of Income Distribution, Poverty and Usage of State Services (1987) found that families with children faced a higher risk of poverty than other households (Expert Working Group, 1993). In the other countries of the European Union, there has also been a growing awareness of similar changes in the composition of the low income and vulnerable population, characterized as the growth in 'new poverty' (Room, Lawson, and Laczko, 1989; Laczko, 1990).

While the precise factors associated with these developments differ between countries, there appear to be a number of broadly common influences. These include increases in the number of lone parent families in the population and in their reliance on means-tested benefits or social assistance, as well as increases in the level of unemployment among families with children. Labour markets have changed, with increases in the extent of part-time work and casual and atypical employment. It has also been suggested that the increase in the proportion of families with two earners has led to a widening of the gap between these groups and lower income families with one or no earners (Cantillon, 1994). At the same time, the relative economic status of older people has improved on average, due to the maturation of public pension systems and the growth in incomes from occupational and private pensions.

It has been suggested that these developments may lead to the possibility of inter-generational conflicts over resources, particularly as the demographic ageing of the population will require a shift in total resources further towards the older population. Thompson (1989) has argued that 'modern welfare states are failing to behave equitably over time . . . the inability or unwillingness to operate intergenerational exchanges fairly is now revealed on such a scale as to seriously endanger the continued consensus for collective welfare programmes . . . The suspicion is that overall public expenditures on free or subsidised services has shifted from areas which most benefit the young to those favoured by the aged' (pp. 35, 44).[1]

These issues are clearly of major significance to debates about future developments in public policies in developed countries. This chapter is intended to contribute to this ongoing debate by providing a new analysis of the economic circumstances of children in ten developed societies — Australia, Canada, France, (the Federal Republic of) Germany, Italy, Luxembourg, the Netherlands, Sweden, the United Kingdom, and the United States — using data from the Luxembourg Income Study (LIS). We first present analyses comparing the level and distribution of household disposable cash income for children in the ten countries. However, the material wellbeing of children (and other population groups) can be affected by a number of factors, not all of which may be 'visible' in standard analyses of cash disposable incomes. In the second part of this chapter, therefore, we present results based upon income concepts which incorporate the value of 'noncash' benefits. These are benefits provided by governments in the form of health and education programmes, by employers in the form of health insurance coverage, and the benefits derived from the ownership of housing. The level and distribution of this broader measure of resources is analysed, using the same methods applied to the income data, and the affects of using this measure of living standards on the economic position of children is assessed. The final section draws out the most important implications of our findings and relates them to the introductory discussion above.

Measuring Living Standards

How can the living standards of children be compared across societies? The first question arising from this relates to the meaning of the term 'living standards'. In common with most previous comparative analysis, we are interested in material living standards. While some might regard this as an overly narrow focus, there are many complexities involved with even this restricted definition. A theme common to much of the comparative literature on living standards is the extent to which international comparisons can be affected by apparently minor methodological or technical choices (see for example Atkinson, 1990; Whiteford and Kennedy, 1995). To review these issues is beyond the scope of this chapter (see Whiteford, Kennedy and Bradshaw, forthcoming), but is important to stress that given these uncertainties the results presented below should be regarded as broadly indicative rather than definitive of the relative circumstances of children in different countries.

The methodology employed in this analysis is that used by the United Kingdom Department of Social Security in its *Households Below Average Income* (HBAI) series (Department of Social Security, 1990; 1992; 1993; 1994). The HBAI approach is conceptually similar to the methods used in previous studies which have used LIS data. Having said this, the HBAI approach has a number of distinctive features. These relate to the unit of analysis, the units who are assumed to pool income, the unit used in describing the results, the equivalence scales used to adjust for the different needs of different units, and the relative income standard. These are described briefly below.

The Income Unit and the Unit of Analysis

The unit assumed to share income in the HBAI approach is the household. Choosing the household as the income sharing unit means that non-dependent children

Table 11.1: Average income of children compared to average income of population, by income group, selected countries, mid 1980s

| | **Average income as per cent of average income[1] of total population** | | | | |
| | | **Lowest quintile** | **Highest quintile** | | **Gini** |
	All children	**of children**	**of children**	**Range[2]**	**Coefficient**
Australia	88	38	158	4.2	0.29
Canada	89	40	155	3.9	0.26
France	92	45	171	3.8	0.28
Germany	89	51	150	2.9	0.23
Italy	94	41	176	4.3	0.31
Luxembourg	91	55	158	2.9	0.23
Netherlands	87	49	144	2.9	0.22
Sweden	99	63	138	2.2	0.16
United Kingdom	89	39	160	4.1	0.28
United States	83	27	165	6.1	0.33

Notes: [1] These are 5 per cent trimmed means for each group of children and for the total population.

[2] The range is the trimmed mean of the highest quintile divided by the trimmed mean of the lowest quintile.

Source: Estimated from LIS data files

living with their parents or older persons living with their adult children, for example, are assumed to benefit from joint consumption and share to some extent in their income.[2] While the HBAI approach assumes that income is shared among household members, the unit whose well-being is analysed is the individual.

Equivalence Scales

All the results below are expressed in terms of 'equivalent income'. Equivalent income is income adjusted to take account of the relative needs of the members of the household sharing that income. The equivalence scales used in the analyses below were developed by McClements (1977) and have been the subject of a range of criticisms (Muellbauer, 1979; Bardsley and McRae, 1982; Townsend, 1991). However, no single set of equivalence scales commands universal acceptance (Whiteford, 1985), and the McClements scales are not extreme when compared with other scales (Department of Social Security, 1992). Having said this, it should be stressed that international comparisons of living standards can be highly sensitive to the choice of equivalence scale (Buhmann *et al.*, 1988).

Poverty, Relative Low Income and Measures of Well Being

Studies of poverty predominate in the comparative income distribution literature. The results shown below are closely related to this literature, by estimating the proportion of the child population in different countries with incomes below various fractions of average income. However, in order to provide a more comprehensive account of children's wellbeing, the analysis below uses additional relative measures, including the average household incomes of children as a percentage of mean incomes for the population as a whole, and measures of income inequality including the Gini coefficient.

The LIS Data

Until recently, international comparisons of income distribution have been severely limited by the lack of truly comparable data. This has been substantially remedied with the development since 1983 of the Luxembourg Income Study (LIS) database, a set of broadly comparable income surveys held at the Centre for Population, Poverty and Policy Studies at Walferdange, Luxembourg.

In the analysis presented below, the European Union (EU) countries included are the United Kingdom, France, (West) Germany, Italy, Luxembourg and the Netherlands, and outside the EU, countries analysed are Australia, Canada, Sweden and the United States. The dates of the surveys included in LIS range between 1984 in France and Germany to 1987 in the Netherlands, Canada and Sweden.[3]

Children and Household Disposable Cash Income

The first set of results of this analysis are shown Table 11.1, which compares the average disposable household cash income of all children in each country.[4] The average income of children in each case is divided by the average income for the total population, to provide a standard measure across countries.[5] On average, children have access to the highest relative household incomes in Sweden, and the lowest in the United States. The remaining countries fall closer together. These averages cover different distributions, however. Children in low income families are best off in Sweden and Luxembourg and worst off in the United States. The best-off quintile of children have the highest relative position in Italy and France, and the lowest in Sweden.

Income inequality among children is measured by comparing the income range and Gini coefficients. The income range is calculated as the ratio of the average income of the richest quintile of children to that of the poorest quintile. On both measures, the United States has by far the highest level of income inequality, followed by Italy, Australia and the United Kingdom. Inequality in the household incomes of children is low in Germany, Luxembourg and the Netherlands, and very low in Sweden (Table 11.1).

Table 11.2 shows how children in different types of two-parent family fare on average. For example, in all countries average household income falls with the number of children, with the gap between large and small families being greatest in the USA, Italy and Australia and least in Luxembourg. The number of earners in the household also has a major impact on relative status, with the difference between children in families where no adults worked and where two or more adults worked

Table 11.2: Average income of children in two-parent families as per cent of average income of population, by number of children, number of earners and age of youngest child, selected countries, mid 1980s

| | Couple, 1 child | Couple, 2 children | Type of family and age of youngest dependent child | | | | | |
			Couple, 3+ children	Couple, no earners	Couple, 1 earner	Couple, 2+ earners	Couple, child < 6	Couple, child > 6
Australia	117	98	77	32	76	106	89	94
Canada	108	98	77	34	73	101	91	95
France	103	102	79	48	76	113	93	95
Germany	100	91	79	90	85	98	90	91
Italy	109	96	72	46	77	120	98	91
Luxembourg	99	95	81	59	85	109	95	90
Netherlands	101	90	77	56	84	109	89	87
Sweden	113	102	89	64	76	104	99	101
United Kingdom	108	97	77	45	86	113	87	97
United States	113	98	72	31	79	97	87	96

Source: Estimated from LIS data files

Table 11.3: *Average income of children in lone parent families by number of earners and age of youngest dependent child, as per cent of average income, selected countries, mid 1980s*

	Average income as % of overall average income				
	All lone parents	**No earners**	**One or more earners**	**Lone parent, child < 6**	**Lone parent, child > 6**
Australia	64	43	84	54	71
Canada	61	40	70	55	65
France	77	45	86	72	79
Germany	67	58	73	57	72
Italy	87	46	97	69	91
Luxembourg	85	76	91	88	94
Netherlands	75	70	94	84	71
Sweden	92	69	95	88	94
United Kingdom	73	63	93	68	78
United States	53	30	63	68	78

Source: Estimated from LIS data files

being greatest in Australia, the USA and Canada. The difference is least in Germany, but this is a consequence of the apparently extremely high average income of couples with no earners. It can also be noted that single income couples are on average best placed in the UK, while children in dual earner families are relatively most well off in Italy, the UK and France. It is also notable that in Germany and the United States, two income families have disposable cash incomes less than the population average. There are also differences according to the age of the youngest dependent child in the family, although these are not as great as the differences associated with the number of children or the number of earners. In most countries, families with pre-school children are not as well-off on average as families without such children, presumably because of the effects on labour force participation of mothers. These differences are greatest in the UK and the USA and least in Germany and Sweden. It can also be seen that in Italy, Luxembourg and the Netherlands, families with younger children are apparently better-off on average, a pattern it is difficult to explain.

In Table 11.3 it can be seen that in all countries, children in lone parent families are on average substantially worse off than in other families with children, with the difference being greatest in the United States, Canada and Australia and least in Italy, Luxembourg and Sweden. It is interesting to note, however, that with the exceptions of France, Germany, Italy and the USA, children of lone parents who are not working are estimated to be better-off than couples where there are no earners. This difference is most marked in the UK, where children of not-working lone parents are estimated to have equivalent incomes nearly 50 per cent higher than children of not-working couples. Not unexpectedly, children of working lone parents are uniformly better-off than children of those not working. The difference between children of working and not working lone parents is greatest in the USA and Italy, although in the USA children of working lone parents are relatively worse placed than in any other country, while children of working lone parents are relatively best placed in Italy.

Table 11.4: Percentage of children in families with incomes below fractions of average income, selected countries, mid 1980s

| | Per cent of average income | | |
	40%	50%	60%
Australia	10.6	19.5	27.5
Canada	10.0	17.7	26.7
France	6.9	14.6	25.9
Germany	3.4	9.3	20.9
Italy	9.7	17.6	27.8
Luxembourg	1.9	6.1	17.8
Netherlands	5.2	9.7	19.2
Sweden	2.2	4.4	7.4
United Kingdom	8.3	16.7	28.6
United States	21.9	29.6	37.9

Source: Estimated from LIS data files

Table 11.5: Percentage of children in families with incomes below 50 per cent of average income, by type of family, selected countries, mid 1980s

| | Type of family | | | |
	Couple, 1 child	Couple, 2 children	Couple, 3+ children	Lone parent
Australia	8.2	10.5	23.6	47.1
Canada	8.4	10.1	22.3	45.8
France	11.4	10.0	17.7	29.7
Germany	4.6	7.3	13.3	33.1
Italy	13.3	14.8	28.2	25.5
Luxembourg[1]	3.8	5.1	7.8	13.4
Netherlands[1]	5.8	5.9	16.4	15.8
Sweden	3.4	4.1	5.8	4.7
United Kingdom	10.5	14.4	22.7	17.2
United States	12.0	14.4	33.8	60.0

Note: [1] Subject to high relative standard errors
Source: Estimated from LIS data files

Lone parents with at least one pre-school child have lower average incomes than those only with older children. The difference for lone parents is greater than for couples, however. The Netherlands is once again an anomalous case, with lone parents with a pre-school child apparently being substantially better off than those with older children.

Children in Poverty

Tables 11.4 to 11.7 provide details of the proportion of children with low household cash incomes. Table 11.4 shows the percentages of children below three 'poverty thresholds' — 40, 50 and 60 per cent of average income. The most striking result is that the extent of poverty, whatever the threshold chosen, is much greater in the United States than any other countries. The proportions below 40 and 50

Table 11.6: Percentage of children in families .with incomes below 50 per cent of average income, by number of earners, selected countries, mid 1980s

	Type of family and number of earners				
	Couple, no earners	Couple, 1 earner	Couple, 2+ earners	Lone parent, no earner	Lone parent, 1+ earners
Australia	91.5	17.6	9.0	81.0	20.4
Canada	90.3	26.5	7.6	83.4	31.8
France	60.8	16.4	4.4	69.8[1]	19.1
Germany	28.5	8.9	3.2	44.5[1]	26.7[1]
Italy	70.7	23.2	5.8	74.6[1]	12.2[1]
Luxembourg	46.8[1]	6.1[1]	2.1[1]	21.7[1]	7.9[1]
Netherlands	31.5[1]	8.7	5.0[1]	15.7[1]	15.8[1]
Sweden	21.4[1]	11.5	3.2	24.5[1]	2.1[1]
United Kingdom	63.1	15.0	3.5	22.5	8.8[1]
United States	88.4	31.3	15.5	94.6	46.8

Note: [1] Subject to very high relative standard errors
Source: Estimated from LIS data files

Table 11.7: Percentage of children in families with incomes below 50 per cent of average income, by type of family and age of youngest child, selected countries, mid 1980s

	Type of family and age of youngest dependent child			
	Couple, child < 6	Couple, child > 6	Lone parent, child < 6	Lone parent, child > 6
Australia	16.6	14.9	59.7	38.5
Canada	16.0	12.1	53.8	40.6
France	11.2	15.1	36.5[1]	26.7
Germany	9.0	7.1	56.9[1]	28.1
Italy	14.4	19.1	46.7[1]	21.9
Luxembourg[1]	4.8	6.1	15.1	12.6
Netherlands	7.0[1]	11.1	3.3[1]	22.0[1]
Sweden	4.3	4.6	6.1[1]	3.9[1]
United Kingdom	19.0	14.2	17.5[1]	17.0
United States	25.4	16.5	73.8	47.4

Note: [1] Subject to very high relative standard errors
Source: Estimated from LIS data files

per cent of average income are also substantially higher in Australia, Canada, the UK, Italy and France than in the remaining countries. The extent of poverty among children seems markedly less in Sweden than elsewhere.

The European Commission has recently adopted less than half average national average income as a working definition of 'social exclusion' (European Commission, 1993). Tables 11.5 to 11.7 therefore indicate the proportion of children in different family types in poverty on the basis of a poverty threshold set at 50 per cent of average income. As one would expect from the earlier results, the poverty appears to increase markedly with the number of children and is generally much higher among lone parents than among two parent families, although there are exceptions. While the extent of poverty varies substantially across countries and household types, there are a number of patterns that can be mentioned. For example, while the proportion of all children with equivalent incomes below 50 per cent of the average is relatively low in Germany, the poverty rate for lone parents in Germany is considerable, they being four times more likely than all children on average to have incomes below half the average. Once again, economic circumstances are associated with the number of earners, with the risk of poverty being particularly high for couples without any earners. It is also notable that nearly half of all working lone parents in the USA have incomes below 50 per cent of the average, while the corresponding figure for Sweden is only 2 per cent.

It would be possible to draw out any number of comparisons across family types or countries, but the main implication of these and earlier results is that there appear to be very substantial differences in the relative economic circumstances of children in different countries. Within this diversity there are some common patterns — such as those related to the number of children, the number of parents present, the number of earners, and the presence of young children — but even so, there are striking exceptions to these patterns, which are difficult to explain.

Children and Older People in Poverty

In the introduction we referred to the debates that are beginning to be heard about inequity in intergenerational exchange. Welfare systems typically attempt to reconcile a number of different objectives (such as smoothing out income over the life cycle, provision of security against certain contingencies, or enabling individual independence), but in recent years calls for greater 'targeting' of welfare spending (see, for example, Department of Health and Social Security, 1985) is often interpreted as suggesting that a higher priority should be attached to the objective of poverty alleviation (but see Atkinson, 1993, for a discussion of the relationship between targeting and poverty alleviation. See also Hills, 1993). If we take the somewhat narrow view that poverty alleviation is the primary objective of welfare policy, then this may be taken to imply that the degree of 'commitment' to the welfare of different population groups by a particular Welfare State can be measured by comparing the extent of poverty among these groups. In this section therefore we compare the poverty rates for children and older people.

Here we define 'older people' as those over the current State pension age in the United Kingdom (65 for men, 60 for women).[6] Figures 11.1 to 11.10 below present for each country the percentage of children, older people and the total population below three thresholds — 40, 50 and 60 per cent of mean equivalent income. In the United Kingdom and the United States, children are clearly more at risk of poverty than older people. Poverty rates are also higher for children in France, the Netherlands, and Canada (when the threshold is at 40 or 50 per cent). In contrast, older people have a higher risk of poverty in Luxembourg, and in Australia the proportions of older people are far more likely than children to be in poverty (at the 50 and 60 per cent threshold at least). In Germany, Italy and Sweden, however, the variation in poverty rates between these groups is far less than

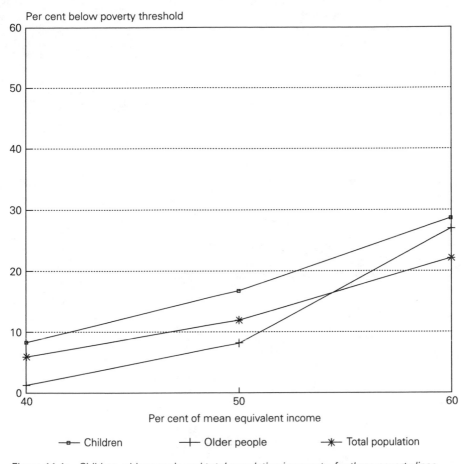

Per cent below poverty threshold

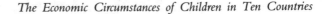

Figure 11.1: *Children, older people and total population in poverty, for three poverty lines, United Kingdom, 1986*
Note: Older people are women aged 60 and over and men aged 65 and over.
Source: Estimated from LIS data files

in the other countries. On the basis of the somewhat narrow criterion of poverty alleviation, therefore, it would appear that the assertion that welfare states are failing to treat different generations equitably may not be universally applicable.

Broadening the Concept of Resources

The analyses presented above compared the living standards of children in terms of cash disposable incomes. However, as the arguments put forward by Thompson (1989) recognize, the activities of the Welfare State are not limited to redistributing cash incomes. Material 'living standards' are determined by a wide range of factors which may not be incorporated into the 'standard' cash disposable income measure.

Per cent below poverty threshold

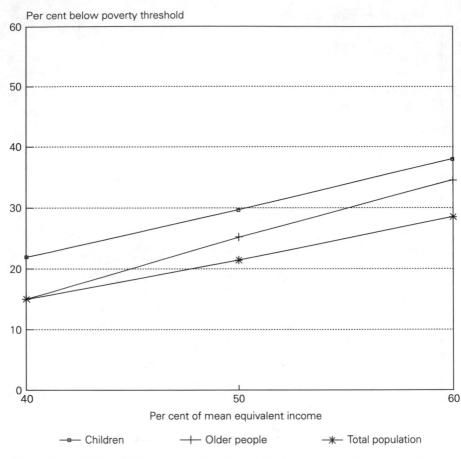

Per cent of mean equivalent income

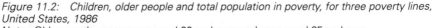

—■— Children   —+— Older people   —✳— Total population

*Figure 11.2:   Children, older people and total population in poverty, for three poverty lines,
United States, 1986*
Note: Older people are women aged 60 and over and men aged 65 and over.
Source: Estimated from LIS data files

'Noncash' benefits include a wide range of government and non-government activities that contribute to individuals' command over resources and their living standards. Potentially, these resources can be self-produced, as in the case of imputed income from domestic labour and child care; they could be purchased (the flow of services from ownership of consumer durables); or they could be provided by government through health, education, and housing programmes; they could be provided by employers; or they could be market-produced, as in the case of imputed rent from owner-occupied housing.

Noncash benefits in their various forms may make a significant contribution to the living standards of all population groups in developed societies. The case for taking account of these benefits is compelling, particularly when making comparisons across countries where the composition of the package of resources of households,

Per cent below poverty threshold

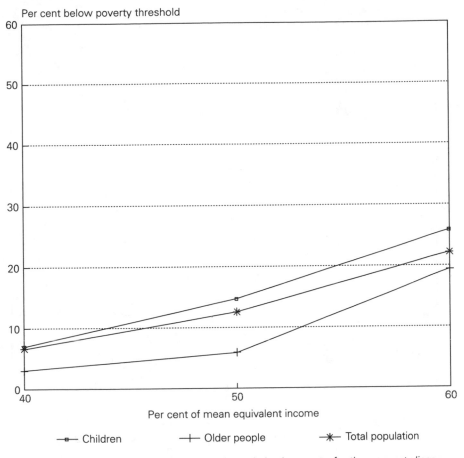

Per cent of mean equivalent income

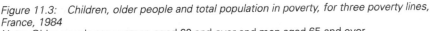

Figure 11.3: Children, older people and total population in poverty, for three poverty lines, France, 1984
Note: Older people are women aged 60 and over and men aged 65 and over.
Source: Estimated from LIS data files

and the relative weight given to cash and noncash social expenditures, may differ substantially. In the remainder of this chapter, therefore, we present results based upon a broader concept of living standards which includes noncash benefits in addition to cash incomes.

The range of noncash benefits that could potentially be estimated is much wider than the resources actually allocated here. Ideally, the full range of noncash benefits should be included in any analysis, but there are very significant problems of data and evaluation affecting the practicality of such a project. For example, domestic labour in the form of child care and other forms of care is quantitatively very important but difficult to value. In summary, we have included spending on the two major government noncash programmes — health and education. In the United States, we have also included employer-subsidized health care. The analysis

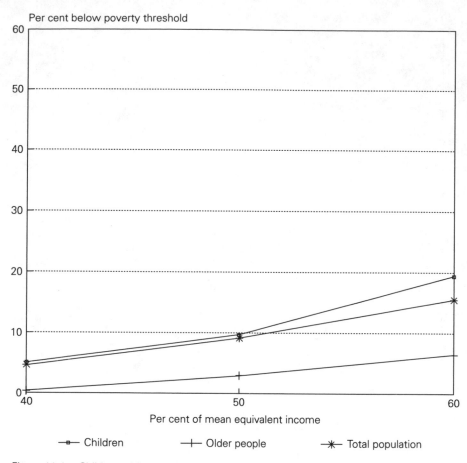

Per cent below poverty threshold

Per cent of mean equivalent income

—■— Children　　　—+— Older people　　　—*— Total population

Figure 11.4:　Children, older people and total population in poverty, for three poverty lines, the Netherlands, 1987
Note: Older people are women aged 60 and over and men aged 65 and over.
Source: Estimated from LIS data files

also includes the value of imputed income from owner-occupied housing, as well as noncash housing subsidies, in selected countries.

Methodology and Imputation Rules

The analysis which follows largely adopts the approach used by an earlier study using the Luxembourg Income Study datasets (Smeeding *et al.*, 1992). With respect to education, we allocated spending according to average per pupil expenditures, by level of education, and the number of children in the relevant age ranges in each household.[7] For health, we estimated average per person expenditures, by age and sex, using data on aggregate expenditure by health care sector and utilization data.

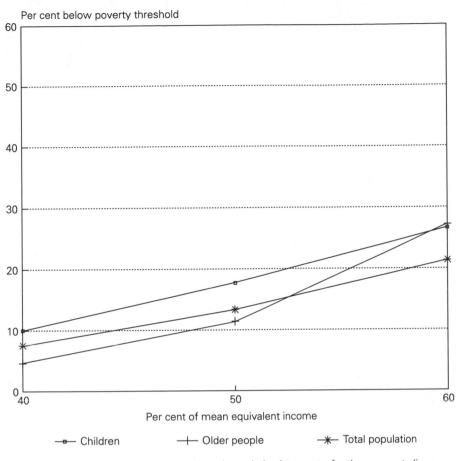

Per cent below poverty threshold

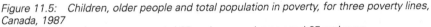

—□— Children   —+— Older people   —*— Total population

Figure 11.5: Children, older people and total population in poverty, for three poverty lines, Canada, 1987
Note: Older people are women aged 60 and over and men aged 65 and over.
Source: Estimated from LIS data files

Amounts were then allocated to individual households according to the age and sex of members, and according to their eligibility for coverage (note that this is important in the case of countries where public health care is not universal, such as the United States and Australia). For housing, we include both noncash subsidies to renters in public sector housing, and imputed income for owner-occupiers.[8] In the case of public renters, we used data on the incidence of subsidies (measures as the difference between rent paid and 'market' rent). For owner occupiers, data limitations forced us to adopt two approaches to estimating imputed income. For some countries, imputed income is measured as implicit rental income minus the costs of owning (mortgage interest, maintenance and repair costs), whereas in others it is measured as a rate of return on housing equity.[9]

For each household, the total amount of noncash health, education and (for

159

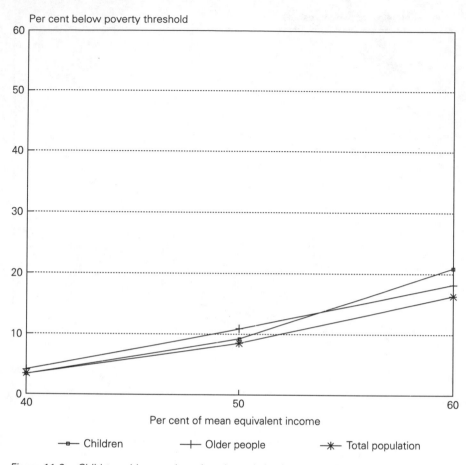

Figure 11.6:   *Children, older people and total population in poverty, for three poverty lines, West Germany, 1984*
Note: Older people are women aged 60 and over and men aged 65 and over.
Source: Estimated from LIS data files

those countries where the relevant data was available) housing benefits was estimated. The total amount of noncash benefit received was then adjusted using the same equivalence scale applied to the cash income data, and added to net disposable cash income to yield 'final income' (see below). It should be stressed that the methods used for valuing and imputing these noncash benefits are not uncontroversial. For a more in–depth discussion of the rationale for including noncash benefits in the definition of income, and a detailed description of the approach adopted, the reader is referred to Whiteford and Kennedy (1995).

The inclusion of these noncash benefits in the definition of income can be expected to have a number of obvious distributional consequences. With respect to health care spending, older people are likely to benefit most since health care utilization among this group is substantially higher than for younger age groups. However,

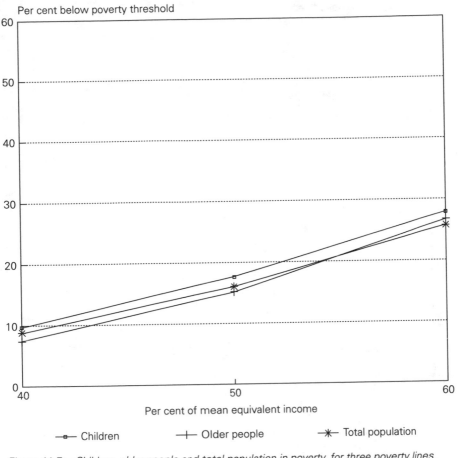

Per cent below poverty threshold

Per cent of mean equivalent income

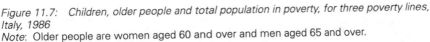

—■— Children   —+— Older people   —✳— Total population

Figure 11.7:   Children, older people and total population in poverty, for three poverty lines,
Italy, 1986
Note: Older people are women aged 60 and over and men aged 65 and over.
Source: Estimated from LIS data files

analysis of utilization data also shows that children, especially young children, and women of childbearing age also use health services disproportionately in comparison to working age men (see Whiteford and Kennedy, 1995). This suggests that the inclusion of health spending would result in a shift in overall resources away from prime age individuals without children towards older people and, less strongly, towards families with children. In addition, because the allocated benefits are the same for all members of the same age–sex groups, health spending is more equally distributed than cash disposable income, and can therefore be expected to reduce measured inequality.

The redistributive impact of public health care spending is also likely to be somewhat greater in Australia and the United States than in the other countries analysed. This is because in these countries public health care is specifically targeted

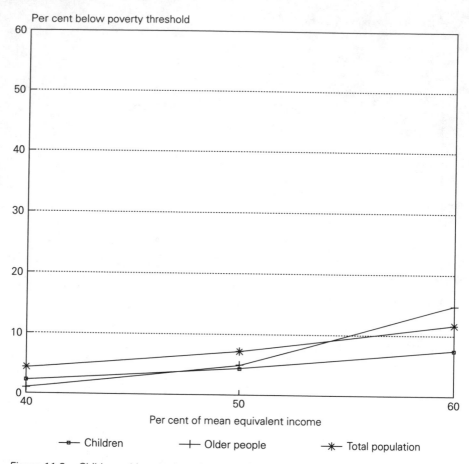

Per cent below poverty threshold

Per cent of mean equivalent income

—■— Children   —+— Older people   —*— Total population

Figure 11.8: Children, older people and total population in poverty, for three poverty lines, Sweden, 1987
Note: Older people are women aged 60 and over and men aged 65 and over.
Source: Estimated from LIS data files

on low income groups. However, in the United States at least, overall health benefits are in fact very unequally distributed, since the equalizing effect of public health care spending is more than offset by the value of employer-funded health insurance (which tends to favour higher income groups).

Education benefits can also be expected to have obvious distributional effects. The position of families with children will obviously improve relative to other groups, but in addition we can expect that inequality among families with children will be reduced. This is because, like health spending, education benefits are the same for each recipient in the same age group.

The overall impact of noncash housing benefits is less predictable, however. Rent subsidies for tenants in public housing can be expected to reduce inequality (since these groups tend to have lower incomes), but imputed income from owner-

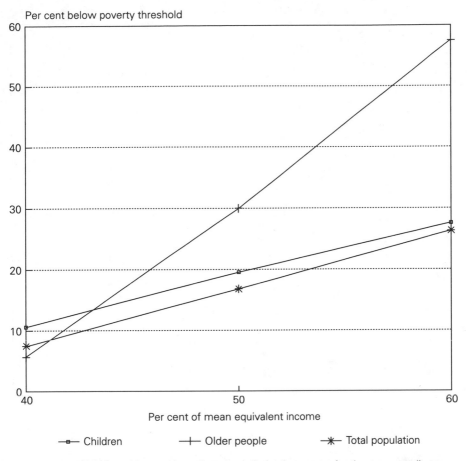

Per cent below poverty threshold

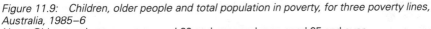
—■— Children   —+— Older people   —✳— Total population

Figure 11.9: Children, older people and total population in poverty, for three poverty lines, Australia, 1985–6
Note: Older people are women aged 60 and over and men aged 65 and over.
Source: Estimated from LIS data files

occupied housing is far more important quantitatively in most countries (although there are large differences between the level of home ownership in different countries). Imputed income can be regarded as the rental income that owners could receive from this form of wealth, less the expenses involved in 'earning' that income — mortgage interest payments and maintenance costs, for example. This means that imputed income from housing can be negative for households at an early stage of purchase, since mortgage interest payments may exceed imputed rent. Thus this form of income tends to be redistributive across the life cycle and is of most benefit to those who own their homes outright. This means that the position of older people improves, while families with children may lose ground somewhat.[10] Having said this, housing wealth (and the level of owner-occupation) tends to increase with income, so the overall redistributive impact of owner-occupation is complex.

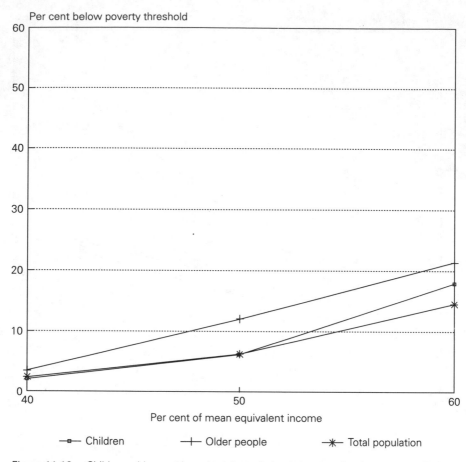

Figure 11.10: Children, older people and total population in poverty, for three poverty lines, Luxembourg, 1985
Note: Older people are women aged 60 and over and men aged 65 and over.
Source: Estimated from LIS data files

The obvious question that arises from the above discussion is whether an analysis based on a broader measure of incomes would change conclusions reached about the wellbeing of children and other population groups and the extent of redistribution. It is to these results that we now turn.

The Impact of Noncash Benefits

Tables 11.8 and 11.9 present the results of our broadening of the concept of income. The tables are the same as those above giving results for disposable cash income, but are restricted to a narrower range of countries for which the additional income components have been imputed.[11] Results are presented for each of three income concepts:

- Income 1 is cash disposable income, as given in the previous tables, but repeated here so that the changes can be readily apparent;
- Income 2 is cash disposable income, plus the value of health and education benefits for each country; and
- Income 3 is Income 2, plus the value of imputed income from owner-occupied housing and government noncash housing benefits.

Table 11.8 shows the effects of broadening the income concept for children generally. In all these countries, the average incomes of children increase when health and education benefits are added, and the difference between countries narrows somewhat. Imputed income from housing is either neutral in its effect or reduces the average position of children (Australia, the USA), because costs exceed benefits. It can also be seen that health and education disproportionately benefit low income families with children, with the average incomes of the lowest quintile of children increasing by between 15 and 22 percentage points, compared to an average increase for all children of between seven and nine percentage points. The income ranges and Gini coefficients indicate a reduction in inequality in all countries, although Sweden maintains its position as having the most equal distribution of income between children and the USA remains the most unequal.

Table 11.9 shows how estimates of the extent of poverty vary by income concept. The use of the broader income concepts has a stronger effect on these measures than on the average position of children, for the reasons just outlined. The extent of relative low income drops dramatically, although the differences between countries do not change to the same extent. Some specific points may be of interest. In many cases, the USA remains the clear outlier, with the extent of relative low income remaining significantly higher than in the next nearest country, be it Canada, Australia or the UK.

Conclusion

This chapter has sought to compare the economic circumstances of children in ten countries. It has shown that there is considerable variation in their economic circumstances and in particular the proportion living in poverty between countries. Regardless of definition and family type the economic circumstances of children are worst in the United States and best in Sweden. The relative position of children in the other countries varies according to the definition of resources, the threshold employed and also by the type of family, employment status of the parents and the number and ages of the children.

Why is this? The results that we have observed are the product of the interaction of a complex of demographic factors, labour force participation and unemployment rates, earnings levels, income tax and transfer policies, and the value and

Table 11.8: Average income of children compared to average income of population, by income concept and by income group, selected countries, mid 1980s

| | Average final income as per cent of average final income of total population | | | | | | | | | | | | | | |
| | All children | | | Lowest quintile of children | | | Highest quintile of children | | | Range | | | Gini coefficient | | |
	1	2	3	1	2	3	1	2	3	1	2	3	1	2	3
Australia	88	95	92	38	55	55	158	151	148	4.2	2.8	2.7	.29	.22	.22
Canada	89	96	96	40	58	57	155	149	147	3.9	2.6	2.6	.26	.20	.20
Germany	89	97	–	51	66	–	150	148	–	2.9	2.3	–	.23	.19	–
Sweden	99	106	–	63	79	–	138	133	–	2.2	1.7	–	.16	.13	–
United Kingdom	89	97	97	39	58	58	160	155	155	4.1	2.7	2.7	.28	.21	.21
United States	83	92	91	27	49	49	165	163	159	6.1	3.3	3.2	.33	.26	.26

Source: Estimated from LIS data files

Table 11.9: Percentage of children in families with incomes below fractions of average income by income concept, selected countries, mid 1980s

| | Per cent of average income by income concept | | | | | | | | |
| | 40% | | | 50% | | | 60% | | |
	1	**2**	**3**	**1**	**2**	**3**	**1**	**2**	**3**
Australia	10.6	4.2	4.2	19.5	7.0	7.0	27.5	15.4	14.8
Canada	10.0	2.6	2.7	17.7	5.6	6.3	26.7	12.5	14.5
Germany	3.4	0.9	–	9.3	3.0	–	20.9	8.3	–
Sweden	2.2	0.2	–	4.4	1.6	–	7.4	3.1	–
United Kingdom	8.3	3.7	3.5	16.7	6.5	6.3	28.6	12.1	13.3
United States	21.9	7.0	6.9	29.6	14.8	14.2	37.9	25.1	26.0

Source: Estimated from LIS data files

structure of noncash benefits. This is not therefore a simple question to answer. Bradshaw *et al.* (1993) have made a comparison of the package of measures that represent the financial support provided by the state for families with children. That study is more up to date than the LIS data and covered all the ten countries in this chapter except Canada. They found that the relative value of the child benefit transfer package varied according to the income of the family, the family type and the number and ages of the children and also according to whether the comparison was made before or after housing costs. However, overall, the most generous transfers were in Luxembourg, Sweden and France, and the least generous in the United States. The other countries were bunched in between with Germany, the UK and Australia rather more generous than the Netherlands and Italy. Thus we can tentatively suggest that the outcomes observed in terms of the percentages of children in poverty may be related to the generosity of the child benefit package. France is perhaps the country where there is the greatest discrepancy between child poverty rates and the value of the child benefit package. A possible explanation for this is that in France support for children is motivated, to a greater extent than in other countries, by concerns other than poverty alleviation — in particular fertility.

It should also be remembered that the results presented in this chapter relate to the situation in the mid 1980s, and the circumstances of children may well of course have changed considerably since then. Indeed, in the United Kingdom, for example, we know that the proportion of children living in households below half average income increased from 24 per cent in 1987 to 32 per cent in 1991/92 (Department of Social Security, 1994). Given the increases in child poverty rates throughout the developed world noted in the introductory discussion, it is not unreasonable to assume that a more up to date comparative analysis would show a further deterioration in the economic circumstances of children elsewhere.

The task of relating the outcomes of social policy to the inputs that generate them is one of the great challenges for comparative policy research. Clearly, much work still has to be done, but the potential of comparative research to inform our understanding of the determinants of living standards is considerable. If governments are serious about tackling child poverty, the lessons to be learned from other countries might point the way towards effective policy responses.

Notes

1   This analysis is based on the experience of a number of countries, but draws particularly from that of New Zealand. It should be noted that Thompson's arguments have been subject to a range of criticisms. See Hills (1992).

2   For a critique of this assumption and suggestions for alternatives, see Jenkins (1991). For a discussion of how the choice of income unit can affect estimates of the extent of low incomes, see Johnson and Webb, 1989.

3   The LIS data are available in a number of 'waves' — the first wave covered surveys conducted at the beginning of the 1980s — between 1979 and 1983 — while the second wave (used in this analysis) included surveys between 1984 and 1987. Results are now becoming available for the third wave (around 1990), but the number of countries included will be restricted for at least the next few years.

4   The income concept employed in this section is as follows. Income from wages and salaries, self-employment and property sum to 'factor incomes'. Factor incomes plus occupational and private pensions give 'market incomes'. Public transfers, private transfers, and any other cash income, when added to market income, produce 'gross income'. Gross income minus personal income tax and employees' social security contributions gives 'net cash disposable income'. Following HBAI practice, negative incomes are reset to zero.

5   These are the '5 per cent trimmed means' for each group of children and the total population. This means that the top and bottom 5 per cent of all cases are not included in the calculation, in order to avoid the distorting effect of extreme outliers, while at the same time incorporating much more of the sample information than would have been included in a comparison of medians, for example. The Gini coefficients are calculated over the entire sample, however.

6   While this definition might appear somewhat arbitrary, it should be noted that because pension ages differ across countries, comparisons on the basis of any single age threshold will include varying proportions of people still in work in some countries, while in other countries people who have actually retired will be grouped with those who are still working.

7   Despite the importance of public spending on higher education in some of the countries concerned, our analysis is restricted to primary and secondary schooling. This decision was taken partly because the LIS data for some countries does not allow us to separately identify students in higher education, and also because most of the income surveys used exclude those living in institutions such as halls of residence.

8   For Sweden and Germany, however, adequate data to estimate noncash housing benefits could not be obtained.

9   These two measures may not necessarily coincide. It should therefore be stressed that the final income measure incorporating noncash housing income may not be strictly comparable.

10   The magnitude of this redistribution towards the older population can however be influenced by changes in tenure patterns over time. In the United Kingdom, for example, the levels of home ownership have increased substantially in recent years. Most of the increase has been among younger age groups, however; the increase has yet to 'feed through' to older age groups. In contrast, in countries where home ownership has been encouraged for longer (the United States, for example), levels of owner-occupation peak later in the life cycle.

11   This is mainly due to the fact that the data required to estimate the value of noncash

benefits and to allocate these amounts to households is not available for all the countries. Nevertheless, the countries included — the United Kingdom, West Germany, Sweden, Australia, Canada, and the United States — represent a range of welfare states with radically different welfare arrangements.

References

ATKINSON, A.B. (1990) *Comparing Poverty Rates Internationally: Lessons from Recent Studies in OECD Countries*, Welfare State Discussion Paper WSP 53, London, STICERD, London School of Economics.

ATKINSON, A.B. (1993) *On Targeting and Social Security: Theory and Western Experience with Family Benefits*, Welfare State Discussion Paper WSP 99, London, STICERD, London School of Economics.

BARDSLEY, P. and McRAE, I. (1982) 'A test of McClements' method for the estimation of equivalence scales', *Journal of Public Economics*, **17**, pp. 119–22.

BRADSHAW, J. (1990) *Child Poverty and Deprivation in the United Kingdom*, Innocenti Occasional Papers, Economic Policy Series, Number 8, Florence, UNICEF.

BRADSHAW, J., DITCH, J., HOLMES, H. and WHITEFORD, P. (1993) *Support for Children: A Comparison of Arrangements in Fifteen Countries*, Department of Social Security Research Report No. 21, London, HMSO.

BUHMANN, B., RAINWATER, L., SCHMAUS, G. and SMEEDING, T. (1988) 'Equivalence scales, well-being inequality and poverty: Sensitivity estimates across ten countries using the Luxembourg Income Study (LIS) database', *The Review of Income and Wealth*, June, pp. 115–41.

CANTILLON, B. (1994) 'Family, work and social security', in FALKINGHAM, J. and BALDWIN, S. (Eds) *Social Security and Social Change*, Hemel Hempstead, Harvester Wheatsheaf.

DEPARTMENT OF HEALTH AND SOCIAL SECURITY (1985) *Reform of Social Security*, Cmnd. 9517, London, HMSO.

DEPARTMENT OF SOCIAL SECURITY (1990) *Households Below Average Income: A Statistical Analysis, 1981–1987*, London, HMSO.

DEPARTMENT OF SOCIAL SECURITY (1992) *Households Below Average Income: A Statistical Analysis, 1979–1988/89*, London, HMSO.

DEPARTMENT OF SOCIAL SECURITY (1993) *Households Below Average Income: A Statistical Analysis, 1979–1990/91*, London, HMSO.

DEPARTMENT OF SOCIAL SECURITY (1994) *Households Below Average Income: A Statistical Analysis, 1979–1991/92*, London, HMSO.

ESPING-ANDERSEN, G. (1990) *The Three Worlds of Welfare Capitalism*, Cambridge, Polity Press.

EUROPEAN COMMISSION (1993) *Towards a Europe of Solidarity*, Brussels, European Commission.

EXPERT WORKING GROUP (1993) *Interim Report of the Expert Working Group on the Integration of the Tax and Social Welfare Systems*, Dublin, Department of Social Welfare.

HAVEMAN, R. and WOLFE, B. (1993) 'Children's prospects and children's policy', *Journal of Economic Perspectives*, **4**, Fall, pp. 153–74.

HILLS, J. (1992) *Does Britain have a 'Welfare Generation'?: An Empirical Analysis of Intergenerational Equity*, Welfare State Discussion Paper WSP 76, London, STICERD, London School of Economics.

HILLS, J. (1993) *The Future of Welfare: A Guide to the Debate*, York, Joseph Rowntree Foundation.

JENKINS, S. (1991) 'Poverty measurement and the within-household distribution: Agenda for action', *Journal of Social Policy*, **20**, 4, pp. 457–84.

JOHNSON, P. and WEBB, S. (1989) 'Counting people on low incomes: The effect of recent changes in official statistics', *Fiscal Studies*, **10**, 4, pp. 66–82.

KUMAR, V. (1993) *Poverty and Inequality in the UK: The Effects on Children*, London, National Children's Bureau.

LACZKO, F. (1990) 'New poverty and the old poor: Pensioners' incomes in the European Community', *Ageing and Society*, **10**, 3, pp. 261–77.

McCLEMENTS, L. (1977) 'Equivalence scales for children', *Journal of Public Economics*, **8**, 2, pp. 191–210.

MUELLBAUER, J. (1979) 'McClements on equivalence scales for children', *Journal of Public Economics*, **12**, pp. 221–31.

PRESTON, S. (1984) 'Children and the elderly: Divergent paths for America's dependents?', *Demography*, **21**, 4, pp. 435–57.

ROOM, G., LAWSON, R. and LACZKO, F. (1989) '"New Poverty" in the European Community', *Policy and Politics*, **17**, 2, pp. 165–76.

SAUNDERS, P. and WHITEFORD, P. (1987) *Ending Child Poverty: An Assessment of the Government's Family Package*, Reports and Proceedings No. 69, Sydney, Social Policy Research Centre, University of New South Wales.

SMEEDING, T., SAUNDERS, P., CODER, J., JENKINS, S., FRITZELL, J., HAGENAARS, A., HAUSER, R. and WOLFSON, M. (1992) *Noncash Income, Living Standards, and Inequality: Evidence from the Luxembourg Income Study*, LIS Working Paper, Luxembourg, CEPS/INSTEAD.

THOMPSON, D. (1989) 'The Welfare State and generational conflict: Winners and losers', in JOHNSON, P., CONRAD, C. and THOMPSON, D. (Eds) *Workers versus Pensioners: Intergenerational Justice in an Ageing World*, Manchester, Manchester University Press.

TOWNSEND, P. (1991) *The Poor are Poorer: A Statistical Report on Changes in the Living Standards of Rich and Poor in the United Kingdom, 1979–1989*, Bristol, Statistical Monitoring Unit, Department of Social Policy and Social Planning, University of Bristol.

WHITEFORD, P. (1985) *A Family's Needs: Equivalence Scales, Poverty, and Social Security*, Research Paper No. 27, Canberra, Department of Social Security.

WHITEFORD, P. and KENNEDY, S. (1995) *Incomes and Living Standards of Older People: A Comparative Analysis*, Department of Social Security Research Report No. 34, London, HMSO.

WHITEFORD, P., KENNEDY, S. and BRADSHAW, J. (forthcoming) *Comparing the Living Standards of Children and Families across Countries: A Methodological Perspective*, Social Policy Report series, Social Policy Research Unit, University of York.

Chapter 12

'Family', State and Social Policy for Children in Greece

Theodore Papadopoulos

Introduction

This chapter examines certain aspects of welfare support for the family in Greece. The working definitions of the terms family and family policy are presented, followed by a description of the pattern of family arrangements and the attitudes towards families in Greece. The level of family benefits and tax allowances for a number of 'model' families is examined. An evaluation of the overall support for the family provided by the Greek Welfare State follows, as the Greek child benefit 'package' is compared with the 'packages' of fourteen countries inclusive of all the European Union countries, Australia, Norway and the USA. The comparison reveals that the Greek Welfare State provides very limited support for families with children. These findings highlight the central role that the family plays in providing care for children in Greece. Furthermore, they raise questions about the intra-family relationships that are legitimized and reproduced as a result of Greek family policy, an issue that will be discussed in the second part of the chapter.

The 'Family' and Family Policy: Working Definitions

The term 'family' has been used in sociological, political and social policy contexts in various ways to include both a variety of social arrangements and ideological constructions.[1] In this study, the concept of family refers both to a social institution and a social process and includes material and ideological aspects. It is defined as a 'structure' in Giddens' terms within which the different types of social relationships between men, women and children refer not only to 'the production and reproduction of [a] social system but also to resources — the means, material and symbolic, whereby actors make things happen' (Giddens, 1994, p. 85). As a fundamental working assumption of this study it is accepted that a welfare state via its family policy has a direct effect in maintaining, legitimizing and changing the relationships within different family types. Moreover, family policies affect the extent to which certain notions of 'the family' are re-enforced and reproduced as ideological constructs and, consequently, certain family types are encouraged or discouraged in a given society.

For Wilensky *et al.* (1987, p. 422) the term 'family policy' refers to an 'umbrella' of different policies and programmes aiming to provide for a variety of persons, i.e., 'the young and old, transition singles (divorced, separated or widowed) and women temporarily separated from the labour market due to maternity'. Kamerman and Kahn (1978) applied a more critical approach to family policy by arguing that the term is a disguise for a series of programmes of population, labour-market and health policies. Other authors placed the term within a gender perspective giving emphasis to the special relationship that women have to the Welfare State and its interaction with social class, 'race' and age. (Ginsburg, 1992; Langan and Ostner, 1991; Dominelli, 1991; Gordon, 1990) The very concept of 'the family' is so heavily ideologically laden that one could argue that the term 'policy for families' is probably more adequate as it refers to different forms of the family. In this study, the term family policy in practice refers to welfare state policies which implicitly or explicitly support a particular ideological notion of 'the family' and, consequently, the particular role that certain family types, in agreement with this notion, play in a given society.

For Wennemo (1992) family policy consists of three components: family legislation, social services targeted to families and income transfers to families. This study will focus on the last two components, especially on the elements that constitute welfare support of families with children. Policies under investigation include: income transfers to families with children in the form of benefits, tax allowances, subsidies and services in kind related to health, education and housing policies. Their overall income value constitutes, what will hereafter be called, the Greek child benefit 'package'.

Families with Children in Greece: A Comparative View

It is often argued that Greeks, as well as other southern Europeans, are strongly attached to family. A good starting point to explore this claim is to examine comparatively the composition of families in Greece. The distribution of families with children by number of children in eleven European Union countries is presented in Table 12.1. It can be observed that, compared with the other countries, Greece has the lowest proportion (10.9 per cent) of lone parent families and the highest percentage of couples with children (89.1 per cent). The percentage of lone mothers with one child is the lowest amongst the rest of the European Union countries. The first indication that attachment to the nuclear family is strong can be illustrated by the fact that Greece has the highest proportion of married couples with two children compared to the other European Union countries. However, when it comes to couples with three or more children, Greece occupies a position close to the average, as it has a similar percentage of couples with three or more children to Belgium, Italy, Portugal and the UK. When it comes to couples with four or more children, Greece is amongst the countries with the lowest percentages of these types of

Table 12.1: Families with children (%) by number of children in eleven* Member States of the European Union

Types of Family	BE	DK	FR	DE	GR	Countries IE	IT	LU	NL	PT	UK
One-parent Families	21.2	22.0	16.1	18.6	10.9	18.4	13.5	18.6	15.8	13.1	22.95
– Fathers with 1 child	3.1	2.9	1.6	2.2	1.4	1.6	1.4	2.9	2.8	1.1	2.1
with 2 children	1.1	0.7	0.5	0.6	0.6	0.8	0.6	1.4	0.8	0.4	0.7
with 3 children	0.3	0.1	0.15	0.1	0.1	0.5	0.1	–	–	0.2	0.2
with 4 children or more	0.1	–	0.06	–	0.05	0.3	0.05	–	–	0.1	0.05
– Mothers with 1 child	10.7	12.0	8.6	11.2	5.4	7.6	7.4	10.0	7.2	6.6	11.2
with 2 children	4.4	5.3	3.5	3.6	2.7	4.1	3.0	2.9	3.7	3.1	5.5
with 3 children	1.2	0.9	1.1	0.7	0.6	1.9	0.73	1.4	0.9	1.0	1.8
with 4 children or more	0.4	0.1	0.5	0.2	0.15	1.6	0.22	–	0.3	0.6	0.7
Couples with Children	78.8	78.0	83.8	81.4	89.1	81.6	86.5	81.4	84.2	86.9	84.2
– Couples with 1 child	33.8	32.3	33.3	38.1	33.6	19.3	35.7	35.7	29.0	38.1	30.2
with 2 children	30.2	35.2	32.0	32.7	42.3	24.8	37.4	32.8	38.5	33.8	32.9
with 3 children	10.6	8.7	13.1	8.2	10.7	19.0	10.9	10.0	12.7	9.6	10.9
with 4 children or more	4.2	1.8	5.4	2.4	2.7	18.5	2.5	2.9	4.0	5.4	3.8
Total (in thousands)	1,812	768	9,898	13,635	1,766	613	12,095	70	2,450	1,936	9,709

Note: *Data according to the categories used in the 1990/1991 censuses. Data for Spain are not available.
Source: Calculated from Eurostat (1994a, p. 8)

Table 12.2: *Selected demographic indicators (EUR12)*

Countries	Divorces per 1,000 population 1993	% of births outside marriage (1,000) 1993	Average number of children per woman 1977	1993
Belgium	2.1	11.3	1.71	1.61
Denmark	2.4	46.4	1.66	1.75
France	1.9	33.2	1.86	1.65
Germany	1.7	14.6	1.40	1.30
Greece	0.7	2.7	2.27	1.38
Ireland	–	18.0	3.27	2.03
Italy	0.4	7.2	1.98	1.21
Luxembourg	1.8	12.9	1.45	1.70
Netherlands	2.0	13.1	1.58	1.57
Portugal	1.2	17.0	2.45	1.53
Spain	0.7	10.0	2.65	1.24
UK	3.0	30.8	1.69	1.82

Sources: Eurostat (1994b, p. 4; 1992, p. 23)

families. Thus, in Greece the predominant type of family is the typical nuclear family, a couple with two children.

The claim that in Greece attachment to the nuclear family is strong can be supported by the examination of selected demographic indicators (Table 12.2). Greece has the second lowest divorce rate in Europe, although the legal and religious regulations for getting a divorce are not as stringent as in countries with a Roman Catholic tradition.[2] In addition, the percentage of births outside marriage is the lowest in Europe (2.7 per cent). Attempts to explain the latter phenomenon often refer to the 'stigmatization' of lone parenthood and the fact that access to abortion in Greece is relatively unrestricted. However, economic factors have also to be taken into account. It will become apparent from this analysis that welfare support for lone parents in Greece is very limited. This lack of support reflects and reproduces certain attitudes and social practices with regard to the institution of marriage and the nuclear family. An examination of the social values and attitudes held by Greek men and women sheds light on the issue.

Family as a Social Value and Attitudes towards Family Policies in Greece

In the Eurobarometer report on the Europeans and the family (CEC, 1993), Greeks appear as the most strongly attached to, and supportive of, the institution of 'the family'. In response to questions concerning the order of values, an overwhelming 99.4 per cent of the Greek respondents placed the family as their top priority on the value scale, the highest figure in Europe (EU average: 95.7 per cent). Indeed, similar views have been observed in a recent public opinion survey where 69.2 per cent of male and 75.5 per cent of female interviewees agreed respectively with the statement that 'the family is the basis for a healthy society'.[3] In addition, 46.3 per cent of men and 55.8 per cent of women strongly agreed with the statement that 'life without family is meaningless'.

However, despite the strong ideological attachment to the institution of the family, a series of ideological changes have taken place in respect of social roles within families. They relate to a series of structural changes, often defined as 'modernization', which has occurred in Greece since the early 1960s. Modernization refers to the shift from an economy based on agriculture to an economy based on services and (to a lesser extent) industry; the expansion of Greek statism and the intensification of 'intra-middle-class conflicts for access to the state machinery' (Petmezidou-Tsoulouvi, 1991, p. 40); the phenomena of rapid urbanization and migration; the cultural and economic impact of tourism; the increase in accessibility to higher education; the increase in women's labour force participation (small though it was); and last, but by no means least, changes in family legislation which preceded entry into the European Community. Directly or indirectly these changes have influenced the social structure of families in Greece, especially gender roles within the household. Lambiri-Dimaki (1983) observed that a shift from traditional to more egalitarian gender roles has taken place while Kouvertaris and Dobratz have noticed a gradual detachment from the traditional roles within families 'as a less permissive society [was giving] way to a more permissive one' (1987, p. 155). Similarly, in a study by Georgas on the change of family values in Greece it has been suggested that contemporary attitudes towards family are characterized by the gradual 'rejection of the collectivist values and the gradual adoption of individualist values' (1989, p. 90). This trend is accompanied by a transition from an extended family system to a nuclear family system, a transition which is currently more observable in the non-urban areas. In the urban areas, such transition has been, to a large extent, completed.

The change in attitudes reflects and, at the same time, reinforces the shift towards smaller families, as is shown by the data in Table 12.2. The total fertility rate has fallen, in a period of sixteen years from 2.27 to 1.38, one of the lowest in Europe, with further decreasing trends.[4] Attempting to explore the causes behind this spectacular falling, Dretakis (1994) investigated the changes in the levels of income of couples in the period between 1981–91. He found that, during this period, when couples per capita income (without children) lost 16.4 per cent of its purchasing power, couples increasingly tended to delay having children. It was observed that during the same period when the average income of couples with one child lost 7 per cent of its purchasing power, couples stopped having children after the first child or postponed having further children. Dretakis concluded that there is an urgent need to take serious measures to alleviate economic inequalities amongst Greek families and most importantly to increase welfare support of children, for example the level of child allowance. Indeed there is increasing public dissatisfaction with the results of Greek family policy. In the Eurobarometer survey (CEC, 1993, p. 119), 36.9 per cent of Greek respondents mentioned the level of child allowance as one of the most important issues on which the government should act to make life easier for families. As an indicator of dissatisfaction with the Welfare State support for children this is the highest in the European Union and far beyond the EU average level of dissatisfaction (22.5 per cent).

Simulation of the Effects of Policies for Families with Children in Greece: A Comparative Perspective

In order to explore in more detail the level of welfare support for families with children in Greece it was considered appropriate to examine the Greek child benefit package in comparative perspective. Despite the fact that attempts to make comparisons between family policies have been made in the past (Hantrais, 1993, 1994; Wennemo, 1992; CEFAM, 1992; Dummon *et al.*, 1991; Rainwater *et al.*, 1986; Kamerman and Kahn, 1978, 1981, 1983; Bradshaw and Piachaud, 1980) this type of research is still relatively underdeveloped. To a large degree, this underdevelopment can be explained by the problems of 'methods and objectives' which any attempt to compare family policies inevitably encounters.[5] The method and data employed in this study, which derive from a comparative research project by Bradshaw *et al.* (1993), aims to overcome these problems.[6] The project is a comparative analysis of the simulated impact that the child benefit package has on the disposable income of ten model families (horizontally) and eight income categories (vertically) in fifteen countries, inclusive of all the European Union countries, Australia, Norway and the USA.[7] Income data used in this study refers to the situation in May 1992.

There are at least three advantages in adopting a simulation approach. Firstly, it is not that costly because it does not incur the expense of a survey. Secondly, problems related to the accuracy of statistical data on social expenditure are avoided because what is examined is the simulated effect of a policy on families' incomes and not the overall expenditure on family policy. Thirdly, the concept of the package overcomes the problems of explicit–implicit family policies because it includes different benefits, tax allowances and even some quantified benefits in kind. A disadvantage of the method is that what is represented is a simulation and not what happens in reality. As Bradshaw *et al.* (1993, p. 23) have remarked 'it produces a description of the way the system *should* work, rather than how it necessarily *does* work'. In other words, problems related to the implementation of family policies are not addressed. However, this method proves to be very useful in exploring two of the most important questions in the sociology of welfare policy: namely the *ideological assumptions* behind a family policy and, consequently, the kinds of social relationships which are implicitly or explicitly reproduced by such a policy.

The Level of Family Benefits

A good starting point in exploring the inherent characteristics of the Greek child benefit package is to focus on the level of family benefits and the types of families that are supported by the system.[8] When examining family benefits, a distinction has to be made between *non-income related* family benefits and *income-related* family benefits. Both systems of benefits operate in Greece although the non–income related family benefits are allocated to specific types of families. They are given to families with three or more children in an attempt to increase the (low) birth rate. In addition, other types of non–income related benefits provide some extra help to lone parent families and to families with children with learning disabilities. In terms of the real value of benefits Greece performs poorly compared to other European Union countries operating similar schemes (Bradshaw *et al.*, 1993, pp. 34–6). In the case of a couple with four children Greece provides the second lowest non–income related family benefit among the fifteen countries. With regard to lone parent families with one, two and three children Greece occupies the bottom position. In the case of a lone parent family with four children Greece performs slightly better, ranking higher than Ireland and Portugal.

When it comes to income-related family benefits the Greek system of family benefits works clearly in favour of two parent families. For instance, while the allowance for lone parent families is decreasing or remains low as earnings level increases, the opposite happens for couples with children. This is due to the fact that, although child allowances are fixed, spouse allowances are proportional to salary.[9] Hence, the system not only favours couples but favours the couples with earners on high salaries. This is in sharp contrast with arrangements in all the other countries, where, as the earnings level increases, the income-related family allowance for couples with children ceases, or decreases.[10] In Greece, in the case of two parent families, income-related family benefits rise steadily as earnings increase.

A snapshot of the overall level of family benefits for different types of families in one income category is presented in Figure 12.1. The figure shows a comparison of the level of both non–income and income-related benefits for lone parent and two parent families with one or two children, with one earner in the household on 0.5 average male earnings. It is adjusted by Purchasing Power Parities (PPPs) to a common currency (pound sterling).[11] Focusing on the lower income category and on the most common types of families the figure illustrates how the family benefits system should perform in relation to families close to each country's relative poverty line. In Greece, similar to Germany, Italy and the USA, lone parent families receive lower amounts of benefits than two parent families. As far as the overall level of family benefits received is concerned, Greece ranks second lowest after Spain in the case of a lone parent family with one child, while for a couple with one child it ranks last. Greece's performance slightly improves in the case of a couple with two children, ranking above Portugal and Spain. However, in the case of a lone parent family with two children Greece occupies the bottom position.

A comparison of the benefits system of Greece with those of other countries revealed that the system of family benefits works clearly in favour of two parent families, especially those with higher incomes. However, unless the tax and social security contributions are included the picture is not completely accurate. For instance, it will be shown that although in the system of family benefits lone parent families are at a disadvantage compared to couples, when income tax and social security contributions

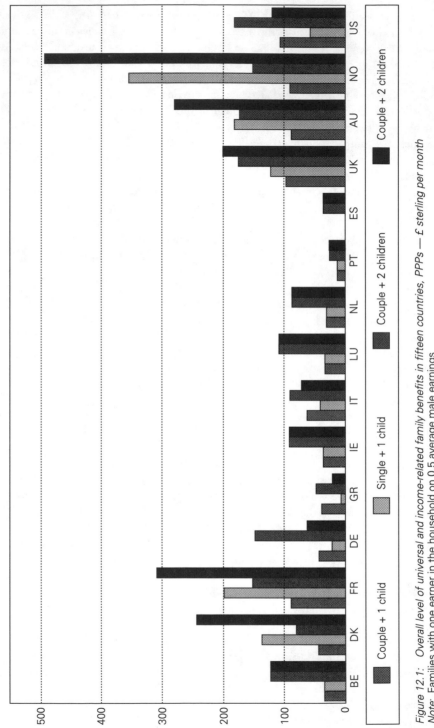

Figure 12.1: Overall level of universal and income-related family benefits in fifteen countries, PPPs — £ sterling per month
Note: Families with one earner in the household on 0.5 average male earnings
Source: Bradshaw et al. (1993, p. 37)

Table 12.3: Value of tax concessions and family allowances by family type in selected countries as a percentage of average male earnings

Tax concessions and family allowances	Lone parent with (number of children)				Couple*	Couple with (number of children)			
	1	2	3	4		1	2	3	4
Denmark	5.7	10	14.3	18.6	8.0	2.5	5.0	7.5	10.0
France	10.2	23.8	45.3	58.6	5.4	2.5	9.2	26.3	35.1
Germany	7.2	11.2	18.5	27.0	7.3	3.4	6.8	14.8	21.6
Netherlands	6.5	11.0	15.5	21.1	2.7	3.2	7.7	12.2	17.8
UK	8.6	11.4	14.2	17.0	3.0	3.5	6.3	9.1	11.9
Greece	1.1	2.9	5.6	7.7	0.2	0.4	1.3	3.5	4.6

Note: *Signifies a couple with no children
Source: Bradshaw *et al.* (1993, Table 5.6)

are included this results in a slight improvement in the financial gains of lone parent families.

The Effect of Income Tax and Social Security Contributions

Comparisons of the systems of tax and social security contributions can be made in two ways, vertically and horizontally. Both ways examine the redistributive capacity of the systems. A comparative examination of how *vertically* progressive a system is reveals the extent to which redistribution from higher incomes to lower incomes occurs. A comparison of how *horizontally* progressive the system is reveals the extent to which a redistribution of income according to the number of children in the family is achieved.

Both vertically and horizontally, the Greek system of tax and social security has been found to be one of the least progressive (Bradshaw *et al.*, 1993, pp. 39–44). There is minimal vertical redistribution because of the way the tax system operates: as income increases, there is little variation in tax rates, while contributions remain the same. It has been found that, horizontally, the Greek system's redistributive efforts towards larger families are minimal.

In Table 12.3 estimates of the relative value of tax concessions *and* family allowances by family type, (with one earner in the household on average male earnings) are presented for selected countries. The estimates are expressed as a proportion of the average gross male earnings and represent the sum of the value of tax concessions and the value of family allowances. Tax concessions for lone parent families are calculated as follows: 'the difference between the income tax paid by lone parents with one or more children and the income tax paid by a single person in the same gross earnings'. For couples, tax concessions are calculated as 'the difference between the income tax liabilities of a couple without children and the corresponding liabilities of couples with children' (Bradshaw, 1993, p. 43). The value of family allowances is calculated as a proportion of average male earnings.

179

Two observations can be made at this point. Firstly, it can be clearly observed that, in comparison to other systems, the Greek system of tax concessions and family allowances is horizontally one of the least progressive. Secondly, in Greece the overall value of tax concessions and family allowances is higher for lone parents rather than couples although comparatively it is still quite low. This is due to spouse allowance being considered as an integral part of income and, therefore taxable. Within the European Union, Greece and the Netherlands are the only countries in which the system results in lone parents being taxed less than couples who have the same number of children.

An Evaluation of the Greek Child Care Package Inclusive of all Components

Next, the Greek child care package (inclusive of all its components) is placed in a comparative perspective, in order to assess its overall value. Firstly, the net disposable incomes of families with children is calculated by taking into account the following: earnings, family benefits (both non-income and income-related), tax allowances, social security contributions, housing, health and education costs and subsidies. However, comparing only the net disposable incomes of families with children has certain limitations. For example, it may be the case that income taxes in a particular country are low for all families, regardless of having children or not. The aim therefore is to calculate the difference in the net disposable incomes between childless families and families with children *at the same earnings level*. This additional income includes all the benefits, allowances and subsidies given to families with children which a childless couple will not receive. It provides a clear indication of the effort that a welfare state makes in order to support families to cover the costs of children.

The method used in this study is a comparison of the *horizontal redistributive effort* of the different countries. A country's horizontal redistributive effort is an estimate of the additional net disposable income which a family with children enjoys compared to a childless couple when both are at the same earnings level. It is calculated as a percentage of the net disposable income of a childless couple at the same earnings level. Table 12.4 presents the efforts of fifteen countries for a couple with two children at three earnings levels. It has been found that housing costs and subsidies are important factors in determining the net disposable income of a family (Bradshaw *et al.*, 1993, p. 45). Therefore two comparisons were applied for every earnings level: before and after housing costs.

It is notable that, in most cases, as earnings increase the horizontal redistributive effort decreases. The majority of countries make their greatest horizontal redistributive effort towards families with children at the lowest earnings level. However, when it comes to the Greek case, the opposite is true. Before housing costs are included, a couple with two children with one earner on *half the average male earnings* is expected to have 1 per cent additional disposable income over a childless couple at the same earnings level. The Greek system makes at this earnings level its least redistributive effort. This is contrary to all other systems which, as we can observe, make at

Table 12.4: Additional net disposable income of a couple with two children as a proportion (%) of the net disposable income of a childless couple before and after housing costs at various earnings levels, in fifteen countries

	One earner on half the average male earnings		One earner on average male earnings		Two earners, one on average male earnings and one on 0.66 average female earnings	
	Before housing costs	After housing costs	Before housing costs	After housing costs	Before housing costs	After housing costs
Belgium	27	34	18	20	12	13
Denmark	14	35	8	11	6	-1
France	20	33	14	18	10	10
Germany	45	88	10	4	7	3
Greece	1	-17	2	-9	1	-6
Ireland	14	14	2	-2	1	-2
Italy	13	13	5	4	1	0
Luxembourg	17	17	14	13	11	11
Netherlands	14	17	9	8	5	5
Portugal	11	1	8	3	6	2
Spain	4	5	1	1	1	0
UK	34	58	8	8	6	6
Australia	31	40	5	7	2	3
Norway	29	74	16	10	11	6
USA	38	29	0	-25	0	-15

Source: Bradshaw et al. (1993, Tables 9.2, 9.3)

this earnings level their greatest effort. If housing costs are included, the position of lower income families in Greece worsens dramatically. A couple with two children with one earner on half the average male earnings is expected to have 17 per cent less net disposable income compared to a childless couple at the same earnings level.

Furthermore, a couple with one earner on *average male earnings* is expected to have 2 per cent additional net disposable income over a couple without children at the same earnings level, while a couple of *two earners* will enjoy only 1 per cent additional income. If housing costs are included, the Greek system makes in both cases negative horizontal redistributive effort, second only to the USA.

To summarize the findings at this stage: compared to other European and western countries Greece ranks very low in terms of its welfare state support for children. The Greek child care package is, comparatively, one of the least generous when it comes to making a redistributive effort in supporting families with children. It is also one of the least vertically progressive when it comes to tax arrangements. Given that the inequality in income distribution in Greece was found to be the highest in Europe,[12] it is understandable why several Greek authors talk about the non-existence of a Greek Welfare State. Petmesidou-Tsoulouvi (1991, p. 39), for instance, maintained that 'it is questionable whether any consistent redistributive social policies have ever existed at all', arguing that 'a welfare state has scarcely been formed in Greece' (p. 36), while Fotopoulos (1994, p. 9) referred to the 'non existent Greek welfare state'.

State, 'Family' and Policies for Children in Greece: A Discussion of the Effects

From the analysis undertaken it became apparent that despite the strong attachment of Greeks to 'the family', the Welfare State support for children in Greece is almost non-existent. This inconsistency is illustrative of the socio-economic role that the family performs in Greece in providing welfare for its members. This role is based upon a web of relationships, a special mix of solidarity and dependency, which the family policy of the Greek Welfare State — via its *inaction* — implicitly nurtures and, thus, reproduces. Commenting on family policy as inaction Barbier argued that

> the absence of a generalised system of family benefits may have a com-
> pletely different significance in a modern welfare state such as the United
> States, or in a state in which private solidarity and informal networks are
> important [. . .] All national contexts do not call for the same public inter-
> vention. A truly complete comparison of policies cannot afford to over-
> look this primary consideration as regards scope: the role of exchanges and
> informal networks in traditional family functions (child-rearing, bringing
> up children, taking care of elderly persons in particular, informal transfers of
> many types, inheritance and property practices and so on) [. . .] An inter-
> national comparison of family policies must take into account the social and
> cultural situations which themselves are at the origin of these policies but
> which are also a product of them. (Barbier, 1990, pp. 331–4)

In Greece, the absence of welfare state support for the family results in 'the family' itself undertaking a very important role in ideological, material and even political terms. According to a study of contemporary Greek society by Tsoukalas (1987, p. 268), the Greek family as a social institution is almost 'possessed' by the idea of social mobility. As an ideological driving force, the belief that the family is the main vehicle for social mobility is embodied in the social practices of almost all social classes through a system of attitudes, visions and expectations.

An expression of this belief can be observed in the attitudes and practices related to the education of children. Greek society is characterized by a 'generalised practice of familial educational investment' (Tsoukalas, 1987, p. 270). According to the same author 'Greek families do not only "hope" for the upward mobility of their children but believe in it and, thus, are doing everything possible in order to "program" it' (p. 268). According to a recent study (Katsikas *et al.*, 1995) the total amount that Greek families spent on their children's education is almost 1 billion Drachmae (2.5 million pounds) per day. This is a massive expenditure given the number of Greek children in education and in numerous cases implies the sacrifice of a better standard of living.[13] As an intergenerational family investment, it has both symbolic and material aspects. At the symbolic level there is the expectation of an enhancement of family image and status, as children 'continue forward' and become 'better' than their parents. At the material level, higher levels of education result in well paid employment (although this pattern has changed in recent years) which accordingly is translated into additional family income and property. The latter advancements do not necessarily benefit a *paterfamilias*, but all the members of a family and especially children since in the future they will inherit family property.

Expectations of mobility crystallize in social practices which produce a special kind of solidarity within the family collective. One could argue that the Greek family functions internally as a co-operative while competing with other families in a society dominated by the idea of social mobility. 'Familial solidarity' remains primarily in the private sphere of the nuclear family, as a kind of intergenerational responsibility towards the family. Although several Greek scholars point to this type of family ideology as one of the main reasons why the Greek Welfare State is so underdeveloped (Maloutas, 1988), it seems unclear whether family ideology is the cause or the effect of this underdevelopment. What is clear, however, is that since solidarity rarely expresses itself in the public sphere, the development of notions of social responsibility or social solidarity encounter enormous obstacles. Thus, the creation of a sustainable ideological base for expanding the residual Welfare State in Greece is weak. In this context, it can be argued that the ideological assumption which characterizes welfare arrangements in Greece is that 'the family' operates as the primary provider of welfare support. I define these arrangements as 'Greek familism'.

The Characteristics of Greek Familism in Terms of Gender and Youth

Familial solidarity is an integral part of the Greek familism. However, it is by no means the only type of relationship that is reproduced by the *inaction* of Greek family policy. If Greek familism is analysed in terms of gender and youth a pattern of dependency and power relationships among the members of Greek families emerges. Attempting a 'gendered typology' of welfare regimes, Lewis (1992) categorized western European countries into strong male-breadwinner countries, modified male-breadwinner countries and weak male-breadwinner countries. Greece fits all the criteria for the first type.

> Strong male-breadwinner states have tended to draw a firm dividing line between public and private responsibility. If women enter the public sphere as workers, they may do so on terms very similar to men. It is assumed that the family (that is women) will provide child care and minimal provision is made for maternity leaves, pay and the right to reinstatement. (Lewis, 1992, p. 164)

This view can be supported by examining the Greek female activity rate.[14] Greece still has one of the lowest female activity rates in Europe, 34 per cent compared with 40.6 per cent which is the average for the European Union (Eurostat, 1992, p. 78). In addition, Greece pays the lowest maternity benefits compared with the other EU countries (Eurostat, 1993, p. 6). Social spending on maternity benefits in Greece consists of only 0.05 per cent of Gross Domestic Product, which is again the lowest in the EU, a figure far behind that of Denmark (0.52 per cent), the highest spender on maternity benefits in the EU.

The Greek family is still patriarchal in its structure and despite any legislative rhetoric the dependency of women upon men continues. The inaction of Greek family policy results in reinforcing the role of women as the sole carers of children by nurturing, reproducing and legitimizing their dependency on men, a reality observed by several Greek researchers (Stassinopoulou, 1993; Labropoulou, 1990; Maloutas, 1988). Thus, a shift from private to public patriarchy (Walby, 1990, Ch. 8) has not yet occurred in Greece. Similar to Ireland (Mahon, 1994), the residual family policy of the Greek Welfare State reproduces the structure of private patriarchy.

However, this is not the only type of dependency that is reproduced. Another type, that Greek social scientists have only recently begun to research (Makrinioti, 1993), concerns the dependency of children on families and especially young people upon parents. Children and young people are still conceptualized within the legislative and policy context as totally dependent on family and a notion of 'child as a partner' or participants in decisions (Qvortrup, 1990, p. 35) is totally absent. Since welfare support is left to families the dependency of young people on parents is reinforced and thus reproduced and legitimized. In a comparative study of the difficulties that young Europeans encounter during their transition to adulthood it was found that in Greece, 'leaving home and living independently of one's parents is almost always associated with marriage [. . .], or with becoming a full time-student' (Burton et al., 1989, p. 63). Since it is almost impossible for a young person to survive independently outside the family context, due to high housing costs, high youth unemployment, lack of income support and with no access to the limited welfare state services, a large number of young people, especially women,[15] often choose to marry in order to 'escape' from the family environment, not least because creating a new family is in most cases 'rewarded' with gifts of very significant value, such as houses,[16] cars or cash. And, thus, a new circle starts again.

To summarize, as the system of family policy operates in Greece, the family is compelled to play an important socio-economic role in providing welfare for its members and, in particular, supporting children. This in turn results in the reproduction of a web of social relationships within families, characterized by a special mix of solidarity, dependency and power. If independence and equality are selected as the criteria to evaluate family arrangements it can be argued that in Greece women and children are particularly badly off. In this context, given the way in which the Greek system of welfare support to families operates, there is a need to explore new modes of structuring family policy in which issues of interdependence, equality and solidarity will be central.

Notes

1   For an extensive presentation of the different perspectives concerning the concept of the family see Williams (1989, pp. 117–46).
2   The vast majority of population in Greece follows the Orthodox Christian denomination. It is generally accepted that on issues such as divorce or abortion the Orthodox Church

has not exerted the same moral pressure as the Catholic Church. Therefore, to perceive Greece as a country where Catholicism is strong is incorrect (see for instance Leibfried, 1993, p. 141).

3   The survey was conducted by MRB HELLAS and reported in *Eleftherotypia* (Greek daily), 11 July 1994.

4   Interestingly, a similar dramatic drop in fertility rates has occurred in all the 'peripheral' EU countries, that is Portugal, Spain, Italy, Greece and Ireland.

5   For a detailed presentation of the methodological problems of comparative family policy see Barbier (1990) and Hantrais (1994). For a more general account of the research issues related to the comparison of family policies see Ginsburg (1992).

6   Bradshaw J., Ditch J., Holmes H., Whiteford P. (1993) *Support for Children: A Comparison of Arrangements in Fifteen Countries*, London, HMSO. The research project was undertaken by the Department of Social Policy and Social Work and the Social Policy Research Unit (SPRU) of the University of York. It was funded by the Department of Social Security (UK). Countries studied include all the EU country members plus Norway, Australia and the USA. The author was the national respondent for Greece.

7   The ten model families of the study include single people and couples without children, lone parents with one, two, three and four children and couples with one, two, three, and four children. The eight income categories of the study include three categories for one earner families, three categories for two earner families, one category where one parent is on average male earnings and the other is unemployed and one category where both parents are unemployed. For a full account of the methodology and a detailed description of family types, earning categories and assumptions see Bradshaw *et al.* (1993, pp. 23–8).

8   Readers who are interested in a recent description of the Greek child care policy system can refer to Papadopoulos (1993).

9   Fixed rates for child benefits apply in the wider private sector. In the public sector and in some parts of the private sector (e.g., banks), income-related child allowances are proportional to the salary and are not fixed, a system again favouring those with high salaries.

10   In France, for instance, the income-related family allowance increases only for lone parent families.

11   Purchasing power parities (PPPs) are used for expressing the actual value of a currency in terms of purchasing power. A PPP is an estimate of how much a basket of goods and services costs in a country. Normally, it is converted into a common monetary denominator which in this study is one pound sterling. As Bradshaw *et al.* (1993, p. 25) point out 'purchasing power parities are more satisfactory than exchange rates in that they take account of differences in the price of a common basket of goods and services in each country'.

12   The Gini coefficient is used as a measurement of the distribution of household and individual income in a society. Lane and Ersson (1987, p. 83) calculated the Gini coefficients of fourteen European countries. Greece was found to have the highest coefficient among the fourteen countries (0.460).

13   In the Eurobarometer survey (CEC, 1993, Table 6.5) the cost of educating children was placed at the top three major issues of concern by Greek respondents (39.2 per cent against an EU average of 33.6 per cent).

14   Female activity rate is calculated as the proportion of women aged 20–59 employed and registered unemployed to the total number of women of this age.

15   In Greece, the average age of women at time of first marriage is the lowest in the EU, 23.8 compared to an EU average of 25.1 years (Eurostat, 1993, p. 4).

16   According to Katrivessis (1993, p. 613), 41.7 per cent of houses transferred from parents
to children consists of houses bought/built for children when they get married.

References

BAILEY, J. (Ed) (1992) *Social Europe*, London, Longman.

BARBIER, J.C. (1990) 'Comparing family policies in Europe: Methodological problems', in the *International Social Security Review*, **3**, pp. 326–41, Geneva, ISSA.

BRADSHAW, J. and PIACHAUD, D. (1980) *Child Support in the European Community*, London, Bedford Square Press.

BRADSHAW, J., DITCH, J., HOLMES, H. and WHITEFORD, P. (1993) *Support for Children: A Comparison of Arrangements in Fifteen Countries*, London, HMSO.

BURTON, P., FORREST, R. and STEWART, M. (1989) *Growing up and Leaving Home*, Dublin, The European Foundation for the Improvement of Living and Working Conditions.

CAMPBELL, J.K. (1983) 'Traditional values and continuities in Greek society', in CLOGG, R. (Ed), *Greece in the 1980s*, London, Macmillan.

COMMISSION OF THE EUROPEAN COMMUNITIES (1990) *Childcare in the European Community*, Luxembourg, Office for Official Publications of the European Communities.

COMMISSION OF THE EUROPEAN COMMUNITIES (CEC) (1993) *Europeans and the Family: Results of an Opinion Survey*, Report prepared by Malpas, N. and Lambert, P., Brussels, Eurobarometer 39.0.

DOMINELLI, L. (1990) *Women across Continents*, London, Harvester and Wheatsheaf.

DOUMANIS, M. (1983) *Mothering in Greece: From Collectivism to Individualism*, New York, Academic Press.

DRETAKIS, M. (1994) 'The reduction in income resulted in a reduction in the birth rate', Athens, *Eleftherotypia* (Greek daily), 21 September.

DUMMON, W., BATRIAUX, F. and NUELANT, T. (1991) *National Family Policies in EC-countries in 1990*, V/2293/91-EN, Brussels, Commission of the European Communities.

EUROSTAT (1992) *Women in the European Community*, Luxembourg, Office for Official Publications of the European Communities.

EUROSTAT (1993) *Rapid Reports: Women in the European Community*, **10**, Luxembourg, Office for Official Publications of the European Communities.

EUROSTAT (1994a) *Rapid Reports: Households and Families in the European Union*, Luxembourg, Office for Official Publications of the European Communities.

EUROSTAT (1994b) *Rapid Reports: The Population of the European Economic Area on 1 January 1994*, **4**, Luxembourg, Office for Official Publications of the European Communities.

FOTOPOULOS, T. (1994) 'The end of Welfare State', Athens, *Eleftherotypia* (Greek daily), 9 April.

GEORGAS, J. (1989) 'Changing family values in Greece', *Journal of Cross-cultural Psychology*, **20**, 1, pp. 80–91, Western Washington University.

GESELLSCHAFT FUR FAMILIENFORSCHUNG e.V. (GEFAM) (1992) *Twelve Ways of Family Policy in Europe: National Policy Designs for a Common Challenge*, Bonn, Research Project commissioned by the Federal Ministry for Family affairs and Senior Citizens (Federal Republic of Germany).

GIDDENS, A. (1994) 'Elements of the theory of structuration', *The Polity Reader in Social Theory*, Cambridge, Polity Press.

GILLIAND, P. and MAHON P. (1988) 'Equality of rights between men and women in family policies and family benefits', in *Equal Treatment in Social Security*, Studies and Research No. 27, Geneva, ISSA.

GINSBURG, N. (1992) *Divisions of Welfare: A Critical Introduction to Comparative Social Policy*, London, Sage Publication.

GLASNER, A. (1992) 'Gender and Europe: Cultural and structural impediments to change', in BAILEY, J. (Ed) *Social Europe*, London, Longman, pp. 70–105.

GOLDTHORPE, J.E. (1987) *Family Life in Western Societies*, London, Cambridge University Press.

GORDON, L. (Ed) (1990) *Women, the State and Welfare*, Wisconsin, University of Wisconsin Press.

HANTRAIS, L. (1993) 'Towards a europeanisation of family policy?', in SIMPSON, R. and WALKER, R. (Eds), *Europe: For Richer or Poorer*, London, Child Poverty Action Group.

HANTRAIS, L. (1994) 'Comparing family policy in Britain, France and Germany', *The Journal of the Social Policy Association*, **23**, 2, pp. 135–60.

HEIDENHEIMER, J., HECLO, H. and ADAMS, T.C. (1990) *Comparative Public Policy*, New York, St. Martin's Press.

KAMERMAN, S. and KAHN, A. (1978) *Family Policy: Government and Families in Fourteen Countries*, New York, Columbia University Press.

KAMERMAN, S. and KAHN, A. (1981) *Child Care Family Benefits and Working Parents: A Study in Comparative Policy*, New York, Columbia University Press.

KAMERMAN, S. and KAHN, A. (1983) *Income Transfers for Families with Children*, Philadelphia, Temple University Press.

KATRIVESSIS, N. (1993) 'State housing and social reproduction', *Proceedings Volume of the Third Congress on Social Policy Today*, Athens, Sakis Karagiorgas Foundation editions, pp. 611–21.

KATSIKAS, C. and KAVADIAS, G. (1995) *Inequality within the Greek Education System*, Athens, Gutemberg.

KOUVERTARIS, Y. and DOBRATZ, B. (1987) *A Profile of Modern Greece: In Search of Identity*, Oxford, Clarendon Press.

LABROPOULOU, K. (1990) 'The relationship between the Welfare State and the family: Selective theoretical perspectives with particular reference to Greece', MSc Dissertation, University of Bristol.

LAMBIRI-DIMAKI, J. (1983) *Social Stratification in Greece: 1962–1982*, Athens, Sakkoulas.

LANE, J.-E. and ERSSON, S.O. (1987) *Politics and Society in Western Europe*, London, Sage.

LANGAN, M. and OSTNER, I. (1991) 'Gender and welfare', in ROOM, G. (Ed) *Towards a European Welfare State*, Bristol, SAUS.

LEIBFREID, S. (1993) 'Towards a European Welfare State', in JONES, C. (Ed) *New Perspectives on the Welfare State in Europe*, London, Routledge.

LEWIS, J. (1992) 'Gender and the development of welfare regimes', *Journal of European Social Policy*, **2**, 3, pp. 31–48.

MAKRINIOTI, D. (1993) 'Children as recipients of social policy: Some basic prerequisites', *Proceedings Volume of the Third Congress on Social Policy Today*, Athens, Sakis Karagiorgas Foundation editions, pp. 744–53.

MALOUTAS, T. (1988) *Problems of the Development of Welfare State in Greece*, Athens, Exantas.

MAHON, E. (1994) 'Ireland: A private patriarchy', in *Environment and Planning*, **26**, pp. 1277–296.

MARTIN, G.T. Jr. (1991) 'Family, gender and social policy', in Kramer, L. (Ed) *The Sociology of Gender*, New York, St. Martin's Press.

PAPADOPOULOS, T. (1993) 'The child support system in Greece', in BRADSHAW, J., DITCH,

J., HOLMES, H. and WHITEFORD, P. *Support for Children: A Comparison of Arrangements in Fifteen Countries*, London, HMSO, pp. 112–14.

PETMEZIDOU-TSOULOUVI, M. (1991) 'Statism, social policy and the middle classes in Greece', *Journal of European Social Policy*, **1**, 1, pp. 31–48.

PETRAKI-KOTTIS, A. (1988) 'The impact of economic development of women's labour force participation rates in Greece', *Equal Opportunities International*, **7**, 2, pp. 9–15.

QVORTRUP, J. (1990) *Childhood as a Social Phenomenon: An Introduction to a Series of National Reports*, Eurosocial Report 36.

RAINWATER, L., REIN, M. and SCHWARTZ, J. (1986) *Income Packaging in the Welfare State: A Comparative Study of Family Income*, Oxford, Clarendon Press.

STAMIRIS, E. (1986) 'The women's movement in Greece', *New Left Review*, **158**, pp. 98–112.

STASSINOPOULOU, O. (1993) 'Family, State, social policy', *Proceedings Volume of the Third Congress on Social Policy Today*, Athens, Sakis Karagiorgas Foundation editions, pp. 702–14.

TSOUKALAS, K. (1987) *State, Society and Work in Postwar Greece*, Athens, Themelio.

WALBY, S. (1986) *Patriarchy at Work*, Cambridge, Polity Press.

WALBY, S. (1990) *Theorizing Patriarchy*, Oxford, Basil Blackwell.

WENNEMO, I. (1992) 'The development of family policy: A comparison of family benefits and tax reduction for families in 18 OECD countries', *Acta Sociologica*, **35**, pp. 201–17.

WILENSKY, H.L., LUEBBERT, G.M., HAHN REED, S. and JAMIESON, A.M. (1987) 'Comparative social policy: Theories, methods, findings', in DIERKES, M., WEILER, H.N. and BERTHOIN, A. (Eds) *Comparative Policy Research*, Aldershot, Gower Publishing Company.

WILLIAMS, F. (1989) *Social Policy: A Critical Introduction*, Cambridge, Polity Press.

Chapter 13

The Crumbling Bridges between Childhood and Adulthood

Hilary Land

During the post-war consolidation and expansion of the Welfare State, young people's access to, and opportunities within, the education system and the labour market changed dramatically in the UK. The majority of young people left school in their mid-teens and went straight into full-time employment in the 1950s and 1960s when the minimum school leaving age between 1948 and 1972 was fifteen years. In 1960 only one in six of 16-year-olds and one in twelve of 17-year-olds were still in maintained schools. Six out of seven school leavers took full-time jobs and few experienced unemployment. In July 1961 only 10,000 of the 330,000 unemployed were under 19 years of age. A small but growing minority (11 per cent), continued into further or higher education. Now the picture is very different. In 1990 over a third of 16- to 18-year-olds were in full-time education, one in six were on a government training scheme and under half had full-time jobs. Over 10 per cent of the nearly three million officially unemployed in 1993 were teenagers. 'Unemployment in the UK is highest among the young. In spring 1993 more than one in five economically active males and one in six economically active females aged nineteen and under were unemployed' (Central Statistical Office, 1994, p. 55).

These changes have raised important questions about the claims which young people have both on their families and on the state for financial support and shelter during the period when they cannot be fully self-supporting by participating in the labour market. These questions came to the fore in the early 1980s when rising unemployment hit the large cohort, reflecting the post-war peak of births in 1964, of young people ready to enter the labour market. The recession also reduced many families' ability to support their older teenage children. The government elected in 1979, was committed to reducing public expenditure. Social security was a prime target, accounting in 1979 for 26 per cent of all public expenditure. The government also believed that parental responsibilities for their own children should *and* could be reinforced by withdrawing direct state support. Sir Keith Joseph said, 'In as much as personal responsibility has been eroded by a shift of housing, education and welfare provision excessively to the state, we are going to shift that balance' (*The Guardian*, 19 February 1983).

In this chapter I want to look at the ways in which government policies have withdrawn support both directly from older teenagers and indirectly from their parents during the period in which children make the transition to adulthood and acquire the capacity to earn enough to establish and maintain themselves in their own households. Compared with twenty years ago, even support given to middle and higher income parents (mainly directed at fathers) as well as to their children in further and higher education, has been reduced as the income tax system no longer subsidizes transfers of income between the generations. The value of the student grant has been eroded and students' claims on the social security system have become very restricted. I shall also show that not only has the government deliberately dismantled many of the bridges erected as part of the expansion of the post-war Welfare State but that it has also failed to recognize that, during the same period, much older systems established well over a century ago, which facilitated the transition to adulthood particularly for poorer and more vulnerable children, have withered away. The pattern of demand for juvenile labour and the need for a military presence within the UK and overseas, particularly in commonwealth countries, have changed and declined. The combination of the erosion of these systems of direct and indirect state support with major restructuring of national and international labour markets has left many young people in *all* income groups heavily dependent on the ability and willingness of their parents to support them into their late teens and early twenties.

The relative wages of young and older workers have varied over time. At the end of the 1960s the gap between adult and teenage wages narrowed but in the 1980s widened again. In 1988 the earnings of young men under 18 were half those of adult men aged 21 to 24 years. Those of young women were a higher proportion because women's wages do not increase with age as sharply as those of men. However, young people's wages have always been lower than adults' wages, not only because they are deemed to be less productive (however defined) but also because it is assumed that they are members of someone else's household and can therefore live more cheaply. Today in the UK, the older teenager is most likely to be living with their parent(s). In 1981 three-quarters of 19-year-old women and five in six of young men were living in the parental home. However, there is evidence from the Scottish Young People's Survey that the proportion of young people leaving the parental home while still in their teens has been increasing in recent years. Between 1987 and 1991, the percentage of 19-year-old men who had left home increased from 31 to 37, and the corresponding increase for young women was from 39 to 42. At the same time the proportion of leavers who subsequently returned home doubled to 11 per cent (Jones, 1994). In the past a much higher proportion experienced living away from the parental home and in someone else's household before becoming established in their own. For working class girls, private domestic service was a common destination and this remained so until the beginning of the First World War. Many more jobs than is the case today offered board and lodging (and often little else). Young people whose parents were unable or unwilling to support them by at least providing them with accommodation, were heavily dependent on these occupations. As Helen Bosanquet, an influential member of the Royal Commission on the Poor Laws (1904–8) commented:

One of the chief difficulties which Poor Law Guardians have to contend with in selecting an occupation for the children passing out of their care is that they have no family to live with during the early years of work; the boys are sent to the army or to sea, while nearly all the girls are sent to domestic service. (Bosanquet, 1905, p. 226)

Roy Parker's research (Parker, 1990) on children leaving the care of the Poor Law or voluntary organizations a hundred years ago confirms this. He found that indeed all the girls went into domestic service and a third of the boys went into the army, navy or merchant fleets. (Those not physically fit enough for active service could join up as bandsmen because most workhouses had their own bands.)

After the Second World War, these routes into adulthood for children leaving care were still being used. In 1959 for example, of 1,263 senior boys placed out from approved schools (established under the Children and Young Persons Act 1933, replacing the old industrial and reformatory schools) nearly one in eight went either into the merchant navy or fishing fleet or into the armed forces. (At this time there were still three nautical approved schools in which instruction given was recognized as qualifying boys for entry to the merchant navy). The largest groups went into the building trade and factory work. Very few were unemployed on leaving. Among the 513 senior girls, over one in six went into private or institutional domestic service, nearly a further one in six went into catering, laundry or dressmaking. The largest group became factory workers and 10 per cent were unemployed (Home Office, 1961, p. 109).

Another very important option for those young people with limited opportunities was emigration. Between 1860 and the early 1930s over 16 million people emigrated from the United Kingdom, a disproportionate number of them young men. The State, together with voluntary organizations, developed schemes to enable children whose parents could not or would not support them into adulthood, to emigrate. Canada and Australia were short of domestic and farm labour and their governments were willing to subsidize such schemes. Roy Parker's research in Canada shows that:

In the 50 years before the First World War, some 80,000 separated children left Britain — mainly for placement on such farms. What was described on this side of the Atlantic as child saving was seen in Canada as welcome farm labour. (Parker, 1990, p. 9)

There was far less emigration during the Depression in the 1930s but emigration remained an option for children leaving care in the post-war years. Section 17 of the Children Act 1948 provided that local authorities 'may with the consent of the Secretary of State, procure or assist in procuring the emigration of children in their care' and section 33 enabled the Secretary of State for Commonwealth Relations to make regulations controlling arrangements made by voluntary organizations for the emigration of children unaccompanied by their parents. In the 1950s, just under a total of 300 children emigrated under the provisions of section 17 but over 2,000 unaccompanied children were emigrated to Australia by voluntary organizations in agreement with the Secretary of State (Home Office, 1961, pp. 82–3). Very few unaccompanied children emigrated in these ways in the 1960s. The demand for labour both in the UK and in the 'old' commonwealth countries changed and the philosophies underlying child care practice placed less emphasis on permanently removing children from inadequate or 'bad' parental influences. More recently such policies have been heavily criticized by those who experienced them. Emigration is no longer an escape for those without skills or without parents to support them.

The traditional route for poor children into the armed forces has remained open for longer. Throughout the 1950s the UK's military commitments overseas together with National Service, which removed virtually all young men both from home and the labour market during their late teens, required a large army, navy and air force. British involvement in Korea meant rearming and in 1952 there were well over three-quarters of a million people in the armed forces (the majority of them young men aged under 25 years). The ending of National Service and a shrinking of defence commitments overseas, partly as more commonwealth countries acquired independence, meant a reduction in the size of the armed forces. Defence spending had fallen from 24.5 per cent of public expenditure in 1952 to 16.2 per cent in 1963. In 1965, 43,000 were recruited into the services. By the end of 1968 the strength of the armed forces was 395,000, representing 2.3 per cent of the male working population. It was estimated that in future every year 35,000 recruits would be needed to enter the 'other ranks'. This meant 'recruiting twenty per cent of all men in the age group who are not either unfit or engaged in further education' (National Board for Prices and Incomes (NBPI), 1969, p. 3). At this time it was feared there would be a labour shortage and there would be difficulty in achieving these targets. In 1970 a military 'salary' was introduced. This ended the system of allowances and access to married quarters and other benefits based on age and marital status because there was evidence that this caused hardship among young married soldiers and, more important, was a deterrent to recruitment. 'On grounds of efficiency and in order to encourage recruitment and, more particularly, re-engagement all discrimination against under-aged married servicemen should be removed' (NBPI, 1969, p. 15). At this time many more young men and women were marrying in their teens compared with the decades either before or since. In 1971, 3 per cent of young men and 11 per cent of young women aged between 16 and 19 years of age were married. This compares with 1 per cent and 5 per cent respectively in 1951 and 1 per cent and 3 per cent in 1981.

Recruitment to the armed forces occurred at an early age. In the army there were 'boy entrants' who were recruited as junior soldiers at the age of 15 or 16 with a commitment to serve twelve years counted from age 17 and a half. In 1974 junior soldiers accounted for a third of the total recruit entry and altogether 60 per cent of total recruits were young soldiers, i.e., 18 years or under, on enlistment. At that time every regiment recruited locally and the corps recruited nationally, but recruits were drawn disproportionately from Scotland, the north-east and north-west (45 per cent of other rank recruits in 1973) — areas with higher than average unemployment. Recruits were not only likely to have *no* educational qualifications (in 1973 70 per cent of adult other ranks recruits had no qualifications when they joined the army) but 20 per cent did not meet the required literacy or numeracy skills. Half of these went to the Royal Army Education Corps' School of Preliminary Education where they received excellent remedial teaching (Army Welfare Inquiry Committee, 1974, p. 49). Young men from large families or from children's homes, foster homes or from single parent families were over-represented in the latter group. For example in 1973, 58 per cent came from families of five or more children and 28 per cent came from being in care or from a single parent family (ibid.) The NBPI were right to say that:

> Many men who would not otherwise receive training because of their lack of formal qualifications on entry or because they missed the chance to enter apprenticeship at the right age, are trained by the services and improve their earning capacity. Then the services offer *a substantial second chance* for training and consequent advancement [my emphasis]. (NBPI, 1969, pp. 3–4)

The opportunity for a 'second chance' was reduced abruptly in 1980. Recruitment to the armed forces as a whole fell by half and although it increased again in the mid-1980s, by 1988–9 was only three-quarters of what it had been in the 1970s. Although the size of the army is to be reduced to 120,000 (nearly 40,000 less than its size throughout the 1980s), the Ministry of Defence is planning to increase the annual intake of young soldiers from 12,000 to 15,000 by 1996 (this is still 30 per cent lower than twenty years ago). However, although they are apparently worried about the poor *physical* fitness of recruits and are setting up youth clubs for 11- to 16-year-olds to improve that, there are no reports of any felt need to provide any remedial education. As the proportion leaving school with no educational qualifications had declined (falling from 20 per cent in 1973–4 to 11 per cent in 1980–1 for example), the army has a bigger choice of recruits already sufficiently literate or numerate. Their remedial education service was disbanded in the 1980s. Boys from disadvantaged homes and educational backgrounds are now much less likely to find a bridge to adulthood provided by the armed forces than their fathers, grandfathers or indeed their great great grandfathers.

Unfortunately these young men will not easily find a second chance elsewhere unless perhaps they offend and are committed to a penal institution. There are worrying reports, however, that the privately run 'mini jails' for persistent young offenders will not provide adequate education according to the school standards watchdog, Ofsted (*The Guardian*, 24 March 1994). Few Youth Training Schemes (YTS, now Youth Training, YT) provide remedial education and individual employees are unlikely to show much interest while youth unemployment is so high. It seems very likely that at least some of the teenagers involved in the riots on large, poor housing estates in the early 1990s would, twenty years earlier, have found a place and therefore a second chance in the army. It is clear reading accounts of the background to those riots that many of these teenagers had missed out on schooling for a variety of reasons (see for example Campbell, 1993). Moreover, if the teenage girlfriend of the young soldier became pregnant, after the military salary was introduced in 1970, there was every incentive to marry because the soldier would be entitled to married quarters (fully furnished). She did not become an unmarried teenage mother so reviled by government ministers today. However, as a young mother usually living far from her own family and married to a young soldier frequently absent for long periods of training or tours of duty in Northern Ireland, she did present welfare problems to the *military* authorities. Parenthood after all, particularly if embarked on as a teenager, requires an adequate infrastructure of social support. Because, at the time the armed forces faced a recruitment and retention problem, the Ministry of Defence could not completely ignore their needs. This was one of the reasons why committees of inquiry into the welfare of naval and army families were set up in the early 1970s.

The other major problem with youth training for young people leaving care or whose families cannot or will not support them, is that the level of allowances paid is based on the assumption that the young person is living at home and their parents can afford to subsidize them. When in the inter-war years the government introduced training and job placement schemes for young people, they at least recognized that some would need accommodation, especially if they were to move to areas of the country where employment could be found for them. The Ministry of Labour had powers first introduced in 1928 for boys and a year later for girls, and extended under the Unemployment Insurance Act 1935, to assist the transfer of unemployed juveniles. The boys and girls were met and placed in suitable lodgings and the Ministry were responsible for ensuring there was 'no exploitation, with low wages or dead-end occupations' (Morgan, 1934, p. 35). The Ministry was also responsible through the juvenile employment officer and the local juvenile committee for keeping in touch with the transferee and for seeing that there were proper facilities for recreation. The young people did not receive a wage directly, instead the Ministry of Labour made up their wages to meet the cost of board and lodging and gave them pocket money (four shillings if they were 15, five shillings when they were 16). At the peak of the scheme in 1936 over 9,000 boys and nearly 6,000 girls were transferred to employment in other areas. The scheme ceased at the outbreak of war, but during its ten years or so of operation it had helped 80,000 boys and girls. It did not always work as well as it was intended, and it came in for considerable criticism. Some of the young people had unsuitable jobs and unsatisfactory lodgings. Many were homesick and returned home. Nevertheless there was official recognition that if teenagers were to leave home to find employment elsewhere they were unlikely to earn a wage sufficient to pay for food, clothing *and* shelter, and therefore the government had a responsibility to fill the gap left by low wages and insufficient parental support.

In 1991, in response to the growing evidence that homelessness is a barrier to finding and keeping employment, a pilot scheme of '*foyers*' for young people was set up in England. *Foyers* are based on the French model of hostels which provide accommodation linked to employment and training. The first stage was based on five existing Young Men's Christian Association (YMCA) hostels and funding came mainly from the employment service, employment department and Training and Enterprise Councils. Nearly 300 people were referred in the first six months. At the end of that period 20 per cent were in training and 10 per cent were in work. The scale and success of these *foyers* is so far modest, especially in the context of Shelter's estimate of 150,000 young people becoming homeless every year (see Department of Employment, 1994).

In the post-war social security system, young people, once they reached the age of 16 years, were entitled to claim social security benefits. They were entitled to a means tested benefit in their own right if they were unemployed or sick (then called National Assistance, renamed Supplementary Benefit in 1966) irrespective of the financial circumstances of their parents. However, there were lower rates for teenagers than for adults based on the assumption that if they were living at home they were being subsidized by their parents. However, if they were not living at home they could claim a board and lodging allowance if living in someone else's household. If they had their own household (unlikely unless they were married) young people received the higher householder's allowance. Once they had contributed to the national insurance scheme for a year they were entitled to unemployment or sickness insurance in their own right. For the first time girls received the same level of benefit as boys, although all young people paid a lower rate of contribution (which, unlike now, was flat-rate) and received a lower rate of benefit. However, if they were married or had a child, they were entitled to the adult rate of personal benefits.

As already stated, unemployment did not become a problem facing any but a tiny minority of young people until the mid 1970s. For example in December 1959, only 27,000 out of a total of 2.1 million National Assistance claimants were aged between 16 and 20 and only 6,000 of these were claiming because they were unemployed. In response to the number of unemployed teenagers increasing from 81,500 in July 1974 to 232,900 a year later, the then Labour Government introduced training schemes. At first there was the job creation programme followed by the work experience programme. In 1978 the Youth Opportunities Programme (YOP) was introduced targeted, unlike some of the other schemes, entirely on young people. In return for participating in the programme normally lasting six months, trainees received an allowance. Other training and work experience programmes topped up either benefit or wages. The numbers on YOP increased rapidly from 75,000 to 226,000 in 1981. Young people without a job or place in a training scheme were still eligible to claim means-tested supplementary benefits. However, by the summer of 1983 it was clear that the Treasury favoured cuts in young people's benefits. There were nearly three-quarters of a million unemployed people on benefit and living with their parents. It was estimated that £300 million could be saved if benefits for unemployed young people were 'targeted' on those whose parents were also in receipt of benefit. This meant that parents would receive an allowance for their unemployed teenage child in addition to their own allowances (in the same way that they received additional allowances graduated by age for any dependent child). Parents not on benefit would receive nothing. The advantage to the government was not just the immediate saving of £300 million. By removing an entire group from eligibility to claim benefits, it would be easier in future to remove other groups.

A year later the government removed the rent contribution for teenagers on benefit. The Secretary of State commented, 'A young person without a job, on Supplementary Benefit will often be living in a household with parents who will not need to look to him for a contribution towards housing costs' (quoted by Allbeson, 1985, p. 86). At the same time, it was assumed employed teenagers would contribute more towards their parents' rent. The deductions from housing benefit for contributions from 'non-dependants' was increased: 850,000 families with a young employed, disabled or pensioner relative living at home had their housing benefit reduced in 1985 as a result of this change.

Those young people who left home in search of a job were equally a cause for concern and their rights to claim board and lodging allowances from the Supplementary Benefit system were reviewed. At the end of 1984, 70 per cent of the 163,000 claimants of board and lodging were claiming because they were unemployed. Half of them were 25 years (Social Security Advisory Committee, 1985). Public concern was focused on these young people who, it was claimed, were having seaside holidays at the taxpayers' expense. Controls were introduced in 1985 and young people's rights to claim board and lodging allowance in a particular locality were limited to two, four or eight weeks according to area; if they could not find a job they were expected to move elsewhere or — preferably — return home. Failure to do so resulted in their benefit being substantially cut or stopped altogether. At the same time, their ability to set up an independent household was being reduced in other ways. For example, in the early 1980s furniture grants for Supplementary Benefit claimants were restricted to families: single people could claim only in 'exceptional circumstances'. Ministers justified this by saying that, without this restriction, 'The family unit would not be encouraged. It would instead encourage people to move away from the family after the slightest argument and would be costly' (Rhodes Boyson, quoted by Allbeson, 1985, p. 89).

The Social Security Act 1986 introduced further restrictions on young people's benefits. For the first time those under 25 years of age were deemed not to 'need' as much benefit as older claimants because they were more likely to be living at home. In fact only half of all claimants aged 21 to 24 years were living at home or in someone else's household (Social Security Advisory Committee, 1985, p. 21). Moreover, it was believed that benefit levels were discouraging young people from accepting jobs at rates employers were willing to pay. Young people had priced themselves out of the labour market. As Professor Minford, one of Margaret Thatcher's economic advisers, said reflecting on the Youth Training Scheme (YTS) and the Social Security Act 1986: 'The whole object of these schemes from an economic point of view is to drive down wages. If they don't drive down wages there is no job creation' ('The Welfare Revolution', *File on Four*, Radio 4, 9 February 1988).

From September 1988, 16- and 17-year-olds could *only* get financial assistance if they took a place on the YTS (the successor to YOP extended in 1983 to one year and in 1986 to two years), except when it would cause 'severe hardship'. There was no possibility of being able to claim contributory unemployment benefit because, since April 1988, contributions have had to have been paid for *two* years. The benefit received (in 1993 £29.50 for 16-year-olds and £35.00 for 17-year-olds, the same as when they were introduced) was too low to enable them to live independently except with extreme difficulty.

Meanwhile the government was attacking young people's wage levels in other ways. In 1986 the government abolished the jurisdiction of Wages Councils over workers under 21 years of age and limited their task to setting minimum basic hourly and overtime rates. This, together with the erosion of young people's benefit entitlements discussed above, the Department of Employment believed encouraged 'more realistic levels of youth pay' (Department of Employment, 1988, p. 27). Between 1979 and 1986 the gap between the earnings of young workers and adults widened; from being 60 per cent of average adult pay they fell to 54 per cent. The Employment Act 1989 repealed the restrictions on hours of work for 16- to 18-year-olds, thus opening up further possibilities for exploiting young people.

Changes in the housing market during the 1980s have also increased young people's dependence on their parents. During the 1980s the number of dwellings available for rent from local authorities and New Town Corporations fell by 1.5 million, representing a reduction of 20 per cent of the stock. Young single people were rarely eligible for housing from local authorities but, as a result of the shrinking of this sector, they now faced stiffer competition — and higher rents — in the private sector. The size of this sector has declined too and this, coupled with deregulation, resulted in increased rents. Between 1979 and 1987 the number of rented dwellings in the private sector fell by 1.3 million (Raynsford, 1990, p. 194). Not surprisingly the number of homeless people, including a significant proportion of young people, grew dramatically in the 1980s. Shelter estimated that by the end of the 1980s 150,000 young people experience homelessness every year (*The Guardian*, 1 June 1994). The Department of Environment explains this by stating:

> A major cause [of homelessness] has been the increase in the number of households *wanting* to live separately due to relationship breakdown and the younger age at which people *choose* to leave home [my emphasis]. (Department of Environment, 1991, p. 83)

Nevertheless the government, under considerable pressure from many charities and pressure groups, had to recognize that not all homeless young people left home by choice. In the 1970s physical abuse of children became a public issue, fuelled by a number of public enquiries into the deaths of young children at the hands of their families (usually their stepfather or father), in the 1980s evidence of sexual abuse surfaced and could not be ignored. For some children the family home is a very dangerous place from which some children need to escape. A recent Scottish survey found that a quarter of homeless young people have a step-parent (Jones, 1994). The evidence that these runaway youngsters were at risk not only of destitution but of being forced into prostitution, drug-dealing or thieving just to stay alive was too strong to be ignored completely. In July 1989 young people 'genuinely estranged' from their parents were added to the list of those school-leavers eligible to claim in their own right for a maximum of sixteen weeks. At the same time young people in night shelters were 'automatically' considered for claims of 'severe hardship' and payments made by local authority social service departments were disregarded in assessing benefit entitlement. In 1989, nearly 18,000 young people applied for severe hardship payments. By the end of the first nine months of 1992, this had increased to nearly 77,000 applications, 83 per cent of which were successful. A MORI report of a survey of severe hardship payments conducted for the Department of Social Security in 1991 found that 45 per cent of those claiming severe hardship payments had at some time slept rough and one in ten had been in care (Coalition of Young People and Social Security, 1993, p. 48). Young people from minority ethnic groups were also over-represented. Racism operates to deny young black people access to housing and operates within the housing market where black people have suffered a disproportionate increase in unemployment (McClusky, 1994b, p. 5). During the year 1993–4 the numbers claiming had increased to 141, 644, 87 per cent of which were successful. The Treasury is reported as wanting to introduce 'tough curbs' on these payments which they estimate will soon cost £40 million annually. The Department of Social Security attributes the increase not to laxity but to the failures of the employment service to meet the youth training guarantee (*The Guardian*, 2 June 1994). The number of places on YT fell from 389,244 in March 1988 to 274,000 in 1993 (*The Guardian*, 1 June 1994).

The Children Act 1989 requires local authorities to 'advise, assist and befriend' young people leaving care. This is important for those youngsters because they are particularly at risk of becoming homeless and comprise a significant proportion (as many as a third) of those who do so (McCluskey, 1994a, p. 4). However, if local authorities do not have sufficient resources, this provision of the Act will not improve their situation in practice. Recent research shows that despite the slightly relaxed eligibility rules for benefit, many young people are not receiving the income and assistance they so desperately need from Social Services and housing departments. Under section 20(3) of the Children Act 1989, social service departments also have a responsibility to help homeless young people in general. A recent study of all social service departments in England and Wales found that only 4 per cent felt they had adequate resources to meet the needs of homeless 16- and 17-year-olds, while 69 per cent thought lack of resources was *the* major constraint against helping this group. A third had failed to develop a joint policy with the housing department and nearly half had not developed a joint assessment procedure (McCluskey, 1994a, p. 25).

Those young people who have chosen to stay in the education system have also experienced a reduction in their rights to social security benefits at the same time as the real value of their grants have declined. While unemployment levels were low the likelihood of students claiming benefit because they could not find a vacation job if they wanted one was also low. While young people still at school or taking a full-time non-advanced course at technical colleges or colleges of further education could not claim supplementary benefit in their own right even if over 16 years of age, those studying part-time could claim benefit provided they were participating in courses requiring fewer than twenty-one hours of study per week. With the growth in modular courses with varying teaching hours, the application of the 'twenty-one-hour rule' has become less clear-cut and social security officers are interpreting it in different ways, usually more strictly. It is estimated that currently 100,000 students are taking part-time courses while claiming benefit (*The Guardian*, 11 October 1994). In February 1995 the government announced that they were considering changing to a 'sixteen-hour rule'.

Before 1975 full-time students in higher education could claim benefits only during the vacations if they could not find vacation work and if their parents could not support them. As the Supplementary Benefit Commission (SBC) explained:

The grants paid by local education authorities provide a contribution to maintenance but students are expected to look for additional support to their parents or to vacation work. If this is not available they can claim supplementary benefits in the same way as any other unemployed person because their parents have no legal liability for their maintenance. Any vacation element in their grant is counted as a resource available to the student. (SBC, 1976, p. 47)

By 1975 the number of students claiming in vacations was beginning to concern the SBC. During August 121,000 students made successful claims. Claims made during the Easter vacations had doubled since 1973 to 90,000 in 1975 (ibid.). The Commission explained these rises by the fact that benefit rates had been increased at a faster rate than student grants, that there were fewer employment opportunities for students and that the National Union of Students had run a very successful publicity campaign, increasing students' awareness of their rights. However, their view was that student support was not a 'proper function' of the supplementary benefit scheme and it was preferable that 'the needs of students should be looked at as a whole, in an integrated grant system designed to provide for student vacation as well as term-time maintenance' (SBC, 1975, p. 48). In February 1976 the government announced that students would no longer be able to claim benefit in the short vacations because the vacation grant entitlement from henceforward would include an amount equivalent to a single non-householder's allowance. Those who were householders could continue to claim as could all students during the summer vacation.

State support for students became a much more contentious issue during the 1980s. While keen to increase the numbers of young people going into higher education the government was looking for ways of cutting the cost both to the educational grant and to the social security systems. In 1988 a government White Paper on Education announced that the value of student grants would be frozen and loans introduced from 1990–1 and full-time students would no longer be entitled to income support, unemployment or housing benefit. These measures were implemented in 1990/91. Overall between 1982 and 1992 the value of the maintenance grant fell by 26 per cent. In 1994 the first of three successive 10 per cent cuts to the grant was applied, and 40 per cent of students eligible to take a government loan were doing so. The typical graduate was finishing their course in 1994 owing £2,000. A former chief education adviser estimates that by the year 2000, the typical graduate maintenance debt will be £5,700 (*The Guardian*, 9 November 1994).

At the same time the government was continuing to withdraw support given via the income tax system from parents whose children continued in full-time higher education. Until 1978 tax allowances for children could be claimed by taxpayers with dependent children, dependent being defined as being under 16 years of age or in full-time education or in vocational training lasting at least two years. The older the child the more valuable the allowance, so that, in 1964–5 for example, children over 16 in full-time education raised their father's annual tax threshold by £165 at a time when the single person's allowance was £200 and the married man's allowance £320. Tax allowances and family allowances disappeared in 1978 when they were replaced by a tax-free cash payment called Child Benefit payable normally to the mother until the child is 16 or 19 if still in full-time education.

In 1988 the Chancellor of the Exchequer announced the removal of a tax concession used by parents (and grandparents) to support students, by ending covenants between individuals (but not to charities). These were an advantage to taxpayers because ever since the Income Tax Act 1842 they had been regarded as the taxable income of the recipient and not the payer. As each child has a personal allowance of their own, sums covenanted up to the amount of the allowance attracted no tax with respect to either the donor *or* the recipient. Spouses could not make covenants to each other because their incomes were aggregated. Parents could not make covenants to their children while they were under-age and unmarried, but could do so to adult children. Other relatives were not restricted in this way. Thus, as the Chancellor of the Exchequer explained, an unintended by-product of dropping the age of majority from 21 to 18 years in 1970 was that it became advantageous for parents to make a covenant to their children while they were students, particularly as the student maintenance grant was — and is — exempt from tax. In the mid 1950s only 75,000 covenants were made in favour of individuals but by the mid 1980s these figures had increased to 250,000 parents in favour of adult children and 150,000 in favour of grandchildren, costing £180 million in foregone revenue. The ending of such covenants not only saved revenue but made students more likely to take part-time employment. The Chancellor of the Exchequer hoped they would, since as he told the House of Commons,

> one desirable side-effect of this reform is that future students will no longer be deterred from taking vacation jobs because their covenant income has already absorbed their personal allowance. (House of Commons Debate, 15 March 1988, col. 1002)

This has happened. For example, between spring 1988 and the spring of 1992, the numbers of students working part-time in the hotels and catering industry increased from 99,000 to 144,000. Firms wanting more flexibility than married women can offer, are taking students on in preference. In the spring of 1993, 29 per cent of the 886,000 men working part-time (using their own assessment of part-time) and 33 per cent out of a total of 967,000 non-married women employed part-time, were still at school or were students (Central Statistical Office, 1994, p. 60). Until the mid-1970s young people were more likely to be employed full-time and studying part-time if at all. Now they are more likely to be studying or training full-time and employed part-time if at all.

Families are now expected to support their children throughout their teens and into their early twenties to a greater extent than ever before. The bridges into adulthood which the State for over a century had actively encouraged and supported, albeit as the result of pursuing other wider objectives concerning the maintenance of empire and military strength (in the case of boys) or reducing 'the servant problem' (in the case of girls), have largely crumbled, leaving many of the most vulnerable young people in our society literally destitute. Even the more advantaged who aspire to gaining further and higher qualifications receive less support than even ten years ago and graduate with debts and a greater chance of experiencing unemployment. Many families have become less able to support their children, particularly into their late teens. For example, during the 1980s the proportion of children in households with below half the average income doubled to one in four. However responsible parents feel towards their children (and most do), poverty is a severe constraint on their ability to provide for their children into their early twenties. The effect of deregulated housing and labour markets has put the supports under the bridges to adulthood which even parents with average incomes can provide under greater strain than at any time since the Second World War.

References

ALLBESON, J. (1985) 'Seen but not heard: Young people', in WARD, S. (Ed) *DHSS in Crisis*, London, CPAG.

ARMY WELFARE INQUIRY COMMITTEE (1974) *Report*, London, HMSO.

BOSANQUET, H. (1905) *The Family*, London, Macmillan.

CAMPBELL, B. (1993) *Goliath*, London, Methuen.

CENTRAL STATISTICAL OFFICE (1994) *Social Trends*, London, HMSO.

COALITION ON YOUNG PEOPLE AND SOCIAL SECURITY (COYPSS) (1993) *Four Years' Severe Hardship*, London, Coypss.

DEPARTMENT OF EMPLOYMENT (1988) *Employment for the 1990s*, Cmnd. 540, London, HMSO.

DEPARTMENT OF EMPLOYMENT (1994) *Gazette*, March.

DEPARTMENT OF ENVIRONMENT (1991) *Annual Report*, Cmnd. 1508, HC.

HOME OFFICE (1961) *Eighth Report of the Work of the Children's Department 1961*, HMSO.

JONES, G. (1994) 'Young people in and out of the housing market', in *Findings*, Housing Research 108, Joseph Rowntree Foundation.

McCLUSKEY, J. (1994a) 'Reassessing priorities: The Children Act 1989 — a new agenda for young homeless people', *Benefits*, January.

McCLUSKEY, J. (1994b) *Breaking the Spiral: Ten Myths on the Children Act and Youth Homelessness*, CHAR, August.

MORGAN, A. (1943) *Young Citizens*, Harmondsworth, Penguin.

NATIONAL BOARD OF PRICES AND INCOMES (1969) *Standing Reference on the Pay of the Armed Forces*, 2nd report, Cmnd. 4079, London, HMSO.

PARKER, R. (1990) *Away from Home*, London, Barnardo's.

RAYNSFORD, N. (1990) 'Housing conditions, problems and policies', in MACGREGOR, S. and PIMLOTT, B. (Eds) *Tackling the Inner Cities*, Oxford, Clarendon Press.

SOCIAL SECURITY ADVISORY COMMITTEE (1985) *Fourth Report*, London, HMSO.

SUPPLEMENTARY BENEFIT COMMISSION (1976) *Annual Report 1975*, Cmnd. 6615, London, HMSO.

SUPPLEMENTARY BENEFIT COMMISSION (1977) *Annual Report 1976*, Cmnd. 6910, London, HMSO.

Chapter 14

Teenage Pregnancy: Do Social Policies Make a Difference?

Peter Selman and Caroline Glendinning

Introduction

Much media attention has recently been focused in the UK on young single mothers (Kershaw, 1993; Phillips, 1995), who have variously been accused of being 'wedded to welfare' (Jones, 1993); of contributing, through their lack of a male partner, to increases in crime and delinquency; and of creating a growing financial burden on the Welfare State. Responses to this 'moral panic' have consisted of an unhelpful mixture of realistic policy priorities and ideological rhetoric. For example, on the one hand official health policy targets include a halving in the rates of conception among women under age 16 by the year 2000 (Department of Health, 1992a, 1992b). On the other hand, there has been controversy over the teaching of sex education to younger teenagers and calls for official enquiries into sex education teaching in some schools. There have also been widespread allegations by politicians and the media that the availability of welfare benefits and housing to single mothers actually encourages out-of-wedlock childbearing; therefore, it is asserted, these births could be reduced by reducing access to such welfare provisions (Helm, 1993).

But what evidence is there that social policies do affect levels of teenage pregnancy and parenthood in the UK? And if indeed they do, then what *kinds* of social policies are more likely to have an impact on sexual activity, contraceptive use and decisions about abortion? Plotnick (1993) argues that 'services and incentives provided by social policies significantly affect teenage pregnancy and child-bearing outcomes', a view which has been challenged by Bane and Jargowsky (1988) and by Hantrais (1994), who warns of the complexity of relationship between policies and demographic outcomes.

This chapter examines some of the evidence relating to a range of different policies which may affect levels of pregnancy and births among young women under age 20. Included in the discussion are policies which are directly aimed at influencing teenage sexual behaviour and fertility — sex education, contraceptive provision and the availability of free legal abortion; and policies which may have a more indirect impact, such as the educational and employment opportunities available to young people, and the alleged incentives associated with housing and social welfare provision.

We will argue that policies which emphasize the importance of information about contraception, access to contraceptive services (including emergency contraception) and free legal abortion appear to reduce levels of teenage pregnancies. We will challenge the view that levels of teenage parenthood are influenced by the availability of welfare benefits for young unmarried mothers and argue instead that high levels of teenage pregnancy are more likely to be associated with poverty, unemployment, low self-esteem and lack of hope for the future among significant proportions of young people. If this is the case, then the policies which are most likely to reduce levels of teenage pregnancy and parenthood are likely to be those which aim to increase educational and employment opportunities for young people, rather than those which seek to restrict access to welfare.

Is Teenage Parenthood a 'Problem'?

Teenage pregnancy has often been viewed as a problem for mothers, their children and society as a whole (Russell, 1968; Jones, 1986; Zabin and Hayward, 1993; Hudson and Ineichen, 1991). However, other commentators have questioned this simplistic assumption (Phoenix, 1991; Pearce, 1993; MacIntyre and Cunningham-Burley, 1993; Phillips, 1995) or have warned against exaggerating the negative implications of early motherhood (Furstenberg *et al.*, 1987; Geronimus, 1987; Musik, 1993).

Some of this disagreement arises from a lack of clarity over the definition of 'teenage mother'. Studies of 'teenage' mothers in the UK have variously included all those under age 20 (Simms and Smith, 1986); those aged 16–19 (Phoenix, 1991); those aged 17 and under (Francome, 1993) and those aged under 16 (Russell, 1968). Around two-thirds of UK births to women under age 20 occur to women aged 18 or 19; however there are significant differences between such women and their younger counterparts, with particular problems for women under 16. Care must therefore be taken in comparing such studies, especially where they appear to offer different accounts of the causes and outcomes of teenage pregnancy. Zabin and Hayward (1993) suggest that use of the term 'adolescent' pregnancy, defined as pregnancy occurring to those aged 17 and under, would help to focus attention on those young mothers and their children who are at greatest risk of social, emotional and health disadvantage.

The recent 'moral panic' over teenage childbearing in both the UK and the USA (Lawson and Rhode, 1993) has been rooted in concern about the implications of growing numbers of unmarried teenage mothers for public expenditure and about possible links between absent fathers and juvenile crime. Yet being a teenage mother is not necessarily synonymous with the absence of a father; as will be discussed below, many young mothers appear to be in stable relationships and living with their male partners. In addition, a preoccupation with the undesirability of teenage parenthood overlooks the needs of such young people for social support, economic independence and a range of other service inputs which could optimize outcomes for both the parents and their children.

Table 14.1: Live births to women under age 20, 1951–92

Year	Total births	Rate[1]	Births outside marriage	Rate[2]	Proportion[3] outside marriage
1951	29,111	21.3	4,812	3.7	165
1956	37,938	27.3	6,290	4.8	166
1961	59,786	37.3	11,896	8.0	199
1966	86,746	47.9	20,582	12.2	237
1971	82,641	50.6	21,555	14.6	261
1976	57,943	32.2	19,819	11.9	342
1981	56,570	28.1	26,430	13.2	406
1983	54,059	26.9	30,423	19.7	648
1986	57,406	30.1	39,613	21.3	690
1988	58,741	32.4	44,642	25.3	760
1990	55,541	33.3	44,583	27.4	802
1991	52,396	33.1	43,448	28.0	829
1992	47,900	31.8	40,100		837

[1] per 1,000 women aged 15–19
[2] per 1,000 single, widowed or divorced women aged 15–19
[3] per 1,000 live births
Source: OPCS Birth Statistics, Series FM1

The Demography of Teenage Pregnancy

Before discussing the impact of policies on teenage pregnancy, patterns of teenage fertility in the UK and elsewhere are briefly described. These comparisons will help to disentangle some of the facts from the rhetoric associated with rising levels of pregnancy among unmarried teenage women.

Teenage Births in England and Wales since the Second World War

In line with the maturing of the post-war 'baby boom', the highest number of births to women aged under 20 occurred in 1966. Rates of births to teenage women peaked in 1971, when 11 per cent of all births were to teenagers.

However both absolute numbers and rates of teenage births fell sharply during the 1970s and until the mid-1980s both the numbers and the rates remained well below those of the early 1970s. The further decline in the number of teenage births since 1988 is largely due to the falling teenage population — rates of births to teenage women have changed little and remain higher than most other European countries (see Table 14.3).

In contrast numbers of births to *unmarried* teenage women have increased sharply since the mid-1970s. Rates of births to unmarried teenagers have also more than doubled since 1977. In 1971 only 26 per cent of teenage births occurred outside marriage; by 1992 this had trebled, to 84 per cent. So far as pregnancies among very young teenagers are concerned, the number of conceptions among girls under 16 in the UK have been falling since the mid-1980s, in line with the overall decline

Table 14.2: Extra-marital teenage births (by registration)

Year	Total Births	Registration		[Joint Registration] Address	
		Sole	Joint	Different	Same
		%	%	%	%
1964	17,400	81	19		
1971	21,555	72	28		
1976	19,819	64	36		
1981	26,430	52	48		
1986	39,613	41	59	[26]	[33]
1991	43,448	35	65	[27]	[38]

Source: OPCS Birth Statistics, Conception Series FM1

in the size of this age group. However rates of conceptions among the under–16s rose during the 1980s, and have only recently begun to reverse.

These figures on births to unmarried teenage women are not as straightforward as they might seem. Since 1964 data has been available on whether the mother alone or both parents have registered the birth of a child born outside marriage. In 1964 over 80 per cent of extra-marital teenage births were registered by the mother alone; by 1991 this had fallen to 35 per cent. Conversely, the number of births registered by both parents rose from 6,124 in 1971 to 28,199 in 1991. Furthermore, in a majority of these joint registrations both parents gave the same address (Table 14.2), implying a degree of stability and even cohabitation, at least around the time of the child's birth.

Clearly data on birth registration can only give a hint as to the real nature of the relationships between teenage parents. However it is inappropriate to assume that the 'unmarried' status of a mother necessarily means she is a lone mother without a male partner. This presents a challenge to one popular theory about teenage pregnancy and parenthood, that young women conceive intentionally and instrumentally not as a reflection of a commitment to an ongoing heterosexual relationship, but in order to obtain benefits and housing.

Conventional definitions of marital status may therefore no longer adequately describe the realities of modern teenage parenthood. Much more needs to be known about the nature and the longer term stability of these apparent 'cohabitations' (Kiernan and Estaugh, 1993; McRae, 1993). For example, Haskey (1983) has estimated that up to 50 per cent of teenage marriages are likely to end in divorce. Teenage 'cohabitations' may prove even less stable (Haskey, 1993), although some *may* eventually lead to marriages which prove less prone to breakdown than those entered into at younger ages.

Teenage Pregnancy in Comparative Perspective

Overall rates of fertility among teenage women in the UK are now the highest in western Europe. Birth rates in the early 1990s are higher than in 1977, in contrast

Table 14.3: Live births to teenagers USA, England and Wales and other European countries, selected years: 1971–88

	Births per 1,000 women aged 15–19					
	1971	**1977**	**1980**	**1983**	**1988**	**1990**
USA	66.1	52.8	53.3	51.7	54.8	59.4
England and Wales	*50.8*	*29.8*	*30.9*	*26.9*	*32.4*	*33.3*
Sweden	34.6	22.1	15.8	11.7	11.4	12.7
Denmark	29.3	22.1	16.8	10.6	9.5	9.8
France	27.7	22.1	17.8	13.9	9.5	9.1
Netherlands	22.2	10.1	9.2	7.7	5.6	6.4

Sources: UN Demographic Year Book; Council of Europe

to most other European countries (Table 14.3). England and Wales now occupy a position in between the USA and most western European countries, but trends in the UK have been similar to those in the USA.

Between 1971 and 1977, rates of births to teenage women declined in all the countries in Table 14.3. Thereafter rates in the USA and in England and Wales rose, so that in both countries birth rates among women under 20 were higher in 1988 than ten years before; the other four countries experienced a striking decline during the same period. Consequently, by 1990 rates of teenage births in the USA were six times those of France or Denmark.

The Role of Abortion

During the 1970s in the UK, an increasing number of extra-marital teenage conceptions appear to have been terminated, thereby halting the increase in teenage births. However, from 1977 onwards, numbers of abortions increased alongside out-of-wedlock births. In contrast, in Sweden and Denmark the majority of teenage conceptions still end in termination, compared to only 41 per cent in England and Wales and 46 per cent in the USA (Table 14.4). However, access to and take-up of legal abortion is not the only explanatory factor; the Netherlands and France also have low birth rates despite abortion rates which are lower than Britain.

Regional Variations in Teenage Conception Rates in England

There are significant regional variations in both the rates and the outcomes of teenage conceptions *within* England and Wales (Table 14.5).

In 1990, both the highest conception rates and the highest proportions of conceptions leading to maternity were in the Northern region; the lowest rates were

Table 14.4: Abortions, births and pregnancies to teenagers in USA, England, Wales and Denmark

	Rates per 1,000 women aged 15–19: 1977–88				
	1977	**1980**	**1983**	**1985**	**1988**
Abortion					
USA	37.5	42.9	43.5	43.8	
England and Wales	17.2	18.2	18.6	20.9	23.9
Denmark	25.5	22.7	17.6	16.3	
Births					
USA	52.8	53.3	51.7	51.3	54.8
England and Wales	29.8	30.9	26.9	29.5	32.4
Denmark	22.1	16.8	10.6	9.1	9.5
Pregnancy					
USA	90.3	96.2	95.2	95.1	
England and Wales	47.0	49.1	45.5	50.4	56.3
Denmark	47.6	38.9	28.2	25.4	

Sources: David (1990), OPCS Birth Statistics and Abortion Statistics, UN Demographic Yearbook

Table 14.5: Regional conception rates within England and Wales per 1,000 women aged 15–19, 1990

	Total	Maternity	Abortion	% leading to maternity
Northern	78.8	57.2	21.7	72.6%
North West	81.2	56.1	25.2	69.1%
Yorks and Humber	78.8	55.0	23.8	69.8%
West Midlands	82.4	53.8	28.6	65.3%
East Midlands	69.3	46.8	22.5	67.5%
England and Wales	**68.8**	**43.9**	**22.5**	**63.8%**
East Anglia	58.7	37.3	21.4	63.5%
South East	60.2	33.8	26.4	56.1%
South West	54.8	33.7	21.1	61.5%

Source: OPCS Birth Statistics, Conception Series FM1, No. 20

in the south-east and south-west of England. Rates are even higher in smaller, subregional areas, such as the urban areas of the west Midlands, Tyne and Wear and Greater Manchester, all of which had maternity rates of over sixty per 1,000 women aged 15–19 in 1990. In an analysis of conceptions in 1991, Babb (1994) found the highest levels of teenage conceptions in inner London and other major conurbations; the lowest levels were in mixed urban/rural areas. Rates of births to teenage women also varied, being 30 per cent higher in the northern region in 1991 than in England as a whole; the proportions of these occurring outside marriage were also higher (88 per cent in the north and north-west regions, compared to 83 per cent for England and Wales as a whole). There were even wider regional variations among very young women, whose maternity rates ranged from 3.2 per 1,000 women aged 13–15 in the south-west to 7.3 in the northern region and 8.4 in Tyne and Wear. These inter- and intra-regional differences in rates of conceptions and births indicate that early motherhood may be related to major cultural and structural factors, although only tentative conclusions can be drawn at this stage without further analysis of demographic and other data.

The Impact of Specific Social Policies

This section examines the impact of a number of policies intended specifically to have an impact on teenage birth rates. Most studies of teenage parenthood in Britain indicate that a majority of pregnancies are unplanned and result from the non-use of contraception (Simms and Smith, 1986; Ineichen, 1986; Francome, 1993). Ensuring that young people know about the consequences of sexual activities, about different forms of contraception (including 'emergency', post coital contraception), and about how to obtain and use contraception effectively constitute a nexus of policies which directly address the issue of teenage conceptions and births. Indeed, lower levels of teenage conceptions in Scandinavia and the Netherlands are generally attributed to the more effective use of birth control (David, 1990; Gress-Wright, 1993; Belleman, 1993). In contrast, in Britain and the USA there has been continuous debate about the content and process of sex education and about the rights of teenagers to confidential advice.

What evidence is there, therefore, about the effectiveness of different approaches to education about sex and contraception, and different methods of providing contraceptive services for younger teenagers? In discussing the impact of policies such as these, some of the questions raised in the foregoing review of demographic data will also be explored further: why are teenage conception and birth rates higher in England and Wales than in other western European countries; why did birth rates rise during the 1980s when in other countries they fell sharply; and how might variations in conception and birth rates within England and Wales be explained?

Preventing Teenage Pregnancy or Preventing Teenage Sexual Activity?

There is little satisfactory international comparative data on teenage sexual behaviour. However most commentators (Jones, 1986; David, 1990; Gress-Wright, 1993) have concluded that the lower levels of teenage pregnancy in, say, Scandinavia compared to the USA or UK do not appear to reflect lower levels of teenage sexual activity. Indeed, both Jones (1986) and Hoem and Hoem (1987) have pointed to very high levels of sexual activity among Swedish teenagers. Moreover, British studies (Schofield, 1965; Farrell, 1978; Wellings, 1994; Ford, 1991) also show a steady move to earlier commencement of intercourse; indeed, by the late 1980s, patterns of sexual activity in the UK appear remarkably similar to those reported for Danish teenagers (Wielandt and Boldsen, 1989).

There is therefore little indication that the higher rates of teenage births in Britain and the USA are due to higher levels of sexual activity. However there has been considerable support in both countries for policies which actively discourage early sexual activity (Joffe, 1993). Because such policies are concerned with teenage sexuality rather than teenage parenthood, they may have had a marked impact on the content of sex education and the availability of contraceptive provision for younger teenagers in both countries.

Sex Education

Reid (1982) and Allen (1985) have pointed to the constraints imposed on sex education in British schools because of fears that explicit teaching might encourage sexual 'experimentation'. Similar anxieties have been expressed in the USA (Fine, 1988; Zabin and Hayward, 1993). Yet the Scandinavian and Dutch experiences give no support to this view; indeed, a recent review of literature from across Europe and North America on the impact of sex education on young people's sexual behaviour indicates, if anything, a delay in the start of sexual activity and a more effective use of contraception (Grunseit and Kippax, 1994).

Sex instruction in Swedish schools became mandatory in 1956 and for older students includes information about contraception and visits to local family planning clinics (Boethius, 1984; Hoem and Hoem, 1987; Swedish Institute, 1990). In Denmark, sex education has been compulsory in primary schools since 1970; attempts by parents to remove their children from such classes have been rejected (David, 1990). Moreover, the introduction of visits to family planning clinics into the curriculum has been associated with a decline in numbers of abortions (David, 1990; Segest, 1991). In the Netherlands sex education is a compulsory part of the curriculum, starting in primary school and subsequently involving practical teaching about contraception (Belleman, 1993). All three countries see explicit sex education as central to their success in reducing levels of teenage pregnancy over the past twenty years; indeed, there is evidence of higher levels of knowledge and more effective use of contraception by sexually active teenagers (David, 1990; Swedish Institute, 1990; Segest, 1991; Belleman, 1993) than in Britain and America (Francome, 1993; Gress-Wright, 1993).

In Britain, the 1993 Education Act now allows parents to withdraw their children from sex education lessons. A combination of New Right and Roman Catholic pressures within government have also attempted further to restrict the content of sex education in schools. It is perhaps therefore not surprising that a majority of the young teenagers in Francome's (1993) study felt they had received little or no information about contraception from school; another recent study showed that the main source of sex education for most British teenagers was their peers (Balding, 1994).

Access to Contraceptive Services

In Britain, contraceptive advice and supplies have been available free of charge from specialist clinics and general practitioners (GPs) since the mid–1970s. GPs now see more than twice the number of women who attend specialist clinics for contraceptive advice (Selman and Calder, 1994). However GPs have been less successful in providing services to younger teenagers, for two reasons. First, given their 'family' doctor status, most young people attend the same surgery (and often the same doctor) as their parents, which is likely to inhibit them requesting contraception. Secondly, the Gillick test case created considerable uncertainty during the 1980s about whether doctors could legally provide contraceptive advice to girls under 16 without their parents' consent; this may have affected both the willingness of young women to seek such advice and the willingness of GPs to give it. A recent survey of GPs found that a third still believed they could not give advice to under–16s. A complementary study of pregnant teenagers found that 42 per cent of those who had not been to a GP or clinic thought it illegal to ask for contraception; a similar proportion thought their parents would be told (Francome, 1993).

In contrast, the number of women under 16 attending family planning clinics in England and Wales has increased in recent years (Department of Health, 1993). Although this suggests a greater readiness to approach clinics, nevertheless many sexually active teenagers still do not seek advice and help from contraceptive services (Balding, 1994) and many of those who do make contact have been sexually active and possibly at risk of pregnancy for some time (Hill, 1988).

The official target of the Government of halving the number of pregnancies in the UK among under–16s by the year 2000 has led to many local initiatives intended to increase the acceptability and accessibility of contraceptive services for young people. Another development of potential importance is the growing use of 'post–coital' or emergency contraception. In 1992/3 this was prescribed on about 70,000 occasions in England and Wales; about half of these involved teenagers, including 6,000 under age 16.

Easy access to contraception for unmarried teenagers has operated for many years in Scandinavia and the Netherlands. In Denmark contraceptive advice is freely available from GPs and family planning clinics (Risor, 1989; Segest, 1991) and a telephone advice line for young people was introduced in 1992. In Sweden, doctors are specifically forbidden to inform parents about adolescents' requests for contraception (Jones, 1986), while concern over rising teenage abortion rates in the late 1980s led to new initiatives providing subsidized contraception to young people (Persson, 1994). In the Netherlands, 'medical' methods of contraception have been available free of charge since 1972 (Doppenberg, 1994). Although the Netherlands has fewer family planning clinics than England and Wales, these are targeted more closely at young people (Plotnick, 1993) and doctors are required to keep visits confidential if requested.

In contrast, contraceptive provision for young people in the USA probably deteriorated in the late 1980s, as programme funding was reduced and the lack of consensus about contraceptive services for young people became more evident

(Brindis, 1993). School-based contraceptive clinics have been opposed on grounds of encouraging young people to be sexually active (Pearce, 1993), although Fine (1988) argues that there is substantial evidence of such clinics reducing pregnancy rates. As anti-abortion activity has become virtually inseparable from opposition to birth control and sex education for young teenagers, there have also been attacks on Planned Parenthood, the main family planning organization, as 'anti-life and anti-family' (Joffe, 1993).

The Resort to Abortion

As described earlier, pregnant teenagers in Sweden and Denmark are much more likely to have abortions than in England and Wales, where two-thirds of teenage conceptions end in a live birth. Moreover, in England the proportion of teenagers proceeding to a live birth is larger in poorer regions; in the northern and north-west regions, a clear majority of under-16s choose to continue with a pregnancy. Such differences in the proportion of out-of-wedlock conceptions ending in abortion raise questions about the ease of access to abortion, both within and between countries.

Since the 1967 Abortion Act, most abortions in England and Wales have been carried out on the grounds of risk to the mental or physical health of the woman. The most striking regional variations are in the percentage of abortions which are funded by the National Health Service and are therefore free of charge. In 1992 this ranged from 45 per cent in the north-west to 85 per cent in the north of England, although levels of teenage parenthood are above average in both regions. There seems, therefore, to be no simple relationship between access to free NHS abortion and levels of teenage parenthood, at least in England and Wales.

In contrast, easy access to free, legal abortion does appear to play a major role in the very low rates of teenage births in Sweden and Denmark, where more than 60 per cent of teenage pregnancies are terminated. In Sweden, women have had a clear right since 1975 to abortion 'on demand' in the early weeks of pregnancy; Swedish health services have translated that 'right' into a reality for most women. In Denmark too, free abortion has been available on demand in the first twelve weeks of pregnancy since 1973 (David, 1990; 1992).

Although similar 'rights' have existed in the USA since the 1973 Supreme Court *Roe versus Wade* judgment, the use of public funds has been severely restricted since the Hyde amendment of 1976. For most teenagers, therefore, free legal abortion is far from being available on demand. Plotnick (1993) reports higher rates of abortion in States with less restrictive policies on public funding; recent Supreme Court judgments have however given states further powers to restrict access to abortion.

The Social Context of Teenage Pregnancy

Finally, evidence on the possible links between a wider range of social and economic policies and teenage conception and birth rates are examined. Welfare policies which have been linked to high rates of teenage pregnancy include the provision of benefits to unmarried mothers (Murray, 1990; Gress-Wright, 1993); the absence of educational and job opportunities (Plotnick, 1993); and factors such as dropping out of school, isolation, poverty, unemployment, lower self-esteem and lack of hope for the future (Brindis, 1993).

Welfare Incentives and Teenage Childbearing

New Right politicians and policy analysts in both the UK and the USA have alleged that a range of fiscal and welfare measures currently favour unmarried people and lone parents over the conventional two-parent family (Morgan, 1995). In particular, social security benefits (Aid to Families with Dependent Children (AFDC) in the USA, Income Support in the UK) are alleged to offer financial incentives for poor women (including very young women) to bear and rear children outside marriage. For example, changes in benefit rates are alleged to have 'lifted a large proportion of low income women above the threshold where having and keeping a baby became economically feasible', in comparison with thirty or forty years ago (Murray, 1990). Indeed, additional benefits for lone parents have been accused of providing official encouragement for lone parenthood (Green, 1991). Similar claims have been made in the UK in respect of the allocation of local authority housing which, within the overall context of a severe shortage of low cost rented accommodation currently gives priority to applicants with children. Policy proposals in response have included severe restrictions on the availability and levels of welfare provision: 'Turn back the clock, restoring the benefit system for single mothers that Britain had in the mid-1960s, and there is every reason to think that you will turn back the proportion of babies born to single women to 1960s levels as well' (Murray, 1993). But what evidence is there to support these arguments?

Social Security Policy in Britain

It is certainly true that a number of social security payments in the UK are 'targeted' at lone parents — that is, they are available to families which are headed by a lone parent but not to other categories of welfare claimants. However it is far from self-evident that either access to these benefits or their levels, once received, constitute 'incentives' to conceive and bear children outside a stable heterosexual partnership.

First, a small addition to child benefit was introduced in 1975 (Millar, 1994), in acknowledgment of the extra costs experienced by lone parent families. However this 'one-parent benefit' has always remained at a very low level; currently (1995/6) it is just £6.30 a week, compared to the universal Child Benefit of £10.40 for the first child and £8.45 for subsequent children and the £15.95 (more than two and a half times the amount) which is allowed under Income Support for a child under age 11. Moreover, one-parent benefit is taken fully into account in assessing lone parents' entitlement to Income Support. This means that it is of no actual advantage at all to those who are supposed to be encouraged by it to become lone mothers — women and children who are wholly dependent on means-tested assistance payments.

Within the Income Support scheme, additional payments (or 'premiums') are also payable to certain categories of claimant. For lone parents this premium is £5.20 a week (1995/6). However, comparison with the levels of premiums for other groups of claimants is instructive. For example, a disabled adult claimant is entitled to an additional 'premium' of £19.80 a week on top of his/her other Income Support allowances. If levels of benefit reflect political and popular notions of more or less 'deserving' claimants, then lone parents are already clearly treated considerably less favourably than other groups of assistance claimants. It is also worth noting that these benefits are available equally to lone mothers and to lone fathers.

Indeed, Income Support contains considerable *dis*incentives to early childbearing. Lone parents aged 16 and 17 are entitled to lower personal rates of benefits than those aged 18 and over — only £36.80 a week compared with £46.50 a week for older lone parents (plus allowances for children). Lone parents under 18 who are still living with their parents receive even less — just £28.00 a week. Lone parents under the age of 16 have *no entitlement at all* to claim any means-tested assistance benefits for themselves or their children. It is assumed that they will be entirely dependent financially on their own parents.

Moreover, lone mothers have been as adversely affected by wider changes in UK social security provision as other groups of claimants. Between 1986 and 1988 major changes to the main social assistance scheme were implemented, as well as changes in a number of other means-tested benefits. Independent estimates of the cumulative effects of all the changes in benefits around the mid-1980s put the proportion of lone parents who lost out at 74 per cent, with only 25 per cent likely to be better off (Benefits Research Unit, 1988). Subsequent qualitative and quantitative studies have confirmed that lone mothers were as likely as couples with children to have experienced changes in benefit entitlements which, taken together, left them considerably worse off (Craig and Glendinning, 1990; Evans *et al.*, 1994).

It is also worth noting that lone parent families have always occupied an anomalous position within the British social security scheme. Apart from widows (who were 'protected' by their former husband's contributions), there was no provision in Beveridge's insurance-based scheme for lone parents. Moreover, policies for lone parents have always displayed an ambivalence about whether, as the sole adult within the family, they should be treated primarily as 'breadwinners' or as 'mothers'. Continuing failure to resolve this dilemma has led to considerably greater risks of poverty for lone parent families (and the children in them) than potential advantages (Millar, 1987; 1994).

Housing Policy and Teenage Pregnancy

In Britain, concern has been expressed about teenagers becoming pregnant in order to obtain local authority housing. Coleman (1993) has suggested that the rationing and allocation system for local authority housing may be one reason for the 'relatively high level of non-marital births and teenage childbearing in Britain'. In 1993 the then Housing Minister asked 'How do we explain to the young couple . . . who want to wait for a home before starting a family . . . that they cannot be rehoused ahead of an unmarried teenager expecting her first, probably unplanned, child?'. Such concerns have led to proposals for legislative amendments which would remove the current priority given to families with children in allocating local authority housing.

Yet there is little evidence that young women do seek motherhood in order to obtain housing. Clark (1989) reports that the young unmarried mothers she interviewed were astonished to be asked whether they had become pregnant in order to obtain council housing; nor had any of the young mothers in Phoenix's (1991) study had a baby in order to obtain local authority accommodation. Another recent study found that young unmarried mothers generally did not become concerned about obtaining housing until some months after the birth of their child — for example, when tensions built up within their own parents' home; most had very little knowledge of the criteria used in the allocation of local authority housing until they finally sought advice about their problems (Cameron *et al.*, 1994).

Welfare Incentives in Other Countries

In the United States, the belief that welfare payments are a key factor in maintaining high levels of teenage births outside marriage has been challenged on the grounds, first, that the value of welfare benefits has declined during the same period that births outside marriage have increased; and secondly that studies of relationships between benefit levels and births outside marriage show almost no correlation (Bane and Jargowsky, 1988; Kamerman, 1988). Despite the lack of evidence, this belief has led to a number of changes designed to build disincentives into welfare policy so that teenagers become more aware of the costs of early childbearing. For example, since 1984 under-age mothers living with their parents are assessed for AFDC on the basis of the household's, rather than their individual, resources. The Family Support Act 1988 now also allows states to require minor parents to live with their parent(s) as a condition of receiving AFDC. Teenage mothers are also required to return to school full time (Pearce, 1993). Despite these changes, teenage birth rates in the United States have continued to rise.

In contrast, in countries with lower levels of teenage parenthood support for young single mothers is no less generous than for older women. Instead it appears less reliant on means-tested benefits and is marked by higher benefits for all families (France) or by encouragement for mothers to enter and remain in the workforce (Sweden) (Kamerman, 1988).

Educational and Job Opportunities

The view that welfare benefits encourage teenage parenthood has been challenged by Andrew Blaikie (1994) who asks: 'Why should young women wish to get pregnant in order to be so impoverished as to need welfare?' One explanation may be that they '. . . do it fatalistically because there is little else left in their poor lot that seems worthwhile.' In this last section we briefly examine this 'nothing to lose' hypothesis.

The proportion of pregnant teenagers who proceed to motherhood is signific-antly higher in the UK and the USA than in Sweden and Denmark. This may reflect a perceived lack of alternatives in education and employment (Furstenberg *et al.*, 1987; Gress-Wright, 1993). In Britain, the highest levels of teenage births occur to the most socio-economically disadvantaged (Babb, 1994) and in the poorer urban areas. Young mothers are less likely to have stayed on at school (Kiernan, 1980; Simms and Smith, 1986); Phoenix (1991) reports that 'the scarcity of adequately paid permanent jobs was . . . the context in which young women in this study decided that early motherhood would not be damaging to their lives.'

In the USA, Zabin and Hayward (1993) suggest that few teenage births are planned or wanted and that for women who proceed to motherhood 'an unin-tended birth carries few costs'. Not surprisingly therefore, Plotnick (1993) con-cluded that improvements in educational and earnings opportunities for disadvantaged young people in the USA would '. . . contribute indirectly towards reducing levels of teenage pregnancy and childbearing . . . because better economic prospects [would] lead teenagers to believe that they have something to lose by becoming parents, thus motivating them to defer childbearing.'

In contrast, in Sweden 'the strong emphasis on school and work means that child-bearing is delayed . . . until an average age of twenty-six' (Gress-Wright, 1993). Low levels of teenage births are part of a general postponement of childbearing in a country where overall levels of fertility are now higher than in Britain. Moreover, Swedish family and employment policies are based upon the assumption that the two-breadwinner family is the norm rather than exceptional; conscious efforts have been made to develop policies which facilitate women's entry into the labour mar-ket and their continued attachment to it, at minimal cost to childbearing and childbearing opportunities (Hoem and Hoem, 1987; Lewis, 1992). 85 per cent of lone mothers with dependent children are in the workforce (Kamerman, 1988), a majority of these working full time. In contrast, Hantrais (1994) cites Britain as an example of 'neutral or negative family policy', offering little help to women wishing to combine full time employment and childrearing.

The positive nature of Swedish family and labour market policy, with its emphasis on the support of women as both workers and mothers, may be much more significant in explaining Sweden's lower rates of teenage fertility than the welfare provisions which are alleged to offer incentives to early motherhood in Britain and the USA. To adopt such an approach in Britain would require not only substantial improvements to child-care facilities for working mothers, but also the development of employment and educational opportunities which would make entry into early parenthood a high cost option for young people.

Conclusion

Teenage birth rates in England and Wales have changed little over the past fif-teen years, whereas rates have fallen substantially in most other European countries. Lower teenage birth rates in Denmark and Sweden are likely to be closely linked to their more effective programmes of sex education and, in particular, the linking of sex education to information about the use and availability of contraceptive services. In Britain, the official target of halving rates of conception in women under 16 by the end of the century may seriously be threatened by cuts in family planning services and ambivalence about sex education in schools.

More broadly, there is little evidence that existing welfare and housing policies in the UK or USA offer advantages to young single mothers over their childless peers; nor is there any evidence that they encourage pregnancy in this age group. On the contrary, any reduction in provision for this group would put both mothers and children at even greater risk of physical and social disadvantage, without any probable influence on reproductive behaviour. Only improvements in educational and job opportunities might increase motivation among young women and men to avoid or terminate unplanned births. Indeed the effects of any backlash against sex education, contraception and abortion services, or against social security and housing provision for young parents are likely to have the reverse effects. Recent declines in teenage birth rates may well reverse, with the heaviest prices almost certainly being paid by young mothers and their children.

References

ALLEN, I. (1985) *Education in Sex and Personal Relationships*, London, Policy Studies Institute.

BABB, P. (1994) 'Teenage conceptions and fertility in England and Wales, 1971–1991', *Population Trends*, **74**, pp. 12–17.

BALDING, J. (1994) *Young People in 1993*, Exeter University.

BANE, M. and JARGOWSKY, P. (1988) 'The links between government policy and family structure: What matters and what doesn't', in CHERLIN, A. (Ed) *The Changing American Family and Public Policy*, Washington, DC, Urban Institute Press.

BELLEMAN, S. (1993) 'Let's talk about sex', *The Guardian*, 19 November.

BENEFITS RESEARCH UNIT (1988) *Bulletin of the Social Fund Project*, **1**, Nottingham, BRU.

BLAIKIE, A. (1994) 'Family fall-out', *Times Higher Education Supplement*, 4 March.

BOETHIUS, G. (1984) *Swedish Sex Education and Its Results*, Stockholm, Swedish Institute.

BRINDIS, C. (1993) 'Antecedents and consequences: The need for diverse strategies in adolescent pregnancy prevention', in LAWSON, A. and RHODE, D. *The Politics of Pregnancy: Adolescent Sexuality and Public Policy*, New Haven, Yale University Press, pp. 257–83.

CAMERON, S., GILROY, R., SPEKE, S. and WOODS, R. (1994) *Young Mothers and Housing: Barriers to Independent Living*, York, Joseph Rowntree Foundation.

CLARK, E. (1989) *Young Single Mothers Today: A Qualitative Study of Housing and Support Needs*, London, National Council for One Parent Families.

COLEMAN, D. (1993) 'Britain in Europe: International and regional comparisons of fertility levels and trends', in NI BHROLCHAIN, M. (Ed) *New Perspectives on Fertility in Britain*, London, HMSO.

CRAIG, G. and GLENDINNING, C. (1990) *Missing the Target*, Barnados.

DAVID, H.P. (1990) 'United States and Denmark: Different approaches to health care and family planning', *Studies in Family Planning*, **21**, 1, pp. 1–19.

DAVID, H.P. (1992) 'Abortion in Europe, 1921–1991', *Studies in Family Planning*, **23**, 1, pp. 1–22.

DEPARTMENT OF HEALTH (1992a) *The Health of the Nation: A Strategy for Health in England*, Cmnd. 1986, London, HMSO.

DEPARTMENT OF HEALTH (1992b) *The Health of the Nation. . . . and You*, London, HMSO.

DEPARTMENT OF HEALTH (1993) *Family Planning Clinic Services 1992/93: Summary Information from KT31 (England)*, London, Department of Health.

DOPPENBERG, H. (1994) 'Free pill in the Netherlands: For how much longer?', *Planned Parenthood in Europe*, **23**, 1, pp. 8–9.

EVANS, M., PIACHAUD, D. and SUTHERLAND, H. (1994) *Designed for the Poor-poorer by Design: Effects of the 1986 Social Security Act on Family Incomes*, London, STICERD, London School of Economics.

FARRELL, C. (1978) *My Mother Said . . . : The Way Young People Learn about Sex*, London, Routledge.

FINE, M. (1988) 'Sexuality, schooling and adolescent females: The missing discourse of desire', *Harvard Educational Review*, **58**, 1, pp. 29–53.

FORD, N. (1991) *The Socio-sexual Lifestyles of Young People in South West England*, South West Regional Health Authority.

FRANCOME, C. (1993) *Children Who Have Children*, London, FPA.

FURSTENBERG, F., BROOKS-GUNN, J. and MORGAN, S.P. (1987) *Adolescent Mothers in Later Life*, New York, Cambridge University Press.

GERONIMUS, A. (1987) 'On teenage childbearing and neonatal mortality in the United States', *Population and Development Review*, **13**, pp. 245–62.

GREEN, D. (1991) 'Liberty, poverty and the underclass', Paper presented at PSI seminar, London.

GRESS-WRIGHT, J. (1993) 'The contraception paradox', *The Public Interest*, **113**, pp. 15–25.

GRUNSEIT, A. and KIPPAX, S. (1994) *Effects of Sex Education on Young People's Sexual Behaviour*, Geneva, WHO.

HANTRAIS, L. (1994) 'Comparing family policy in Britain, France and Germany', *Journal of Social Policy*, **23**, 2, pp. 135–60.

HASKEY, J. (1983) 'Marital status and age at marriage: Their influence on the chance of divorce', *Population Trends*, **32**, pp. 4–14.

HASKEY, J. (1993) 'Trends in the numbers of one-parent families in Great Britain', *Population Trends*, **71**, Spring, pp. 26–33.

HELM, T. (1993) 'Find your own homes, lone mothers to be told', *Sunday Telegraph*, 16 December.

HILL, M. (1988) 'Do family planning facilities meet the needs of sexually active teenagers?', *British Journal of Family Planning*, **13**, 4, pp. 48–51.

HOEM, B. and HOEM, J. (1987) 'The Swedish family: Aspects of contemporary developments', *Stockholm Reports on Demography*, **43**, University of Stockholm.

HUDSON, F. and INEICHEN, B. (1991) *Taking it Lying Down: Sexuality and Teenage Motherhood*, London, Macmillan.

INEICHEN, B. (1986) 'Contraceptive use and attitudes to motherhood amongst teenage mothers', *Journal of Biosocial Science*, **18**, 4.

JOFFE, C. (1993) 'Sexual politics and the teenage pregnancy prevention worker in the United States', in LAWSON, A. and RHODE, D. *The Politics of Pregnancy: Adolescent Sexuality and Public Policy*, New Haven, Yale University Press, pp. 284–300.

JONES, E.F. (1986) *Teenage Pregnancy in Industrialised Countries*, New Haven, Yale University Press.

JONES, M. (1993) 'Wedded to welfare', *The Sunday Times*, 11 July.

KAMERMAN, S. (1988) 'Mothers alone: Strategies for a time of change', Dover, MA, Auburn House.

KERSHAW, A. (1993) 'The wonder years', *The Guardian*, 18 December.

KIERNAN, K. (1980) 'Teenage motherhood — associated factors and consequences — the experiences of a British birth cohort', *Journal of Biosocial Science*, pp. 393–405.

KIERNAN, K. and ESTAUGH, V. (1993) *Cohabitation: Extra-marital Childbearing and Social Policy*, London, Family Policy Studies Centre.

LAWSON, A. and RHODE, D. (1993) *The Politics of Pregnancy: Adolescent Sexuality and Public Policy*, New Haven, Yale University Press.

LEWIS, J. (1992) 'Women and welfare', Paper given to SPA Comparative Social Policy Conference on Sweden, City University, London.

MACINTYRE, S. and CUNNINGHAM-BURLEY, S. (1993) 'Teenage pregnancy as a social problem: A perspective from the United Kingdom', in LAWSON, A. and RHODE, D. *The Politics of Pregnancy: Adolescent Sexuality and Public Policy*, New Haven, Yale University Press, pp. 59–73.

MCRAE, S. (1993) *Cohabiting Mothers: Changing Marriage and Motherhood*, London, PS1.

MILLAR, J. (1987) 'Lone mothers', in GLENDINNING, C. and MILLAR, J. (Eds) *Women and Poverty in Britatin*, 1st ed., Brighton, Wheatsheaf Books.

MILLAR, J. (1994) 'Lone parents and social security in the UK', in BALDWIN, S. and FALKINGHAM, J. *Social Security and Social Change*, Brighton, Harvester Wheatsheaf.

MORGAN, P. (1995) *Farewell to the Family: Public Policy and Family Breakdown in Britain and the USA*, London, IEA.

MURRAY, C. (1990) *The Emerging British Underclass*, London, IEA.

MURRAY, C. (1993) 'No point fiddling with welfare at the margin', *Sunday Times*, 11 July.

MUSIK, J.S. (1993) *Young, Poor and Pregnant: The Psychology of Teenage Motherhood*, Yale University Press.

PEARCE, D.M. (1993) 'Children having children: Teenage pregnancy and public policy from the woman's perspective', in LAWSON, A. and RHODE, D. *The Politics of Pregnancy: Adolescent sexuality and public policy*, New Haven, Yale University Press, pp. 46–58.

PERSSON, E. (1994) 'Subsidising contraception for young people in Sweden', *Planned Parenthood in Europe*, **23**, 1, pp. 2–4.

PHILLIPS, A. (1995) 'Teen mums: The whole story', *The Independent*, 13 January.

PHOENIX, A. (1991) *Young Mothers?*, Cambridge, Polity Press.

PLOTNICK, R.D. (1993) 'The effect of social policies on teenage pregnancy and childbearing', *Families in Society*, June.

REID, D. (1982) 'School sex education and the causes of unintended teenage pregnancies: A review', *Health Education Journal*, **41**, 1.

RISOR, H. (1989) 'Reducing abortion: The Danish experience', *Planned Parenthood in Europe*, **18**, 1, pp. 17–19.

RUSSELL, J. (1968) *Early Teenage Pregnancy*, Edinburgh, Churchill Livingstone.

SCHOFIELD, M. (1965) *The Sexual Behaviour of Young People*, London, Longman.

SEGEST, E. (1991) 'How to do requires knowledge, insight and skill', Paper presented to conference on 'Teenage Pregnancy: International Perspectives', London, September.

SELMAN, P. and CALDER, J. (1994) 'Variations in the characteristics of attenders at community family planning clinics', *British Journal of Family Planning*, **20**, pp. 13–16.

SIMMS, M. and SMITH, C. (1986) *Teenage Mothers and their Partners*, London, HMSO.

SWEDISH INSTITUTE (1990) *Family Planning in Sweden*, Fact Sheets on Sweden, Stockholm, Swedish Institute.

WELLINGS, K. (1994) *Sexual Behaviour in Britain*, London, Penguin Books.

WIELANDT, H. and BOLDSEN, J. (1989) 'Age at first intercourse', *Journal of Biosocial Science*, **21**, pp. 169–77.

ZABIN, L.S. and HAYWARD, S.C. (1993) *Adolescent Sexual Behaviour and Childbearing*, London, Sage.

Notes on Contributors

Pam Alldred Lecturer in the Department of Sociology, where she is completing her PhD. She also teaches in the Department of Media and Communications, Goldsmith's College.

Pat Allatt Professor of Sociology at Teesside Business School, University of Teesside.

Jonathan Bradshaw Director of the Institute for Research in the Social Sciences at the University of York and Associate Director of the Social Policy Research Unit.

Julia Brannen Reader in the Sociology of the Family in the University of London and Joint Director of the Centre for Research in Family Life and Employment at the Thomas Coram Research Unit, Institute of Education.

Lynda Clarke Lecturer in Demography at the London School of Hygiene and Tropical Medicine and Senior Research Fellow at the Family Policy Studies Centre.

Caroline Glendinning Senior Research Fellow, National Primary Care Research and Development Centre, University of Manchester; formerly Senior Research Fellow, Department of Social Policy, University of Manchester.

Allison James Lecturer in Applied Anthropology, Department of Sociology and Anthropology, University of Hull.

Chris Jenks Head of the Department of Sociology and Reader in Sociology at Goldsmith's College, University of London.

Deborah Jones Research Assistant in the Department of Sociology, University of East London.

Steven Kennedy Formerly a Research Fellow in the Social Policy Research Unit at the University of York and is now a member of staff in the House of Lords library.

Hilary Land Professor of Social Policy, Department of Social Policy, University of Bristol.

Margaret O'Brien Principal Lecturer and Research Advisor in the Department of Sociology, University of East London.

Theodoros Papadopoulos Sociologist who is currently completing his DPhil in Social Policy at the University of York.

Alan Prout Senior Lecturer in Sociology, Department of Sociology and Anthropology, University of Keele.

Jeremy Roche Principal Lecturer, School of Law, University of East London.

Peter Selman Head of the Department of Social Policy, University of Newcastle upon Tyne.

Anne Solberg Sociologist and Senior Research Fellow at the Norwegian Institute for Urban and Regional Research in Oslo.

Miri Song Lecturer, Department of Sociology, University of Kent.

Peter Whiteford was a Senior Research Fellow at the University of York and is now a political advisor to the Australian Minister of Social Security.

Index